AF478465

Spirituality in Business

Spirituality in Business

Theory, Practice, and Future Directions

Edited by
Jerry Biberman
and
Len Tischler

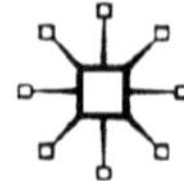

First published in 2008 by
PALGRAVE MACMILLAN™
175 Fifth Avenue, New York, N.Y. 10010 and
Houndmills, Basingstoke, Hampshire, England RG21 6XS
Companies and representatives throughout the world.

PALGRAVE MACMILLAN is the global academic imprint of the Palgrave Macmillan division of St. Martin's Press, LLC and of Palgrave Macmillan Ltd. Macmillan® is a registered trademark in the United States, United Kingdom and other countries. Palgrave is a registered trademark in the European Union and other countries.

ISBN-13: 978–0–230–60371–4
ISBN-10: 0–230–60371–8

Library of Congress Cataloging-in-Publication Data is available from the Library of Congress.

A catalogue record for this book is available from the British Library.

Design by Newgen Imaging Systems (P) Ltd., Chennai, India.

First edition: May 2008

10 9 8 7 6 5 4 3 2 1

Printed in the United States of America.

CONTENTS

LIST OF FIGURES

Margaret Benefiel, PhD, teaches at Andover Newton Theological School in Boston and the Milltown Institute in Dublin, Ireland, and is CEO of Executive Soul, a consulting and training business. Chair of the Academy of Management's Management, Spirituality and Religion group, Benefiel speaks widely, offers consulting services and seminars, and provides coaching and spiritual direction to leaders and organizations. More than 500 executives, managers, and other leaders have participated in her courses and seminars. Author of *Soul at Work: Spiritual Leadership in Organizations*, and weekly syndicated columnist for *United Press International*, Dr. Benefiel has also written for *Leadership Quarterly, Managerial Finance, Journal of Organizational Change Management, Management Communication Quarterly, Personal Excellence, Organization*, and many other periodicals. Her Web site is www.ExecutiveSoul.com.

Jerry Biberman is Professor of Management at the University of Scranton. For twelve years he served as Chair of the Management/Marketing Department at the University of Scranton. He obtained his MS, MA, and PhD from Temple University. He writes, teaches, consults, speaks, and conducts workshops in the areas of work and spirituality, workplace diversity, and organization transformation. Dr. Biberman serves as coeditor of *Journal of Management, Spirituality and Religion*, and has coedited several special editions on work and spirituality for *Journal of Organizational Change Management*. Dr. Biberman is coeditor of *At Work: Spirituality Matters*. He was one of the founders and first chair of the Management, Spirituality and Religion interest group of the Academy of Management.

David Boje holds the Bank of America Endowed Professorship of Management (awarded in September 2006) and has held Arthur Owens Professorship in business administration (June 2003–June 2006) in the

Management Department at New Mexico State University. Professor Boje is described by his peers as an international scholar in the areas of narrative, storytelling, postmodern theory, and critical ethics. He has published nearly 100 articles in various journals, including in the top-tier journals such as *Management Science, Administrative Science Quarterly, Academy of Management Journal, Academy of Manage Review,* and *International Journal of Organization Studies.*

Gerald Cavanagh, S. J. holds the Charles T. Fisher III Chair of Business Ethics and is Professor of Management at the University of Detroit, Mercy. He is the author of more than forty research articles and five books, the latest being *American Business Values: A Global Perspective*, 5th ed. Cavanagh was Academic Vice President and Provost at the University of Detroit, Mercy, and held the Gasson Chair at Boston College, and the Dirksen Chair of Business Ethics at Santa Clara University. He has received honorary doctorates from Loyola of Baltimore and Siena Heights University. He chaired the Social Issues Division of the Academy of Management, and the All-Academy of Management Task Force on Ethics. He referees papers for several journals and for national professional conferences. Cavanagh has served on the board of trustees of Fordham, Santa Clara, Xavier, Holy Cross, Loyola University of New Orleans, and the University of Detroit.

David Cooperrider is Professor of Organizational Behavior at Case Western Reserve University. As a co-originator of Appreciative Inquiry, Dr. Cooperrider is an expert in positive organizational change. He is the coauthor of several books, including *Appreciative Inquiry Handbook* and *Appreciative Inquiry: A Positive Revolution in Change.* His work has been covered in *New York Times, Fast Company, Human Resources Executive Magazine,* and *Training Magazine.* In addition, he consults for organizations such as American Express, BP America, and the U.S. Navy. Dr. Cooperrider earned his PhD from Case Western Reserve University.

Kathy Lund Dean is Associate Professor of management at Idaho State University. She earned her PhD in organizational behavior and philosophy from Saint Louis University. Kathy has been an active member of both the Organizational Behavior Teaching Society and the Academy of Management for ten years and was fortunate to be part of the executive board that created the academy's Management, Spirituality and Religion interest group in 1999. Her current research interests lie in nontraditional research methodologies, business ethics and decision making, and spiritual authenticity in the workplace.

Her research has appeared in multiple journals, including *Journal of Management Education*, *Journal of Management, Spirituality, and Religion*, *Journal of Organizational Change Management*, *International Journal of Public Administration*, and *Academy of Management Executive*. She currently serves on the board of MSR at the Academy and is an Associate Editor for *Journal of Management Education*.

Charles Fornaciari is Professor and the Uncommon Friends Chair in Ethics at Florida Gulf Coast University in Fort Myers, FL. He received an MBA in finance and a PhD in strategic management from Florida State University. He has published over a dozen journal articles in areas such as the role of spirituality and religion in management, affective learning techniques, corporate strategic change, and the use of technology in education in journals such as *Journal of Organizational Change Management*, *Journal of Management, Spirituality & Religion*, *Journal of Management Education*, *Journal of Managerial Issues*, *Journal of Business Research*, and *International Journal of Organizational Analysis*. Charles is also a recipient of the Organizational Behavior Teaching Society's prestigious New Educator Award. He currently serves as an associate editor for *Journal of Management Education* and is an editorial review board member of *Decision Sciences Journal of Innovative Education*.

Louis W. (Jody) Fry is a Professor of Management at Tarleton State University in Central Texas (http://www.tarleton.edu/~fry/). He has presented scholarly papers at National and International symposia, served on editorial review boards, and published articles and reviews in respected scholarly journals including *Leadership Quarterly*, *Organization Science*, *Academy of Management Journal*, *Journal of Occupational Behavior*, *Administrative Science Quarterly*, *Journal of Management*, *Journal of Marketing Research*, *Public Choice*, *Human Organization*, *Journal of Applied Psychology*, and *Academy of Management Review*. He is on the editorial review board of *Leadership Quarterly*, coeditor of *Journal of Management, Spirituality and Religion*, and is the founder of the International Institute for Spiritual Leadership (http://www.iispiritualleadership.com/). He received his BS in Industrial Engineering from Southern Methodist University; MBA from American University, Washington, DC; and PhD in Organization Theory and Behavior and Research Methods, The Ohio State University.

Kerry Hamilton has a thirty-year career in management, highlighted by success in both the corporate and entrepreneurial worlds. In her Corporate Retail experience, Kerry contributed to hiring, mentoring, and developing strategic and capable teams for numerous marketing challenges. Throughout her career, Kerry has been interested not only in doing strategically sound, creative, and result-oriented work, but also in analyzing how teams and people have been engaged to do the work. Kerry is interested in the dynamics that lead to individual empowerment, personal and professional growth, creativity, wisdom, and humor. Now, as CEO of Kerry Hamilton, LLC, working as an Executive, Professional, and Personal Coach, Kerry combines her managerial experience and life experience, reputation for personal integrity, excitement for growth and opportunity, and enjoyment of work and people into a dynamic, personalized, and life-enhancing practice to help people get unstuck and realize their personal and professional dreams.

Mary Ann Hazen is Professor of Management in the College of Business Administration, University of Detroit, Mercy. She earned her PhD in Organizational Behavior from Case Western Reserve University. Journals that have published her work include *Human Relations, Journal of Organizational Change Management*, and *Journal of Management Education*. She has published various works and continues to write about dialogue and polyphonic organizations, grief in organizations, and business and social responsibility. She serves as an associate editor for *Journal of Management Education*.

Dennis Heaton, EdD, is Professor of Management, Codirector of the PhD Program in Management, and Dean of Distance Education and International Programs at Maharishi University of Management in Fairfield, Iowa. His previous publications include articles and invited chapters on higher stages of development, leadership, ethics, and peak performance.

Keiko Krahnke is Associate Professor of Management at the Monfort College of Business at the University of Northern Colorado. She received her PhD from Colorado State University. Her professional interests include management and spirituality, Appreciative Inquiry, and management education. She has coauthored articles in *Journal of Behavioral and Applied Management, Journal of Organizational Change Management, Journal of Business and Entrepreneurship*, and *Central Business Review*.

Dr. Marjolein Lips-Wiersma is Senior Lecturer in the Department of Management at the University of Canterbury. She teaches courses in workplace spirituality, research methods, organizational behavior, and leadership. She is former Chair of the Management, Spirituality and Religion interest group of the Academy of Management, current book review editor for *Journal of Management, Spirituality and Religion*, and has published in journals such as *Journal of Organizational Behavior, Journal of Change Management*, and *Journal of Managerial Psychology*.

Charles Manz, PhD, is a speaker, consultant, and best-selling author of over 200 articles and scholarly papers and 20 books including *Mastering Self-Leadership, 4th ed., Fit to Lead, The New SuperLeadership, The Power of Failure, Foreword Magazine* best book-of-the-year Gold Award winner *Emotional Discipline,* and Stybel-Peabody National Book–prize winning *SuperLeadership.* His work has been featured on radio and television and in *Wall Street Journal, Fortune, U.S. News & World Report, Success, Psychology Today, Fast Company,* and several other national publications. He is the Nirenberg Chaired Professor of Leadership in the Isenberg School of Management at the University of Massachusetts. Formerly a Marvin Bower Fellow at the Harvard Business School, his clients have included 3M, Ford, Xerox, General Motors, P&G, American Express, the Mayo Clinic, Banc One, the U.S. and Canadian governments, and many others.

Karen Manz is author and speaker in the area of values, spirituality, and work life. She has spoken nationally and internationally on the language of spirituality and values, virtues in organizations, and on teaching in this emerging field. Manz was the conference coordinator for *Going Public with Spirituality in Work and Higher Education* held at the University of Massachusetts, Amherst, in June 2000. She is an adjunct professor at Hartford Seminary, a consulting editor for *Journal of Management, Spirituality and Religion,* and member of the American Academy of Management and the American Academy of Religion.

Robert Marx is Professor of Management at the Isenberg School of Management, University of Massachusetts, Amherst. He is coauthor of the *Wisdom of Solomon at Work: Ancient Virtues for Living and Leading Today* and the coauthor of *Management Live: The Video Book.* He is the Board Chair of the Organizational Behavior Teaching Society, an international organization focused on excellence in management education, and is the recipient of the 2005 Distinguished Teaching Award at the University of Massachusetts, a lifetime achievement award honoring significant contributions to the teaching mission of the University and beyond. In 2006, he was awarded a grant from the Graduate Management Admissions Council of the Management Education Research Institute to study how AACSB accredited Business Schools prepare their doctoral students for classroom teaching. Professor Marx consults with organizations in both the public and private sector in the United States and abroad on issues of leadership, teamwork, and communication.

Judi Neal, PhD is the President and CEO of the International Center for Spirit at Work. She is a cofounder of the Management, Spirituality and Religion interest group at the Academy of Management, and one of the founding editors of *Journal of Management, Spirituality and Religion.* Her book *Edgewalkers: People and Organizations That Take Risks, Build Bridges, and Break New Ground* is a best-selling business book. Judi is the Academic Director for the Master of Arts in Organizational Leadership program at the Graduate Institute. Her work has been featured in *Wall Street Journal, New York Times, U.S. News & World Report, Business Week, Tokyo Shimbum,* and several other national and international publications. She is President of Judi Neal & Associates, and consults and speaks internationally. Her clients include Hewlett-Packard, General Electric, Pfizer, Unilver, Yale University, and many others.

Dr. Venkataraman Nilakant is an Associate Professor in the Department of Management at the University of Canterbury. He teaches courses in change management and organization theory in the University's undergraduate and postgraduate programs. He has published two books and papers in journals such as *Organization Studies, Journal of Applied Behavioral Science, Journal of Managerial Psychology,* and *International Small Business Journal, Total Quality Management, and Human Systems Management.*

Peter C. Olden, PhD, worked in senior management at several hospitals for fourteen years. Initiating a career change, he earned a PhD in Health Care Organization and Research and joined the University of Scranton where he is now Professor and Director of the Graduate Health Administration Program. Dr. Olden writes and speaks about health care organizations and their management, preventive health, the U.S. health system, and health care management education. His works have been published in journals such as *Milbank Quarterly, Health Services Research, Journal of Healthcare Management,* and *Health Care Management Review.* He has made presentations at meetings of the Academy of Management, American Public Health Association, and Academy Health, and at meetings abroad in Canada, Slovakia, and Georgia. He is active in numerous scholarly and professional associations and provides service to several nonprofit health organizations.

Scott R. Safranski, PhD, is Associate Dean and Associate Professor (Management), John Cook School of Business, Saint Louis University, St. Louis, Missouri. Dr. Safranski has authored one book and authored or coauthored over fifty articles, book chapters, or professional papers. The focus of most of Scott's research has been on the organization-environment interface, particularly in religious and other nonprofit entities. Dr. Safranski has worked with organizations in both the for-profit and nonprofit spheres and on issues ranging from employee benefits to global outsourcing. Clients have included organizations ranging from single-owner small firms to fortune 500 companies and from colleges to a Roman Catholic Archdiocese. Dr. Safranski also serves as a peer reviewer for the Higher Learning Commission of the North Central Association of Colleges and Schools.

Dr. Jane Schmidt-Wilk is currently Associate Professor of Management, Codirector of the Doctoral Program in Management, and Director of the Center for Management Research at Maharishi University of Management in Fairfield, Iowa. She earned her MBA and PhD from Maharishi University of Management. She has recently been appointed editor of *Journal of Management Education* after serving as its coeditor for eighteen months. She also serves on the editorial board of *Journal of Management, Spirituality and Religion*, and has edited special issues of *Journal of Social Behavior and Personality*, and *Journal of Organizational Change Management*. Her teaching and publications explore the relationships between development of consciousness and business management.

David Steingard, PhD, is Assistant Professor of Management and Assistant Director of the Pedro Arrupe Center for Business Ethics in the Haub School of Business at Saint Joseph's University. His teaching, research, and consulting interests include spirituality in business, intentional intelligence, business ethics, and transformational approaches to management. David has published articles in *Journal of Management Inquiry*, *Journal of Management Education*, *Journal of Business Ethics Education*, and *Journal of Organizational Change Management*. He has given conference presentations nationally and internationally.

Len Tischler is Professor of Management and Chair of the Management/Marketing Department at the University of Scranton. He earned his MBA. in strategy and his PhD in organizational behavior at the University of Maryland, College Park. Curious about why some people and organizations become "successful" and others less so, Dr. Tischler's areas of focus in business management are personal development, spirituality in organizations, quality and lean management, and sustainability. Dr. Tischler has consulted to more than 130 companies. He has also published more that twenty-five articles and presented an equal number of papers; he has given more than a hundred speeches, led corporate training programs and retreats, and has presented workshops on such diverse topics as personal growth, individual spirituality, spirituality in organizations, total quality management, lean management, and sustainability.

ACKNOWLEDGMENTS

We would like to thank those people and organizations that have contributed to the development of the field of spirituality and business and have encouraged our work in that field over the past fifteen years. Special thanks to the International Academy of Business Disciplines, and particularly the late Abbass Alkhafaji, for allowing us to have sessions and a track on the topic in the early 1990s, The Management Spirituality and Religion interest group at the Academy of Management, and Yochanan Altman, founding editor and publisher of *Journal of Management, Spirituality and Religion*. We would also like to thank the many academics and managers we have gotten to know over the years who have given us insights about this field of spirituality in business.

We would like to give special thanks Mr. Sura Aparaks, our graduate assistant, who helped us with many hours of work, and our contributing authors who have done a fine job for this book.

CHAPTER ONE

Introduction

JERRY BIBERMAN AND
LEN TISCHLER

The human race seems to be in the midst of a major shift (e.g., Hawken;[1] Hawkins;[2] Toffler[3]), and part of this shift is a shift in spirituality. Part of this larger shift in spirituality is occurring in the workplace. The aim of this book is to offer some insights about this shift in the workplace as of 2007.

We do not believe that we can chronicle the entire shift in one book. According to chaos theory, one cannot fully see the change or predict its outcome while in the midst of a change of state, and we believe that a change of state (we'll later call it "level") is occurring. Our intent is to chronicle some of the changes that have been occurring in this shift so far through the eyes of academics.

What Is Spirituality?

The first question is what is spirituality? There seem to be as many definitions of spirituality as there are articles about it, and even those who write about it seem to shift their definitions over time or are not clear in their definitions. In this book we separate spirituality from religion. In doing so, we agree with the Dalai Lama's distinction:[4]

Religion I take to be concerned with faith in the claims of one faith tradition or another, an aspect of which is the acceptance of some form of heaven or nirvana. Connected with this are religious teachings or dogma, ritual prayer, and so on. Spirituality I take to be concerned with those qualities of the human spirit—such as love and compassion, patience tolerance, forgiveness, contentment, a sense of responsibility, a sense of harmony—which brings happiness to both self and others.

Although all religions began with spirituality and have a spiritual component, in this book we will not focus on religion. Focusing on spirituality instead, we will contend that for most people spirituality is a process that moves them in either or both of the following two (non-contradictory) directions:

- (usually inward) into a deeper, broader experience, toward a Transcendent universality or higher reality (whatever name we give it) and
- toward being intimately, interdependently interconnected with the entire universe and everything/everyone in it.

The result of an individual's growth in spirituality, in the above two directions, takes the form of the behaviors, feelings, and attitudes as indicated above by the Dalai Lama.

Giacalone and Jurkiewicz[5] define workplace spirituality in their *Handbook of Workplace Spirituality and Organizational Performance* as "a framework of organizational values evidenced in the culture that promotes employees' experience of transcendence through the work process, facilitating their sense of being connected in a way that provides feelings of compassion and joy." This definition is essentially the same as ours, and, while mentioning work process, still describes essentially an individual worker's experience. Their definition is thus a definition for the individual level and individual experience. We have not yet seen any definition of group or organizational spirituality.

We might look to Native American tribes and see that even across tribes, even across hundreds and thousands of miles between these tribes, each tribe seems to hold a reverence for the earth and our direct connection with it. Knowing that not all members of a tribe make their spiritual "journeys" or make them successfully, we might be able to say that there is an underlying group spirituality that is independent of a particular person's spiritual experience and that provides a context for each person's spiritual experience. These tribes tend to fall in the second category above: aiming for experiences of an intimate, interdependent, interconnected reality with the world around us. In some ways we can say that modern religions also provide a context within which members have their spiritual experiences. Experiencing Jesus, Mohammad, Krishna, God, the Transcendent, or the Tao appear to be quite different, but each is a deeper, broader experience of or toward a Transcendent universality or higher reality. One can question whether the contexts that each tribe or religion set are simply cultures and belief systems, no different than what we call corporate cultures. As of yet there is no clear answer to this.

Back to the individual level, we can divide the space "spirituality" into spiritual practices, levels, and states.[6] There are a plethora of spiritual practices, including meditations, prayers, dancing, chanting, learning, rituals, and so on. You will see in this book that our authors include appreciative inquiry, discernment, and meditation as practices that deepen managers and bring out their wisdom. The purpose of practices is to bring one to higher levels of awareness or consciousness—to broader awareness, ultimately to the ability to directly experience the Transcendent and to directly experience one's intimate connection with everything and everyone.

Several of our chapters relate to levels directly or indirectly: as simply broader awareness or the rising of inner wisdom, or as permanent changes that affect how we think and act. On the way toward higher levels of awareness most people have "spiritual experiences" or temporary states in which the way they perceive reality changes in some personally significant way. This book does not focus on temporary spiritual experiences.

We also have to recognize that spirituality has inner and outer manifestations. For individuals these come as changes in our inner experiences and ways of seeing and thinking, and in our outer behaviors. For organizations these can come as changes in vision, purpose, values, culture, and programs internally, and as changes in behaviors, structures, and relationships externally.

We can also look at spirituality from the perspective of groups within organizations—for example, work teams or departments—or globally. In our search through all of the empirical work on spirituality and organizations during 1996–2004, we found almost no work done on work groups or on global spirituality.

The Implementation of Spirituality
in Work Organizations

There appear to be several avenues for implementing spirituality in or bringing spirituality to work organizations. Individuals bring their own spirituality with them. On the other hand, organizations can and some do encourage their employees to practice spirituality. As examples, some companies set aside time for prayer at the beginning of meetings, some provide meditation training and meditation rooms, and some provide opportunities for employees to meet with others of similar spiritual or religious persuasion. As mentioned above, companies are increasingly using techniques such as appreciative inquiry, discernment, and meditation as means for deepening their managers' thinking and developing their abilities to think, feel, and act more effectively.

Many would argue that spiritual development without a change in behavior is not true (or meaningful) spirituality. Although he doesn't address spirituality, Hawken[7] demonstrates that some of the kinds of behaviors we expect from more spiritual people—focusing on social justice and assuring that our environment remains healthy—are on the rise worldwide. In fact, these social movements are external forces pushing work organizations not only to act properly externally (in society and with regard to the physical environment), but also to act properly with regard to their own employees. There has been a dramatic shift over the past fifty years or so toward better treatment of employees, and this shift is accelerating.

Finally, organizations are encouraging employees to grow in many ways: personally, professionally, and spiritually. Increased empowerment and teamwork are creating the need to train employees not only in technical areas, but also in interpersonal skills, team skills, decision-making skills, and so on. The pressure to remain competitive is increasing the pressure to increase creativity and innovation in most companies. To do so employees are not only getting training in these skills, but are being given more time and more opportunities to experiment and even fail—more opportunities to learn how to learn. As employees gain these skills, they are finding that they need to do more reflecting, more inner work, to become better at these skills. This is in the same direction as doing spiritual work (inner, deeper, broader, and more connected).

The rise of spirituality in organizations leads to a variety of questions, many of which are addressed in the chapters in this book. These questions include

- How best can spirituality be implemented or used in organizations?
- How is it currently implemented or used in organizations?
- What value is spirituality creating for organizations?
- What value is spirituality creating for people connected with organizations?

- What value is spirituality creating for society?
- How does spirituality relate to other processes or techniques used in organizations?
- Are there negative effects or implications of using or implementing spirituality in organizations?
- Are there other positive effects beyond effects on organizations using it?
- In what direction is spirituality in organizations moving?
- What might organizations do to improve their engagement with spirituality?

A Model for Understanding and Researching Spirituality in Organizations

Most of the academic writing and research on spirituality in business to date has its origins in the positivistic social science paradigm exemplified by psychology and other social sciences. This approach emphasizes the importance of objectivity and the tools and approaches of the scientific method.

When we attempted to summarize and organize the research that has been done so far in the area of spirituality and work, we found that theory development in the field of management, spirituality, and religion in organizations to date had been hampered by the fact that the research has not been able to build on itself, making emergent theory from the research difficult to develop and extant theory difficult to test. In an attempt to change this situation, we proposed a map of the territory in which most research on spirituality in organizations is done, offering researchers an opportunity to focus or segregate their research in specific areas that can be compared with other studies.[8] Based on reviewer reaction and discussion of the model, we revised the model and then tested this model (with Charles Fornaciari) using the 187 peer-reviewed empirical journal studies in the field from 1996 to 2004.[9]

We would now like to briefly present and explain that revised model and the results of our test of the revised model.

The Model

The purpose of this model is to map the territory in which most research is done on the topic of spirituality in organizations. The purpose of

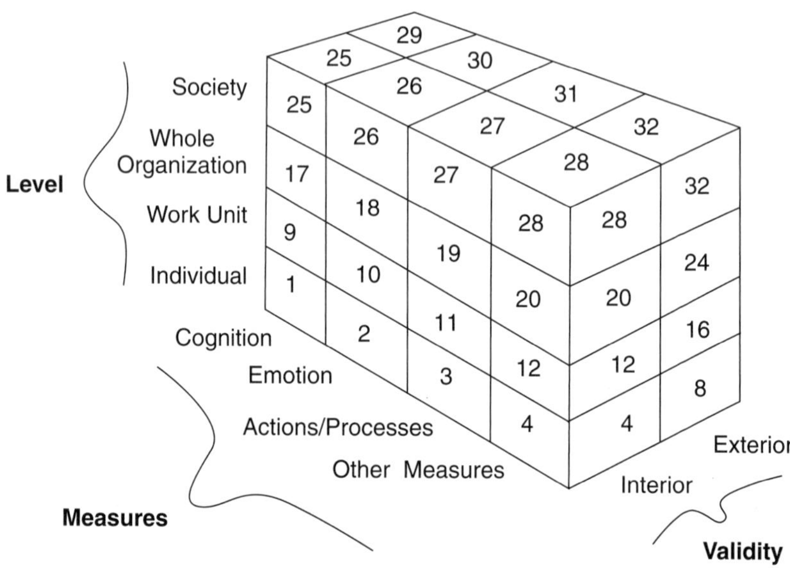

Figure 1.1 A Model of Areas of Research: Spirituality in Organizations

such a map is to parse spirituality research into definable areas that are comparable so that each study can build on previous studies in the same part(s) of the map. Figure 1.1 presents the model visually.

The model can be broken down into three main dimensions—level, measures, and validity. "Level" refers to the level of analysis of the study, and is divided into individual, work unit, whole organization, and society. The first three are the standard levels used in organizational research,[10] while the fourth is found in fields such as economics, public policy, and ethics.[11] "Measures" refers to the types of data being examined or phenomena being measured by the measurement instruments or procedures used in each particular study; they are described as either measuring cognition, emotion, action, behaviors or processes, or other measures. Finally, "validity" refers to the way in which the phenomenon being studied is validated—as either internally perceived experiences (interior) validated only by the person having or reporting the experience, or externally observable or measurable phenomena (exterior) that can be "objectively" validated. This three-dimensional model results in thirty-two possible combinations. The dimensions of the model are more fully described elsewhere.[12,13] See table 1.1 for the definitions of each category.

Table 1.1 Definitions of Model Dimensions

Dimension	Definition
Individual level	Something about a single individual is measured.
Work unit level	The work unit can mean an ad hoc or permanent work team or one's department.
Organization level	Organizational level would include any level of a whole organization including a division, a strategic business unit, a subsidiary, or a conglomerate corporation.
Society level	This can include measures of the national or world economy, of a local community in which the firm does business, of the firm's customers, of nations in which the firm does business, of behaviors or impacts on society as a whole at the national or global level, of impacts on the physical environment.
Cognitive	Cognition has to do with thinking, knowledge, and perception. We will also include intentions and attitudes in this category (although they also have an emotional component).
Emotional	Questions about how an individual subject feels about something, or about how work unit's or firm's members experience the unit's or firm's culture would be included in this category.
Actions/Processes	Any kind of observable physical behavior is included in this category, as well as an individual's, team's, or organization's systems or processes.
Other	This category is meant to capture all other measures. One kind that we can anticipate is measures of profitability, market share, and other organizational or business outcomes. At the individual level, promotions and pay hikes could be the measures in this category. Researchers might also study or compare membership of people in professional groups or other groups: how a more amount or a less amount of spirituality affects some aspects about the profession.
Interior validation	When questions are asked of individuals that elicit how the individual, firm, or unit thinks or feels about something or perceives a situation, or about an inner experience; these statements can only be validated by questioning each individual and testing them for truthfulness. One cannot know what another person is thinking, feeling, or perceiving.
Exterior validation	If the answer to a question can be validated by observation or other objective means, it would fit into this category of exterior validation.

The $4 \times 4 \times 2$ three-dimensional map provides thirty-two boxes within which we can define and focus research in this field. A given study may fall into one or more of these boxes.

Classifying the 187 empirical studies published in the field from 1996 to 2004 using the model showed those areas of research that have received the most and the least amount of research attention.[14] Most of the studies reported were at the individual level. There were few studies at the organizational level and very few reported at the work group or unit level and society level. With regard to measures, most of the studies reported using surveys to measure cognitive and action/process variables. Those studies that were done using interviews, focus groups, and other types of qualitative techniques were most likely to measure a combination of cognitive, emotional and action/process variables. In terms of validity, most of the studies used interior validity from some type of self-report.[15] The results of testing the model suggested that future research should be conducted at all levels, particularly at the work unit and organizational levels, and should involve more attempts at external validity using measures that go beyond self-report to more externally observed measurements such as direct observations or externally measured behaviors or processes.

Limitations of Our Model and
of the Newtonian Paradigm

The model we have presented so far is based on commonly accepted constructs and norms familiar to almost any management doctoral student or practicing researcher. However, given the inherently unique nature of research on spirituality in organizations, and the fact that it is often difficult to measure, quantify, or observe spirituality-related phenomena, there are other considerations for systematizing this research. These alternate systemizations, suggested largely by Ken Wilber's work,[16,17] might take some years to create agreement around. We will briefly describe two of them. They are as follows.

Levels of human development can be organized around differences in worldview or levels of consciousness. Worldview levels range from self-centered (puts the individual at the center of his or her universe), to focus mostly on my family, my neighborhood, my race or religious group, my country, my company, and so on, to universal (seeing the world as fully interconnected and interdependent). If we think of levels of human development in terms of levels of consciousness, we can take an Eastern or Enlightenment view and divide the territory into three general levels: waking consciousness, awareness with the witness, and unity consciousness in which the Transcendent and material universe are unified. The idea behind developmental levels, and of determining which level is "higher" and which is "lower," rests on the concepts of transcend and include, and depth and span.[18] Each higher level transcends the lower level while it also includes it. Each higher level also has greater depth but less span. The issue with worldview or with level of consciousness is that many spiritual traditions very clearly suggest that the world is perceived and acted on very differently at each level. We have found that almost none of these studies clearly distinguish among the levels of worldview or consciousness. We would propose that some kind of hierarchical level model would probably be helpful to improve research in this field. This might fit into our model within "intention or attitude" or could be a separate model or a separate dimension of the current model.

Lines of human development[19] describes proxy variables such as cognitive development, psychological development, socioemotional development, moral development, physiological development (low skin resistance, more coherent brain waves), and so on that can be used to measure an individual's spiritual progress. We expect highly spiritual people to be developed multidimensionally. Most people develop very well along one or several lines but not others. What are we to make of measures of the different lines of development? How can we compare a study that measures development of one line with a study that measures development of another? Is the development of the higher reaches of spirituality possible without some development of some of the "lines"? Do we need to develop along all of the "lines" if we are to develop our consciousness fully? Wilber[20] counts up to twenty-four lines of development. Our model organizes these into three general categories—cognitive, emotional, and behavioral.

More fundamentally, the results of testing the model highlight the ongoing tensions within workplace spirituality concerning logical-positivistic methods and less commonly accepted forms of behavioral and social scientific investigations. The concentration of the studies was on a comparative few areas, such as individual levels and cognitive and action/process measures using interior validity assessments. This is perhaps a direct result of both the training and the publication process of workplace spirituality scholars. Likewise, the relative lack of investigations at the organization and societal levels, using emotional and other measures with exterior validity methods perhaps also reflects upon a field struggling to progress to maturity. Scholars who are able to integrate, or resolve, the positivistic/alternate methods dilemmas in the research are likely to find great success in helping the field to move forward.

As Hawkins[21] points out, this linear positivistic approach is an extension of the Newtonian scientific paradigm, which values content over context and fails to adequately address spiritual experiences or concepts. Specifically, the approach does not adequately address transcendence, nor does it adequately address nonlinear influences. These tensions are evident even in Giacalone and Jurkiewicz.[22] While its opening chapter argues for a hard-line empirical linear approach, most of the chapters in their book are neither empirical nor take a hard-line positivistic approach.

As we mentioned above, Wilber's model attempts to bridge this gap or go beyond a strict positivist approach when he talks about interior states and experiences and talks about levels and lines. However, Wilber defends his model in a linear way, and mostly cites linear research and concepts in explaining the elements of his model.

Sandra Waddock[23] argues that spirituality, emotion, and community have received little attention in management thinking, research, and practice, calling spirituality the "ghost in the machine." We agree, and will return to these concerns in our closing chapter.

Summary of Chapters and How They Fit into Our Model

As do most current researchers, the authors of the chapters in this book also take a mostly positivistic approach to the subject of workplace spirituality, and thus we are able to fit their chapters into our model. We will now summarize each chapter and show where each fits within our model.

Appreciative Inquiry as Spiritual Practice

Appreciative Inquiry (AI) provides a way to move mankind beyond the machine model of human organizations toward a model of unleashing the wisdom within us, collaborating, and cocreating a reality that we envision. Through (appreciative) inquiry change automatically occurs: by going more deeply inside about issues people begin to see things differently and act differently. By going most deeply inside, the changes are even more profound. This can be done on an individual basis or collectively. There already is a positive force within each of us and it is at the deepest levels of life. We simply need to tap into this by inquiring deeply within to unleash it. The ultimate inquiry is who are we, where did we come from, and where are we going?

Using our model, we would classify this chapter as describing individual and group level, cognition, emotion, and actions/processes with interior and exterior validity.

Sustainability, Spirituality, and Discernment
or Discernment Upholds Sustainability

Spiritual discernment supports sustainability: the practice of discernment during decision making will lead decision-making groups to be more apt to reach decisions that are sustainable socially and environmentally. Discernment is one of the major spiritual practices of the Jesuits, founded in 1540. It involves going beyond discussing the issues and arguing for one's viewpoint, which is what happens in most decision-making meetings. Discernment adds a couple of processes in the meeting:

- People no longer bring their opinion to the meeting, but more of the facts and ideas they have uncovered.
- After open discussion, bringing out all the facts and ideas people have offered, the meeting quietens down so that each person can quietly introspect to see how their feelings and intuition interact with what they heard. They pay attention to their bodies and feelings for this.
- This is followed by sharing what happened inside and more ideas, and then by more interior work as needed.

Such a decision-making process yields decisions with more attention to side effects and with fewer negative side effects. More is taken into account by accessing our inner wisdom than by restricting our decision making to our rational thinking and our argumentative/persuasion skills.

Using our model, we would classify this chapter as group level, cognition, emotions, and actions/processes with interior validity.

Practical Compassion: Toward a Critical
Spiritual Foundation for Corporate Responsibility

Research and practice of spirituality in organizations has been tied to the positivistic, bottom-line approach. That is, the underlying purpose of allowing or encouraging spirituality in one's organization, from a managerial perspective, has often been to enhance productivity. Also, research has almost always proposed adding spirituality to an organization's activities or culture because of its effects on productivity. Spirituality's raison d'etre has been the bottom-line benefits it can create. This chapter proposes that this is wrongheaded: spirituality should be entered into for its own sake, because it is the right thing to do, and because it is good for people.

Using our model, we would classify this chapter as describing organizational level, actions/processes with interior validity.

Spirituality in Health Care Organizations

Spirituality in Health Care: increasing numbers of patients now ask for some kind of spirituality as part of their treatment. Research is demonstrating that this seems to have positive effects on patients' health care. Hospice and pastoral care have been growing significantly in recent decades, but in addition health care organizations are gradually finding that they need to integrate spirituality into patients' treatment. This necessitates new training for staff in all professions and also necessitates some structural changes within health care organizations. Using our model, we would classify this chapter as describing organizational level, actions/processes with exterior validity

Intentional Intelligence: How the New Mind of
Leadership Manifests Success in Business and Life

Intentional Intelligence: achievement is based on action, action is based on thought, and thought is based on a flow of connection between mind and "The Field." By enhancing this connection between mind and The Field, one's thinking, actions and achievement are enhanced. The focus is on individual achievement. Being intentionally intelligent begins with interior mindfulness and includes embodied presence and experiencing life as interconnected to a larger force, source, and so on.

Using our model, we would classify this chapter as describing individual level, cognition, with interior and exterior validity.

Spiritual Leadership: State-of-the-Art and Future Directions for Theory, Research, and Practice

Spiritual Leadership is an emerging concept that describes how a leader's inner life (developed by spiritual practices), through the concomitant development of hope/faith, vision, and altruistic love, positively impacts effort, performance, and reward. These latter three are the underpinnings of motivation and success. Adding vocational calling (making a difference, life has meaning) and the feeling of organizational membership (being understood and appreciated) for all members of the organization, individual and organizational outcomes are further enhanced. Using our model, we would classify this chapter as describing the individual and organizational levels, cognition and emotions, with a mix of interior and exterior validity.

Awakening the Leader Within: Behavior Depends on Consciousness

This chapter demonstrates that human development is needed for leadership development to have its intended impacts. Human development at its most advanced stages is associated with spiritual intelligence, which can come from systematic cultivation of the Transcendent. This chapter describes the benefits to individual leaders who cultivate the Transcendent. Using our model, we would classify this chapter as describing individual level, and actions/processes with interior validity.

Infinite Leadership: The Power of Spirit at Work

Action research began with Kurt Lewin and includes "action science" of Argyris and Schon, "cooperative inquiry" of Heron and Reason, and "action inquiry" of Torbert. Two in-depth examples are given here: a company developing by openly sharing and learning with leaders of other companies, and a manager developing through open sharing and learning with a coach. In both cases it is by suspending the normal rational thinking process—by going more deeply inside to notice and reflect on the subtleties of experience during action—that allows participants to learn more deeply, to develop new ways to frame concepts, issues, and situations, and to decide and act differently. In both cases this suspension occurs on the basis of the players being given a safe space in which to more deeply inquire and openly share what they find. An iterative process of experience and reflection allows this inquiry process to dive deeply and bring out deeper wisdom about oneself and one's situation. Using our model, we would classify this chapter as describing individual, group and organizational level, cognition, emotion, and actions/processes with interior and exterior validity

Critical Theory Approaches to Spirituality in Business

Critical theorists have often been critical of spirituality—in and of itself, as part of formal religion, and as it relates to business. This chapter demonstrates that critical theory (CT) and spirituality in business can cohabitate. The problems CT has with spirituality in business, as with many management practices, include

- It has led to employees being abused: overworked and overstressed in order to benefit the company and its already-rich stockholders.
- It is used to serve the purposes of the company, and companies have historically been predatory and destructive in their practices toward society and the environment.

This chapter points out that these abuses (at the individual or corporate level) are not necessarily due to spirituality itself. Spirituality can also seek equality, social justice, and plurality in ways that benefit business and society. This is the only chapter to examine actions/processes at the whole organization and societal level with exterior validity.

The Ethics of Spiritual Inclusion

Within the field of spirituality in business, differences (diversity) among traditions, practices, and beliefs can make it difficult for managers to make inclusive, ethical workplace decisions. Examples of problems include the following:

- managers pushing one tradition or practice over another;
- how to handle an individual's rights to express or practice their spirituality versus how the individual's practice or behavior affects others at work (productivity, other employees, or customers),

- management using spirituality as a means for increased productivity or profit (rather than as a good in itself),
- employees shunning those with different beliefs and so on.

These break down to two arenas of difficulty: individual versus individual and individual versus firm.

On the other hand, religious discrimination disputes still tend to be "handled with the least aggressive, retaliatory, and public path." What is needed is that individuals and firms should be "authentically flexible" with each other. Using our model, we would classify this chapter as describing individual and whole organization level, and actions/processes with exterior validity.

Teaching about Spirituality and Work:
Experiential Exercises for Management Educators

Students (in schools and organizations) are often timid about discussing or engaging in spirituality issues. This chapter provides exercises for introducing spirituality in a nonintimidating manner. We would categorize it as describing individual and group level actions/processes with interior validity.

Future Directions

Following these chapters, our concluding chapter will examine the need to expand our model into nonlinear areas, and whether, in order to do so, it is necessary to come up with a totally new paradigm, or, conversely, whether it is possible to do so within the confines of the current paradigm. We will conclude with an expanded model, and will attempt to answer the question of what a non-ego organization would look like.

Notes

1. Hawken, P. 2007. *Blessed unrest: How the largest movement in the world came into being and why no one saw it coming.* New York: Viking Press.
2. Hawkins, D.R. 2002. *Power vs. force.* Carlsbad, CA: Hay House.
3. Toffler, A. 1972. *Future shock.* New York: Bantam Books.
4. Dalai Lama XIV. 1999. *Ethics for the new millennium.* New York : Putnam. 22.
5. Giacalone, R.A. and Jurkiewicz, C.L. 2003. Toward a science of workplace spirituality. In Giacalone, R.A. and Jurkiewicz, C.L. (eds.), *Handbook of workplace spirituality and organizational performance.* Armonk, NY: M.E. Sharpe. 3–28.

6. Wilber, K. 2000. *A brief history of everything*. Boston: Shambala.

7. Hawken, P. 2007.

8. Tischler, L., Biberman, J., and Altman, Y. 2007. A model for researching about spirituality in organizations. *Business Renaissance Quarterly*, 2(2): 23–39.

9. Tischler, L., Biberman, J., and Fornaciari, C.J. 2007. Conference on the development and test of a research model for management, spirituality & religion in organizations. Academy of Management, Philadelphia, PA, August 3–8.

10. Klein, K.J. and Kozlowski, S.W.J. 2000. *Multilevel theory, research and methods in organizations*. San Francisco: Jossey-Bass.

11. Lawrence, A.T., Weber, J., and Post, J.E. 2004. *Business and society: Stakeholders, ethics, and public policy*. 11th ed. Boston: McGraw-Hill College.

12. Tischler, L., Biberman, J., and Altman, Y. 2007.

13. Tischler, L., Biberman, J., and Fornaciari, C.J. 2007

14. Tischler, B., Biberman, J., and Fornaciari. C.J. 2007.

15. Ibid.

16. Wilber, K. 2000.

17. Wilber, K. 2001. *Sex, ecology, spirituality: The spirit of evolution*. 2nd rev. ed. Boston: Shambala.

18. Ibid. 28–33.

19. Wilber, K. 2000.

20. Wilber, K. 2005. Leadership workshop. Boulder, CO. July.

21. Hawkins, D.R. 2002.

22. Giacalone, R.A. and Jurkiewicz, C.L. 2003.

23. Waddock, S.A. 1999. Linking community and spirit: A commentary and some propositions. *Journal of Organizational Change Management*, 12(4): 334, 335, 323–344.

CHAPTER TWO

Appreciative Inquiry: Inquiring New Questions and Dreaming New Dreams

KEIKO KRAHNKE AND
DAVID COOPERRIDER

Ap-pre'ci-ate, v., 1. valuing; the act of recognizing the best in people or the world around us; affirming past and present strengths, successes, and potentials; to perceive those things that give life (health, vitality, excellence) to living systems. 2. to increase in value, e.g. the economy has appreciated in value. Synonyms: VALUING, PRIZING, ESTEEMING, AND HONORING.

In-quire' (kwir), v., 1. the act of exploration and discovery. 2. to ask questions; to be open to seeing new potentials and possibilities. Synonyms: DISCOVERY, SEARCH, AND SYSTEMATIC EXPLORATION, STUDY.[1]

The Need for Repositioning

We are living in a critical period of time and may be on the brink of a major shift in human consciousness. Long-held management philosophies based on fragmentation, extreme competitiveness, seeing human and nonhuman resources as exploitable and expendable assets, and rigid command and control methodologies are being challenged. We are now recognizing that organizations are products of human interactions and that we have lost something fundamentally important by applying the machine model to human organizations.

As we see organizations more as living systems, we begin to recognize our interconnectedness and interdependencies across individual, organizational, societal, and national boundaries. We see the whole instead of parts, and notice patterns of change rather than static images.[2] Although technology and science have improved the quality of our lives, the level of our consciousness and wisdom has not kept pace. How can we navigate through complex challenges and choose a path that leads to a positively significant future? Some of the environmental and social-sustainability challenges that we face are so serious that they might bring irreversible consequences.

Raffi Cavoukian, a singer and song writer well known for children's songs, developed a paradigm called child honoring. Child honoring is a "vision of hope and renewal in response to a time of unprecedented social and ecological breakdown worldwide"[3] and "a global credo for maximizing joy and reducing suffering by respecting the goodness of every human being at the beginning of life, with benefits rippling in all directions."[4] Seeing our children's physical and emotional well-being is a good measure of our generativity, and considering the conditions in which many children are raised, we realize that we have not done well on a global scale.[5] When we dream, hope for, and design our future, we cannot do so without honoring our responsibility for the future generations. Raffi calls this movement a "compassion revolution." As Raffi believes, the benefits should ripple in all directions. Nonviolence and compassion are central to human emotional, and even spiritual, maturity.[6] When we truly understand the wholeness and interconnected nature of humans as spiritual beings, it would be impossible to hurt other humans and sentient beings. It is time for us to reconnect our fragmented selves so we can see the consequences of our own actions and their impact on others. We will then be able do a great deal to reduce the suffering felt at all levels of life.

Peter Drucker once said, "The best way to predict the future is to create it." Creating our future is not so much about needing more goods or technology; but rather, it is about bringing change in our consciousness. Humanity has yet to learn a lot about collaborative capacity in creating our future—a future that can sustain the rich and diverse life on the planet and a thriving human spirit. It appears to us that the essential question before humanity, and its various systems and institutions, is this: How can we each rediscover and unleash our wisdom within us, collaborate with each other, and cocreate a reality that we envision?

We believe humans have larger capacities than most of us have been led to believe. Uncovering that capacity and seeing the interconnectedness of life with the physical world are necessary for us to face our complex challenges.[7] Appreciative Inquiry (AI) is "about the coevolutionary search for the best in people, their organizations, and the relevant world around them."[8] It is about discovering what gives life to a living system. It often takes courage to focus on the positive and on the power to create our own reality. Creating our own reality means that we have to believe in something intangible that hasn't happened yet, and that is very different from the more common belief that reality is only based on tangible evidence. It takes a great deal of faith to be unconditionally positive, to choose to see potential rather than obstacles, and to align strengths to make an impact. AI is known to mobilize a magnitude of change because it taps into the best of who we are. Real change can only occur within us. Just as "strange attractors," inherent in chaotic systems, bring order to natural systems such as snowflakes or weather patterns, AI helps us to remember the "hope" within us hidden underneath real and imagined problems. Even though we may sometimes feel confused and have doubts about the meaning and purpose of our lives, there is always present somewhere deep within us a pull, a yearning, a hope, or even a knowing that life's meaning and purpose somehow must be findable.

In this chapter we explore ways in which AI helps individuals and organizations tap into the deeper levels of consciousness and discover meaning in their individual and organizational lives, and thereby manifest the collective capacity to build a future that we envision. This chapter addresses AI as a model of possibilities, the role of hope, the power of thought and language, collective learning and wisdom, and finally as a way of being.

AI as a Model of Possibilities

The traditional mode of organizational inquiry is problem-oriented. It is based on the deficit model, and the common notions of this model are "closing the gaps," "gap analysis," and "knowledge gaps." It is about measuring people and human performance against the norm. Organizations have measured outcomes, closed gaps, and made incremental changes to improve their performance. We have valued deficit-oriented approaches with which we try to identify weaknesses so we can fix them. Many organizations have stories and vocabularies of why they fail, but not of those that lead to successes. We are accustomed to focusing on problems and problem-solving. When we focus on problem solving in an organization, the basic assumption is that the organization is a problem to be solved rather than a mystery to embrace. Over 90 percent of the articles published in psychology journals focus on problems, and the media prefers negative news to positive. Since the science of psychology has focused on what is wrong, it has provided us with little information about human strengths.[9] We have studied problems and failure as if we could achieve excellence by avoiding what leads to failure. The opposite of failure, however, is "not failing," which is far from excellence. Marcus Buckingham[10] makes it clear that we cannot learn about excellence by studying failure. We cannot learn about happiness or joy by studying sadness, and about health by studying sickness.

In the past decade, we have seen some evidence that the process of thinking about organizations has begun to move away from the paradigm of analyzing problems and fixing them. A new and radically different approach is to build on strengths and emphasize generativity. Organizations are increasingly shifting from deficit models to a strength-based approach with successful results in performance. When people connect with their positive core and engage in a collaborative exploration of the vision of the group, they cocreate a sense of community and a shared vision. AI is based on the assumption that every organization and every person has a strength. Through dialogue, these strengths are discovered and developed. "It involves the discovery of what gives 'life' to a living system when it is most effective, alive, and constructively capable in economic, ecological, and human terms."[11]

One of AI's principles is the poetic principle. The heart of this principle is the infinite possibilities of the future. "An organization's story is constantly being coauthored."[12] Just as we find in poetry, there are endless possibilities of topics to study human experience and ways to study it in organizations. It's not that there is a "world out there" that we can objectively study, but it is constructed in a social process. Jaworski has also noted, "Cognition is not a representation of the world 'out there' but rather a 'bringing forth of the world through the process of living itself.'"[13] He also points out that we need to change if we want a larger system such as an organization and society to change. "We are essential to its coming forth. We evoke a potential that is already present. Because things cannot exist as observable phenomena without us in the quantum world, the ideal of scientific objectivity disappears."[14] The poetic principle helps us to reawaken to the power within us, reexamine what matters most, and explore the purpose of human inquiry. We choose what we inquire. The questions we ask matter because they lead us to the focus of inquiry.

Transcending Linear Time

The power of AI becomes evident when a group of people discovers past success and greatness, builds on them, and develops a shared vision. Both the past and the future are brought into the present, and what we do in the present makes a difference in the future—and perhaps even the past or our perception of the past. By uncovering high-point experiences during appreciative interviews, we may rediscover the sense of power and strength we had in the past. The feeling of empowerment can be unleashed, which may lead to a different perception of the past. Storytelling, reflecting, and dialogue help us to assign new meaning to our life circumstances and even reauthor previous weaknesses and downfalls as personal strengths.[15] According to Carr, space for reauthoring is not accessible in traditional deficit models.

Thatchenkery and Metzker call the "ability to perceive the positive inherent generative potential within the present," Appreciative Intelligence; it is the ability and capacity to "see the mighty oak in the acorn."[16] Three components of Appreciative Intelligence are reframing (the present situation), appreciating the positive, and seeing how the future unfolds from the present.[17] The most important of the three is the ability to channel the present strengths to the future and see the future unfold. It is about literally being able to vividly see the future now. Tremendous manifest energy is unleashed when we treat the acorn as if it were the mighty oak.

Just as the quantum field offers all possibilities, visiting the future in the "dream" stage of the AI's 4-Dd cycle helps us to explore different possibilities and scenarios. The 4d cycle is an application of the AI philosophy for organizational change, and the process follows four stages: discovery (what gives life?); dream (what might be?); design (what should be?—the ideal); and destiny (how to empower, learn, and adjust/ improvise?). As AI summit participants go through the 4d process, they work with past successes, present strengths, and infinite future possibilities. Transcending linear time and aligning these creative forces into one workable package open doors never imagined before.

Hope as a Generative Agent for the Future

"Hope" is not a word we commonly hear at work or see in academic literature. It is relatively recently that we started paying attention to hope in an academically rigorous way. Hutson and Perry[18] note that the first scientific mention of "hope" was by Karl Menninger at the American Psychiatric Association in 1959. In his address, Menninger urged his colleagues to rediscover "the validity of Hope in human development,—hope alongside of its immortal sisters, faith and love."[19] Seligman[20] also notes that psychology generally focused for many years on what was wrong and we know little about human strengths. Positive psychology research has revealed that optimists do better in adversarial situations and are physically healthier.[21] It may be because it sounds soft or because it's not easily measurable that hope is often left out of the topics of human elements in an organization. In Studs Terkel's book, *Hope Dies Last: Keeping faith in difficult times,* the interviews tell stories of hopes, dreams, and persistence.[22] If "hope" is in fact the last thing that dies in us, it deserves more serious attention in academic inquiries.

Hope does not exist only in difficult or adversarial situations, and it does not need a clear picture of the future; it thrives in all conditions.[23,24] Hope exists before the future can be seen. Viktor Frankl's story[25] of his life in a concentration camp attests to the powerful force of hope. Joan Chittister, author of *Scarred by struggle; Transformed by hope,* speaks about hope as follows:

> Hope is not a matter of waiting for things outside of us to get better. It is about getting better inside about what is going on out-side. It is about becoming open to the God of Newness. It is about allowing ourselves to let go of the present, to believe in the future we cannot see but trust to God. Surrendering to the demands of the moment, holding on when holding on seems pointless, brings us to that point of personal transformation which is the juncture of maturity and sagacity. Then, whatever the circumstances, how-ever hard the task, the struggles of life may indeed shunt us from mountain top to mountain top but they will not destroy us.[26]

Ludema[27] identifies four qualities of hope: (1) born in relationship; (2) inspired by the conviction that the future is open and can be influ-enced; (3) sustained by dialogue about high human ideals; and (4) gen-erative of positive effect and action. Ludema notes, "Hoping reaches beyond the self: it prospers when people place themselves in service of the other."[28] Stephen Post, who heads the Institute for Research on Unlimited Love at Case Western Reserve University, recently wrote a book called *Why Good Things Happen to Good People,* along with Jill Neimark.[29] In an interview in *Christian Science Monitor,* he shares encouraging findings that show that altruistic love leads to health, longevity, and general mental health.[30] When we care about and give to others, we are also doing good for ourselves. Here are a couple of powerful examples. A study of 100 communities in England revealed that communities with more volunteerism had fewer crimes and happier people. In a study conducted at the institute on the brain, people were asked to put a check mark next to the charity that excites them the most. Post says, "The part of the brain that is deeply emotional lights up—the part that doles out feel-good chemicals like serotonin and dopamine."[31] The brain scientifically and biochemically shifts at mere thoughts of excitement. Post gives many examples of altruistic people receiving physical and emotional benefits. Hope is born in relationship, and hope connected to hope creates change, and strengths connected to strength create change.

Thought Directs Energy and Words Create Worlds

The Power of Thought

We might think the future is unknown and can only be guessed at or predicted. Based on the assumption of AI, however, the future is something we can cocreate. The future is not something that happens to us, and we are not helpless receivers of the fate it brings. The future is created through the mind's anticipatory images, values, and intentions. Social constructionism emphasizes that people participate in creating the perceived social reality and that it is not a reflection of the world out there.[32] Cooperrider and Whitney[33] define constructionism as "an approach to human science and practice which replaces the individual with the relationship as the locus of knowledge, and thus is built around a keen appreciation of the power of language and discourse of all types (from words to metaphors to narrative forms, etc) to create our sense of reality—our sense of the true, the good, the possible."[34]

The power of positive thinking is acknowledged by many, but still have not reached the point where we truly believe we can create our own realities with our thoughts and anticipatory images. We can choose to evolve our consciousness. It is a profound shift from being victims or passive recipient of external forces to having dominion over our lives. By using the word "dominion," we do not mean "exercising power over others" or "controlling others." It is about taking responsibility for our thoughts, knowing that our thoughts and actions create the world we choose. Through language and collaborative interaction, humans create meaning. As we talk, we construct the world we live in, and how we talk changes the world.[35,36]

As individuals, we may be living in an atmosphere of negativism because of negative assumptions we make about the world around us. Not being fully aware, we often think of ourselves as victims of unfortunate circumstances. "Creating our own reality" or "the power of positive thinking" may sound to some as though it is a New Age narcissism, but there is a sound physiological basis for the role of positive values in our cognition. When we have repeated thoughts, feelings, and events in our lives, the neurons in our brains create a neurosignature or brain groove.[37] Interconnected neurons in the brain grooves carry specific thought patterns or habits.[38] Giving attention feeds the habit; for example, the more often you think about love or confidence, the more predisposed you will be to think, feel, and experience love and confidence in everything that happens to you.[39] Thoughts you entertain in your brain create chemicals that send these thoughts to other cells, and "emotion-specific" peptides instantly spread throughout your body telling every cell how it should "feel." Interestingly, the more frequently you have a particular "feeling" flushing through your body, the more predisposed all of your cells are to experience that feeling in the future. That is, the more frequently we think about and feel fear, the harder it will be for us to think and feel safe, as opposed to fear. Continued repetition feeds the habit; therefore, feeding positive thoughts would create new positive brain grooves, which will starve the negative ones.[40]

There is more good news from neurobiology. Our conscious intention makes a difference in manifesting our potential. Pert,[41] in *Molecules of Emotion,* notes that peptide receptors exist everywhere in our bodies, which means that our brain or consciousness is not localized in the brain but in the cells all over our body. According to Pert,[42] 98 percent of information exchange occurs at cell receptors, and peptides bind themselves to specific peptides to infuse information. This is where optimism and positive feelings play a critical role. When we feel excited, happy, and optimistic, cells' receptors are more open to life-giving peptides. These life-giving peptides grab hold of receptors and drive out the negative ones, or even viruses. Pert argues that the body and the mind are not separate, and there is an undeniable relationship between positive feelings and health.

We have learned from Humberto Maturana's work on the biology of cognition that we see the world not as it is but as we are. O'Donohue[43] also noted that "the mind is the eye of the world. When the mind changes, the world is different." We humans commonly try to understand how everything is "put together," and the insights and information that we believe we are gleaning from such inquiries are matters that speak to the inner reality of who we are. It means that we are not independent observers of the "way things are." On the contrary, we are an intrinsic part of the universe in all its unfolding, and as such we are reflections and manifestations of those very realms of inquiry. As physicists investigating subatomic particles and wave dynamics have confirmed, the observer and the observed are intimately and factually linked, each being clearly interrelated and interactive.[44]

One of the most powerful pieces of evidence for positive imagery at play comes from the study of placebo responses. The effects of placebo studies have clearly shown that the power of belief plays a major role. A 2005 press release of the result from a University of Michigan study describes the first direct evidence about the brain's pain-fighting chemical that plays a role in placebo effects and reduces pain.[45] Positive imagery actually awakens the healing power of the body.

The Power of Words

Linguists have argued for many decades about the relationship between language and thought. Although they may not agree on the extent to which language influences thought and vice versa, there is an undeniable relationship between the two. The word is not just a means to convey meaning or a symbol. It is something with which we create meaning and, furthermore, create reality. Language is the most powerful tool humans have, and it can be a two-edged sword, and the word we choose can create beauty and instill hope, or implant fear and doubt in others' minds.[46] Words literally create worlds. Ruiz notes that words can hook us, enter our minds, and change our beliefs, and that is why he urges us to be impeccable with our words. By "being impeccable with our words," Ruiz[47] means speaking with integrity, saying what you mean, and not being against yourself. We may be saying to ourselves things that are not in our best interest. For example, we may be subconsciously and continuously saying how frustrated we are or how busy we are. When something becomes a habit, it is like breathing; we don't know we are doing it. Unbeknownst to us, we may actually be projecting certain thought forms, programming them in our brain, and giving a passive consent to manifesting a particular reality, which may not be what we want.

One of the principles in which AI is grounded is "the principle of simultaneity." Inquiry is intervention. The minute we inquire, change occurs; therefore, the way the first question is asked sets the stage of data that are discovered in the inquiry. "The seeds of change are in things people think and talk about, the things that people discover and learn, and the things that inform dialogue and inspire images of the future."[48]

Humans learn from pain, but pain only teaches us to avoid certain things. AI emphasizes the heliotropic nature of humans. Building and sustaining change requires a great deal of positive energy such as hope, excitement, and caring. Therefore, positive questions bring about more sustainable outcomes of change. Peter Senge[49] has noted in *the Fifth Discipline* that many organizational visions fail because they are built on "what to avoid," and such visions convey a message of powerlessness and are often short-lived. When we try to "drive out fear" and use the statement "Don't be afraid," we may find more fear because we are paying attention to it. When we say, "This idea won't work because we don't have enough resources," we have already shut down all possibilities. Daniel Siegel and Ellen Langer have done extensive work on mindful learning. Siegel[50] references Langer's work in *The Mindful Brain* stating that conditional statements such as "might be" or "can be," instead of absolute statements such as "is" or "are," facilitate mindful learning and engagement of the mind. Siegel explains that conditional statements trigger more intricate and complex neural connections so that knowledge can include more possibilities.

The Power of No-Thought and Stillness

Our mind is always thinking about something, and our brain is constantly chattering. Our brain is a goal-seeking, problem-solving entity. It's useful in some situations, but the active brain activity gets in the way of accessing our inner knowing and wisdom because the brain only sees what you're looking for.[51] Silence is a way to still our brain. Once we become silent and turn off the chatter of the brain, mindful awareness becomes possible. Mindful awareness allows us to notice our preconceptions, emotional reactions, and judgments, and eventually to be able to disengage from them. We learn that these emotional reactions and judgments are impermanent and are not part of our core "self."[52] Without habitual thinking and emotional reactions, we become more acutely aware of the present and more "receptive to the things as they are."[53] By being mindfully aware, we will know what we are looking at and be able to discern the underlying meaning instead of automatically reacting to life's situations. This kind of awareness or knowing is increasingly necessary as we continue to evolve our consciousness and navigate through our complex world.

By quieting the chatter of our brain, we can more easily access knowledge and information at a much deeper level and a level where our ego doesn't interfere. Emptying the mind and going to the place of no-thought allow us a glimpse into the "ultimate reality" or the "most fundamental element of reality."[54] This ultimate reality that Laszlo speaks of is the physical vacuum in the universe from which matter emerges. This quantum vacuum is "the subtle energies that underlie all matter in the universe."[55] Just as matter manifests from the quantum vacuum, ideas and information emerge from the place of no-thought.

Collective Learning and Wisdom

Toward an Interdependent Self

The capacity to learn collaboratively is critical in navigating our current challenges in the world. Collaboration doesn't happen naturally in some cultures. In countries such as the United States and Great Britain, one of the primary social values is that of the independent self, and people in these countries tend to think of the self as the dominant unit of society. In the West, it is generally important to be independent, make one's own decisions, and take care of one's self. In this view, people are inherently separate and self-contained, and general positive feelings are associated with independence and interpersonal disengagement. For example, notions such as "realizing yourself" and "being unique" are independent processes. These expressions of individualism are important aspects of the Western selfhood, but we are realizing that it's not possible to live in complete independence in our increasingly complex society.

Martin Buber[56] talks about treating another person as a "Thou" and about having an I–Thou relationship instead of an I–It relationship. When I and you connect with a sense of unity and with fuzzier boundaries, I and you create a "we" and influence each other. In this experience, I and you are both influenced.[57] An I–It relationship is a subject/object relationship. In this relationship, the "I" treats the "It" as an object. Peter Russell urges us to move from a selfish "skin-encapsulated ego" model of self to a "leaky margin" model.[58] The "leaky margin model" has fuzzier boundaries and a greater sense of oneness with the outside world. This selfish model of self or I–It relationship has contributed to societal crisis and environmental degradation.

The Power of Wholeness

We live not only in a fragmented world but also with fragmented thought and a fragmented "self." We make distinctions between body and mind, work and play, science and art, and so on. We try to understand things by isolating them into smaller and smaller units, and this fragmented thinking is pervasive in many academic disciplines and management systems.[59] Fragmentation inherently encourages competition, and it may be the source of many societal and environmental problems we are facing today. We feel disconnected within ourselves, from the environment, and from each other. Palmer notes, "the divided life is a wounded life, and the soul keeps calling us to heal the wound."[60] It is a "failure of human wholeness," and "the costs are immense."[61] Fragmentation is pervasive in organizations as well. Unless we redirect our focus from studying parts and making quick judgments to looking at the larger whole and suspending our assumptions, deep change and innovation cannot happen.[62] There is a hidden wholeness in all things and all living systems,[63,64] and each self-organizing system is a whole with parts that are also whole, making it larger than the sum.

Human systems are living systems. In AI summits, the whole system of an organization participates in the process. Organizational value is created in the dynamic social systems that cross the boundaries of organizational charts.[65] Energy emerges and collaborative capacity increases in the middle of AI tables with a maximum mixture of individuals across all levels and teams participating and exchanging ideas. The future emerges from people of diverse perspectives coming together in a collaborative engagement and exploring questions that matter.[66]

Discussion, Debate, and Dialogue

In order to learn about our individual strengths and collective capacities, free and open sharing of ideas and meaning is vital. As we have mentioned earlier, we have yet a great deal to learn about learning and creating together. We still have little knowledge of and experience with collective capacities. Peter Drucker noted, in an interview by Cooperrider in 2006, shortly before he died, "the task of leadership is to create an alignment of strengths, making our weaknesses irrelevant." When strength connects with strength, it creates a vortex of positive energy that leads to transformation.

How do we communicate and share our thoughts? In the Western Hemisphere especially, we are accustomed to discussing or debating.

Both "discussion" and "debate" have a connotation of a game in which you hit the ball back and forth. Especially in debates, we do not listen to the other in order to understand, but only to counterargue. The purpose of debates is to have a winner and a loser. Humans have been taught early on to take sides, which is unfortunate because taking sides often manifests in rigid assumptions of "either...or" or "good or bad" categorization. When we take sides, debate, or make a narrow assumption, we are cutting half of ourselves off, the half that can only emerge in interdependent interaction with each other. Furthermore, debates do not facilitate deep listening because participants in a debate often spend their listening time thinking about ways to defend their argument, disagree, and to counterargue. Many complex issues that we face today are not "either...or" but require deeper and creative thinking. Furthermore, they require a greater level of collaborative capacity. Learning to suspend our assumptions and judgment would facilitate more meaningful interactions and help us to see the issues from a system's perspective.[67]

The word "dialogue," on the other hand, means "through" (dia) and "word" (logos), and it is a way people participate in common meaning and develop something without competing.[68] Dialogue allows us to see issues from many perspectives, and when individuals suspend assumptions, an open exploration becomes possible.[69] Brown[70] says the purpose of dialogue is "honoring development of individuals and ideas and organizations, at a very deep level. It opens paths to change and clears space for organizational transformation by changing the way we perceive the world, the way we think about cause and effect, the way we conceptualize the relationships among things, and the meaning we ascribe to events in that external world."[71]

Different Ways of Knowing

Epistemological assumptions in the West stress the objective, analytical approach that explains and predicts in a linear manner. The fundamental Anglo-Saxon epistemological paradigm is the monological gaze.[72] It is basically about observing objective behavior of others without tapping into their interior or being involved with their consciousness.[73] It does not require a dialogue or mutual sharing of thoughts and feelings. AI requires a different kind of knowing—knowing that comes from inner knowing and from direct involvement.

Wilber asserts that it is possible to see and experience the world as one, not in fragments and duality, such as "seer and seen," "subject and object," and "fragment and fragment."[74] He talks about "one taste," which is a recognition that you don't see the sky but you are the sky, the wind doesn't blow against you but it blows through you, and you don't see the mountain, you are the mountain. It's not that you are the subject and the world is the object; there is no separation. Wilber says that we don't need to do anything special to make things nondual; it started out as nondual. Perhaps, with our cognitive and scientific analysis, we have made the world dual and separated ourselves from the rest. Wilber uses a Pythagorean term, kosmos, to refer to all domains of existence together in the universe. He believes that we are not in the kosmos but the kosmos is within us and that there is nothing outside of us that we should want or desire. All that we need to know is within ourselves.

Peter Russell notes in *The Global Brain*[75] that change that needs to occur is not external. It's not about needing more material or technology; it is about learning about our consciousness. He points out that we are awakening to our "global brain" and realizing that we are each a unique part of something larger. Imagine the magnitude of positive change we could create by connecting six billion people in the world by tapping into our positive core and aligning our strengths.

AI as a Way of Being

AI is not just a technique that we should add to our organizational development toolbox. It is a way of being. It encourages us to see the world differently when we choose to see goodness and possibility in everything and everybody. "Serious consideration and reflection on the ultimate mystery of being engenders a reverence for life that draws the researcher to inquire beyond superficial appearances to deeper levels of the life-generating essentials and potentials of social existence."[76] Something about tapping into our life-generating core moves us at a deeper level. Participants of AI interviews and summits engage themselves at more levels than just the cognitive, as they might in other meetings. Recalling and telling stories of extraordinary experiences or contemplating on one's dream can be an emotionally charged moment, and it can trigger a major mental shift. William James notes, "emotions that come in this explosive way seldom leave things as they found them."[77]

AI helps us to bring power back to where it belongs, and that is in us and in our wisdom. Knowing our inner strengths and accepting our innate greatness make us resilient. Knowing who we are beyond our brain and underneath our personalities and ego would reveal our true potential. Earlier in the chapter, we described Peter Russell's "skin-encapsulated ego" self and the "leaky margin" self.[78] An example of comparing a hard plastic ball and a sponge ball illustrates the difference and more. A seemingly strong plastic ball has a hard, clear boundary, but it breaks easily by an external force. A sponge ball, on the other hand, is soft and malleable but is resilient. No matter how long we step on it, it bounces back to its original shape because it knows and has the memory of who it is in every cell.

Ultimately, knowing our strengths or positive core means much more than recognizing our skills and our cognitive knowledge. It is about remembering who we really are and our true potential as humans. Perhaps our utmost assignment here on earth is to remember our original greatness.

Conclusion

How can we create such a revolution in our values and consciousness? Contrary to the notion of making change happen by planning ways to overcome difficulties and resistance, Fry and Barrett[79] suggest that we only need to unleash the positive force already present. Positive change emerges from people's positive emotions, stories, and cooperative capacities rather than managed tasks, plans, and meetings.[80] By focusing on solving problems and overcoming resistance, we are perhaps making change more difficult than it should be. We keep looking for solutions outside of ourselves instead of finding and unleashing our inner wisdom.

Strength connected to strength creates change. When an individual connects to another individual and they share each other's life-giving force, it creates positive change larger than the sum of the forces. The key to taking humanity and its systems and organizations to the next level lies in the interdependent relationships and our collective capacities. By deeply looking into ourselves, we are reaching into the very essence of humanity and the depth that generates the consciousness of the whole of humanity, which has the whole of humanity enfolded in it. Understanding the concept of enfoldment and interconnectedness is critical in evolving our consciousness. Laszlo describes the evolution of human consciousness as moving from "ego-bound" to the "transpersonal" form, and transpersonal consciousness would bring about the emergence of higher civilization.[81] "It could produce greater empathy among people, and greater sensitivity to animals, plants, and the entire biosphere. It could create subtle contact with the rest of the cosmos."[82]

AI has a legacy to leave in the cosmic unfolding and must continue inquiring our ultimate search: "who are we, where did we come from, and where are we going?" In order to do so, our modes of inquiry need to shift to another level. We should discover, or rediscover, our consciousness beyond the brain. Having studied patients with near-death experiences, a cardiologist, Pim van Lommel, concludes that consciousness beyond the brain exists.[83] With such consciousness, can we access a realm beyond the material world, a field of interaction called Akashic field where everything connects everything else in the cosmos? Laszlo's poetic vision of the Akashic field is as follows:

> A lightless, soundless, formless plenum. It is filled both with the primeval consciousness that is the womb of all mind and spirit in the cosmos and with the fluctuating energies out of which all things come to exist in space and in time. There is no-thing in this cosmic fullness, yet there is every-thing, in potential. Everything that can and will ever happen is here, in formless, soundless, lightless, quiescent turbulence.[84]

Humanity has repeated the same stories for thousands of years—much like being trapped in a never-ending mobius strip. It is time for us to reposition ourselves, uncover our power and potential, know beyond our brain, and to conavigate toward our future of possibilities. It's time for humanity to inquire about new questions and dream new dreams.

Notes

1. Cooperrider, D. and Whitney, D. 2000. A positive revolution in change. In Cooperrider, D.L., Sorensen, P.F., Whitney, D., and Yaeger, T. (eds.), *Appreciative inquiry*. New York: Stipes Publishing.
2. Senge, P. 2006. *The fifth discipline; The art & practice of the learning organization*. New York: Boubleday.
3. Cavoukian, R. 2006. Introduction: The case for child honoring. In Cavoukian, R. and Olfman, S. (eds.), *Child honoring*, Westport, CT: Praeger Publishers. xvi.
4. Ibid. xix.
5. Olfman, S. 2006. Self, identity, and generativity. In Cavoukian, R. and Olfman, S. (eds.), *Child honoring*, Westport, CT: Praeger Publishers. xvi.
6. Cavoukian, R. 2006.
7. Senge. P. 2006.
8. Cooperrider, D. and Whitney, D. 2000. 5.
9. Seligman, E.P. 2000. Positive psychology. In Gillham, J.E. (ed.), *The science of optimism and hope: Research essays in honor of Martin E. P. Seligman*. Philadelphia: Templeton Foundation Press.
10. Buckingham, M. 2007. *Go put your strength to work*. New York: Free Press.

11. Cooperrider, D., Whitney, D., and Stavros, J. 2005. *Appreciative inquiry handbook.* Berkeley, CA: CROWN Custom Publishing and Berrett Koehler. 3.
12. Cooperrider, D. and Whitney, D. 2000. 18.
13. Jaworski, J. 1996. *Synchronicity: The inner path of leadership.* San Francisco, CA: Berrett-Koehler. 175.
14. Wheatley, M. 1992. *Leadership and the new science.* San Francisco, CA: Berrett-Koehler.
15. Carr, A. 1998. Michael White's narrative therapy. *Contemporary Family Therapy,* 10(4): 485–503.
16. Thatchenkery, T. and Metzker, C. 2006. *Appreciative intelligence.* San Francisco: Berrett Koehler Publishers. 5.
17. Ibid.
18. Hutson, H. and Perry, B. 2006. *Putting hope to work.* Westport, CT: Praeger Publishers.
19. Ibid. 21.
20. Seligman, M. 2003. Foreword: The past and future of positive psychology. In Keyes, C.L. and Haidt, J. (eds.), *Flourishing.* Washington, DC: American Psychological Association.
21. Seligman, M. 2006. *Learned optimism.* New York: First Vintage Books.
22. Terkel, S. 2003. *Hope dies last: Keeling faith in difficult times.* New York: New Press.
23. Ludema, J. 2000. From deficit discourse to vocabularies of hope: The power of appreciation. In D.L. Cooperrider, P. Sorensen, D. Whitney, and T.F. Yaeger (eds.), *Appreciative inquiry,* New York: Stipes Publishing.
24. Bloch, E. 1986. *The principles of hope.* Cambridge, MA: MIT Press.
25. Frankl, V. 1959. *Man's search for meaning.* New York: Washington Square.
26. http://www.csec.org/csec/sermon/Chittister_4613.htm.
27. Ludema, J. 2000. 279.
28. Ibid. 278.
29. Post, S. and Neimark, J. 2007. *Why good things happen to good people: The exciting new research that proves the link between doing good and living a longer, healthier, and happier life.* New York: Broadway Books.
30. Lampman, J. 2007. Researchers say giving leads to a healthier, happier life. *Christian Science Monitor,* July 25, Sec. Living.
31. Ibid.
32. Gergen, K. 1985. *Toward transformation in social knowledge.* New York: Springer-Verlag.
33. Cooperrider, D. and Whitney, D. 2000.
34. Ibid. 17.
35. Cooperrrider, D. 2000. Positive image, positive action: The affirmative basis of organizing. In D.L. Cooperrider, P.F. Sorensen, D. Whitney, and T. Yaeger (eds.), *Appreciative inquiry.* New York: Stipes Publishing.
36. Bushe, G. 2000. Appreciative Inquiry with teams. In Cooperrider, D.L. Sorensen, P.F., Whitney, D., and Yaeger, T. (eds.), *Appreciative inquiry.* New York: Stipes Publishing.
37. Shapiro, P. 2005. *Healing power: Ten steps to pain management and spiritual evolution.* Bloomington, IN: Authorhouse.
38. Ibid.
39. Ibid.
40. Ibid.
41. Pert, C. 1997. *Molecules of emotion: Why you feel the way you feel.* New York: Simon & Schuster.
42. Ibid.
43. O'Donohue, J. 1998. *Eternal echoes: Exploring our hunger to belong.* Auckland, New Zealand: Bantam. 311.
44. Bohm, D. 1980. *Wholeness and implicate order.* New York: Routledge.
45. Zubieta, J., Bueller, J.A., Jackson, L.R., Scott, D.J., Xu, Y., Koeppe, R.A. Nichols, T.E., and Stohler, C.S. 2005. Placebo effects mediated by endogenous opioid activity on μ-opioid receptors. *Journal of Neuroscience,* August 24 25(34): 7754–7762.
46. Ruiz, D.M. 1997. *The four agreements.* San Rafael, CA: Amber-Allen Publishing.

47. Ibid.
48. Cooperrider, D., Whitney, D., and Stavros, J., 2005.
49. Senge, P. 2006.
50. Siegel, D.J. 2007. *The mindful brain.* New York: W.W. Norton & Company.
51. Begley, S. 2007. *Train your mind change your brain.* New York: Random House.
52. Seigel. D.J. 2007.
53. Ibid. 78.
54. Laszlo, E. 2007. *Science and the Akashic field.* Rochester, VT: Inner Traditions. 103.
55. Ibid. 83.
56. Buber, M. 1996. *I and thou.* New York: Touchstone.
57. Zohar, D. 1990. *Quantum self.* New York.
58. Russell, P. 2006. *The global brain.* [Motion picture]. Las Vegas: Elf Rock Productions.
59. Senge, P., Scharmer, O., Jaworski, J., and Flowers, B.S. 2004. *Presence.* New York: Doubleday.
60. Palmer, P. 2004. San Francisco, CA: John Wiley & Sons. 20.
61. Ibid. 7.
62. Senge, P. 2004.
63. Palmer, P. 2004.
64. Senge, P. 2004.
65. Sandow, D. and Allen, A.M. 2005. The nature of social collaboration: How work really gets done. *Society for organizational learning,* 6(2–3): 1–14.
66. Brown, J. and Isaacs, D. 2005. The world café. San Francisco: CA: Berrett-Koehler.
67. Senge, P. 2006.
68. Bohm, D. 1965. *A special theory of relativity.* New York: W.A. Benjamin.
69. Senge, P. 2006.
70. Brown, J. 2007. *A leader's guide to reflective practice.* Victoria, VC, Canada: Trafford.
71. Ibid. 220.
72. Wilber, K. 2000. *A brief history of everything.* Boston, MA: Shambhala Publications.
73. Ibid.
74. Ibid. 207.
75. Russell, P. 2006.
76. Cooperrider, D. and Srivastva, S. 2000. Appreciative Inquiry in organizational life. In Cooperrider, D.L., Sorensen, P.F., Whitney, D., and Yaeger, T. (eds.), *Appreciative Inquiry.* New York: Stipes Publishing.
77. James, W. 1992. *The varieties of religious experience: Human nature.* New York: Longmans, Green and Co. 164.
78. Russell, P. 2006.
79. Fry, R. and Barrett, F. 2002. Conclusion: Rethinking what gives life to positive change. In Cooperrider, D.L., Sorensen, P.F., Whitney, D., and Yaeger, T. (eds.), *Appreciative inquiry and organizational transformation reports from the field.* Westport, CT: Quorum Books.
80. Ibid.
81. Laszlo, E. 2007. 117.
82. Ibid. 118.
83. Ibid.
84. Ibid. 130.

CHAPTER THREE

Sustainability, Spirituality, and Discernment or Discernment Upholds Sustainability

GERALD CAVANAGH, S.J. AND
MARY ANN HAZEN

There is considerable evidence that the climate of the earth has been growing warmer over the past century and is likely to continue to do so.[1] Scientists report that it is caused primarily by the effects of industrialization and the increased use of fossil fuels, especially by those in economically developed countries.[2] Many people believe that with concerted collective effort worldwide, this process of global warming can be slowed, stopped, or even reversed. It is here that the most controversy exists about global warming, as we move from the scientific recognition of past and present climate patterns and the interpretation of what they mean to the realm of social perceptions and political activity. What should we do about it? As weather patterns continue to change, large groups of people are and will be affected by drought, flooding, and destructive storms. Hence, individuals, organizations, and political entities must decide how to respond to these problems in a socially just manner. Making choices about our present and future behaviors, individually and collectively—at the personal, family, organizational, and national levels—is a moral and spiritual process to which we bring our beliefs, values, and imaginations. In this chapter, we describe a method of spiritual discernment developed by St. Ignatius Loyola and used for centuries by his followers in the Society of Jesus and others. We show

how it can be applied by organizations or families to major practical issues facing them. As an example we discuss the decisions taken by organization members that impact global climate change.

Ignatius Loyola's Spiritual Discernment

Insights from Ignatian spirituality are now being applied to many management issues. Business managers have been offered many insights and practical applications from Ignatius's *Spiritual Exercises* and Jesuit practice in recent years.[3,4,5,6,7]

Ignatian discernment is a spiritual method developed by Ignatius Loyola (1491–1556) that has been used throughout the centuries by people on all continents. It is a process that guides a person or a group to make an important decision that is most in accord with their long-term goals and the good of the community as a whole. Ignatian discernment helps decision makers to avoid reaching inappropriate and premature conclusions on insufficient evidence. This method also helps to prevent arguments, taking sides, or trying to convince others that only one point of view is correct. Ignatius's spirituality and discernment is particularly useful for dealing with the issues of our period. Brackley[8] points out, "Ignatius's outlook was revolutionary. While he was a child of his times, he also transcended them. He even transcends our own. According to the great theologian Karl Rahner, Ignatius's originality will be understood only in the future." Ignatian discernment, as both an insight and an application, can today provide tools that are useful for individual and group decision making.

Discernment Leads to Action

Ignatian discernment is geared toward action. It is a process that assists those using it to firmly accept what is true to God and their deepest longings and to firmly reject what is contrary to both.[9,10] Ignatian discernment helps individuals and groups to make objective, long-term decisions on issues that are of major importance. As a supplement to rational analysis, it enables them to choose future attitudes and actions that flow from their most basic goals and values and God's plan.[11,12,13] It is a process that is designed to align people's choices and actions with their true desires and the good of the larger community, or what we often designate as the common good. Discernment demands calm reflection and prayer. It requires time and patience, and this is not always easy for contemporary people. Many are accustomed to and rewarded for making quick decisions. The decisions and actions that are arrived at through the slower process of discernment have a higher probability of being accurate, valid, and of long-term value. Ignatius's process is a subtle but powerful instrument:

> These rules contain the most practically usable instruction in the entire Christian tradition regarding discernment of spirits. In an unparalleled way and precisely because Ignatius has chosen the genre of *rules*, these...directives constitute a uniquely valuable instrument toward making spiritual sense of the movements of our hearts.[14]

Individuals or groups can use these rules as they make decisions that are important to them personally or to an organization.

Ignatian discernment can be either individual discernment—when a person prayerfully reflects on his or her future directions or group discernment—when a group of people prayerfully reflects together on their common future priorities and actions. In this chapter, we focus on the discernment process as it takes place in a group, among people who can meet face to face, such as a small business, a business unit of a larger organization, or even a family, school, church, or neighborhood.

Group Ignatian discernment is a way of being together. It entails a respect for and listening to one another. The process requires that each person in the group listen carefully to each other and to the movements within himself or herself. It is based on the conviction that the group has more wisdom than any individual and that God touches all in subtle and quiet ways. It is not a time to argue or to try to convert others to one point of view. Group discernment is "...very different from the dynamics of a process which aims only at a humanly wise, efficient, administrative decision by a majority vote....Corporation boards of directors or state legislatures are not models for discerning God's will."[15] Moreover, when Ignatian discernment is done in a business setting, there are a variety of prior and parallel steps that would be appropriate, such as establishing a vision for the group, eliciting the best ideas before the process begins, and having as many of the stakeholder participants involved in the process as possible in various forums.[16] Ignatian discernment promises to provide greater peace and harmony to the persons and the organization doing the discernment. But the process does take longer and participants may become impatient.

Discernment demands quiet time. For believers, Ignatius recommends that they spend time in God's loving presence. Christians might imagine Christ on the Cross and ask themselves in Ignatius's words: What have I done for him? What am I doing for him? What should I do for him?[17] More specific questions might be What biases and attachments hold me back from freely making a choice? Am I primarily concerned with my own benefit or my group's welfare, and less concerned for others or for those who might be neglected?

Ignatius warns that we often become hostage to our own self-centered desires of seeking wealth, prestige, and pride. After 450 years, Ignatius's cautions are just as appropriate today. If not compensated for, these conscious or unconscious prejudices can predispose our deliberations and result in selfish, manipulative attitudes and actions. So God invites us to review our past and rectify our attitudes and behavior. Moreover, God is always ready to forgive us.

Consolation and Desolation

The results of discernment may mean that either the person or the organization must change priorities and direction. And change is not easy. Ignatius labels the feelings that people have when anticipating or acting on our choices as consolation and desolation. People experience desolation as they become discouraged when they try to follow new insights and paths. On the other hand, they also experience consolation as joy, enthusiasm, and hope at the prospect of choosing a new path. Attending to such feelings is a delicate and sensitive journey for each person and is frequently a challenge for a group. This process is often a struggle and Ignatius offers us insights and suggestions to help us to determine the most appropriate path. Evil can disguise itself as good and delude otherwise good people into false conclusions. It is humbling to realize some of the brightest and best-educated people have supported racism, fundamentalism, terrorism, and Nazism and initiated wars. Ignatius's "Rules for Discernment" help us to examine these interior dispositions.[18]

Ignatius points out that people who are moving from bad to worse in their moral habits, that is, developing vices, often experience confirmation of their inclinations from "the enemy." For Ignatius the enemy is the evil spirit but it also includes selfish inclinations and habits. Attachments to pleasure or comfort, fear of pain, and the "thrill of commanding people" often push people further into selfish behavior.

At the group level, clinging to ideologies, rigidly holding on to aspects of custom or culture, or giving in to authoritarianism can be the enemy of freely made choices. The Divine Spirit, on the other hand, may sting their conscience with sadness and remorse.

People who are advancing in spiritual and moral maturity, or developing virtue, experience these forces in the opposite way. When a person is trying to reform, "it is characteristic of the evil spirit to cause gnawing anxiety, to sadden, and to set up obstacles. In this way the enemy unsettles these persons by false reasons aimed at preventing their progress" (315). The "enemy" (which may be personal selfish inclinations) thus discourages and stirs fear and sadness when a person perceives the cost of the new path; this is called desolation. On the other hand, the Divine Spirit encourages people, helps them remove obstacles and gives joy, happiness, and peace; this is called consolation. Ignatius suggests that we seek confirmation of our decision by examining its results and how we feel about the decision as we pray in God's presence. We may see good results and experience joy, which probably indicates that we have made a good decision; or we may see poor results, along with sadness and anger, which probably indicates that we have made a poor decision.

The discernment process is a spiritual habit. That is, it can be developed over time with repeated actions and so becomes a habit or virtue.[19] It brings a new freedom and thus liberates the person and lays the foundation for better decisions.

How does all of this apply to larger issues of an organization and the problems that confront it? Immense mistakes and atrocities have peppered human history. But so has human progress, such as education, safe drinking water, health care, democracy, the labor movement, abolition of slavery, and the recognition of the equality of women and minorities in politics and in the workplace. Both evil and good movements grow and develop. Wise leaders, like Mahatma Gandhi, Abraham Lincoln, Mother Theresa, Max De Pree, and Mohammad Yunus help us by their lives and their words, but their lives come to an end. Ultimately, each person, group of people, and organization must mature emotionally, morally, and spiritually.

How to Avoid Stumbling

More than half of all the decisions by managers in organizations fail. Research shows that the principal reasons for this are that managers decide prematurely, invest in the wrong things, and use failure-prone decision-making processes.[20] Ignatian discernment promises to help managers to make more successful decisions. The steps of discernment guide the decision-making process away from the typical exclusive dependence on rational-technical models and toward a more balanced, reflective process leading to greater freedom. A lack of freedom can lead to the above blunders. This lack of freedom is described by Paul in his letter to the Galatians (5:16–21) when he cites the effects of idolatry, strife, jealousy, anger, fornication, factions, envy, and drunkenness. "To this list we might add greed, selfishness, addictions and any other smallness of spirit."[21]

Ignatius proposes three tests for our decisions in the practice of spiritual discernment. The first is to consider a person whom you

Table 3.1   Group Discernment Process

First Step: *Reason*	State the matter clearly.
	Gather all the relevant data that will help in making the decision.
	List the pros and cons of each decision or action.
	Examine the list:
	a. What will be gained? What will be lost?
	b. How will others be affected?
	c. What do you like (dislike)?
	d. What are your motives?
Second Step: *Discernment*	State the matter clearly and consider all the relevant information (from first step).
	Recognize that I (we) are in the presence of God, and be aware of his love for us.
	Lay aside preferences, attachments, and opinions.
	Listen carefully and sympathetically to the data and positions presented by others.
	Be balanced and open to God's will.
	Come to a conclusion by consensus.
	Notice the feelings of consolation and desolation.
	As confirmation, or to check one's conclusions,
	a. Consider someone with the same concern who asks your advice. What advice would you give?
	b. Imagine that you are dying, what decision would you have liked to have made?
	c. Imagine, after death, you are facing God who loves you. What decision would you have liked to have made?

have never seen earlier and who is facing the dilemma of making the same decision. How would you suggest that this person proceed "supposing you wished the best for the person and that the choice be for the greater long-term good? Then follow that same advice yourself" (185). A second test is to imagine yourself on your death-bed. What action would you have wished you had chosen earlier? Then choose that which will give you the most satisfaction and peace when you are about to die (186). The third test is similar to the second, and it is to consider yourself before God at the last judgment. What decision would you have liked to have made? Then make that choice now (187).

The Ignatian discernment process and contemporary decision theory both encourage engagement of those involved. Both urge openness, listening, and an environment in which one can take risks in presenting ideas and proposals. Ignatian discernment also urges an environment of freedom, prayer, and acknowledging the presence of God.

This chapter provides a summary overview of the Ignatian discernment method as it might be used within an organization; for an outline, see table 3.1. In order to effectively engage in this process, individuals and groups should also refer to the principal sources that are cited here.[22,23] Examples of the use of Ignatian discernment may help us better understand how it can be used.

Ignatian Discernment in Organizations

We present three diverse examples of the successful use of Ignatian discernment in organizations: (1) the practice of Ignatian discernment in basic business decisions by Ascension Health and its many hospitals; (2) the use of discernment by a business owner in the decision to sell a pharmaceutical business to a large European firm; and (3) an almost yearlong collective discernment process regarding a decision by a community on how they were going to live.

Ascension Health is a Catholic health network with 100,000 associates and a revenue of $11.4 billion; it operates more than seventy-three major hospitals in twenty states. The managers of the network and individual hospitals use discernment in their major decisions, such as capital asset management, outsourcing, opening and closing hospitals, and partnering with a secular hospital. For Ascension, this discernment is a formal process that initially was developed as ethical discernment and then broadened to include spiritual discernment. In each case the relevant managers at Ascension Health gather the facts, listen to each other carefully, seek objectivity, pray for God's guidance and seek God's will in the decision. Dr. Andre Delbecq is a member of the board of trustees of Ascension Health, serves as a consultant for them, and helped to devise the discernment process for the network and individual hospitals.[24]

Catalytica, a pharmaceutical and energy firm, was founded by Richardo Levi. In twenty-five years it grew to a strength of 1,800 employees with branches at several sites and with a market capital of $750 million. The Dutch pharmaceutical firm DSM sought to purchase Catalytica's drug business. Levi was concerned about what would happen to the employees and customers and also worried whether the section of the business that DSM did not want to purchase could survive on its own.

Just prior to the buyout offer, Levi, a Jew, participated in a pilot course, "Spirituality for Business Leaders," led by Andre Delbecq at Silicon Valley's Santa Clara University. Levi used the discernment skills learned in the course to help him make a decision. He acknowledged that the price had to be right and that writing out all the elements of the decision was an essential first step. But the rational approach alone was not enough to make a good decision. As Levi put it, "Those are subtle issues that don't fit into an Excel spreadsheet. It's not really writing a list on the left and a list on the right." He took the matter to prayer and watched for God's influence on him and his decision. He carefully listened to others and prayed for openness as he gathered data and considered the issues. He then prayed that he would be open to God's will. He did sell the drug business and he continued leading the energy business. He gives the Ignatian discernment process major credit for his coming to a correct decision.[25]

A third example of discernment arose in 1992 when the Jesuit Community at the University of Detroit Mercy was faced with making a choice of how they would live together. Their previous residence was too large and did not meet their current needs. Among the options they considered were purchasing several homes in a residential neighborhood adjacent to the university campus, renovating a section of a current university student residence building, or renovating either a 1926 or a 1962 building.

The group met together weekly, considered the options, examined costs, and made lists. But more importantly, they listened to each other's concerns and prayed together. Each person prayed for objectivity for himself when doing the group discernment decision. Each man found that he was more willing to entertain a wider spectrum of possibilities after listening to the ideas and concerns of others. Placing oneself in the presence of God and asking God to guide the group decision gave the group a unique objectivity and equanimity that it probably would not have had otherwise. After six months of listening to each other and praying together, the group decided to renovate the 1926 building. They then proceeded to the second step in order to decide how that renovation should be done: How large should the rooms be? Should there be individual or family style bathrooms? What kind of common living space was needed? How should the chapel be restored? Again, each individual heard each other's concerns and thus became more objective and open to new possibilities. The result satisfied all, largely because of the Ignatian discernment process. Let us now apply this Ignatian group discernment process to the vital issue of how a small business or a unit of a larger organization might respond to global climate change.

Ignatian Discernment: Does Global Climate Change Exist?

In order to deal with the immense and complex issue of global climate change, it is essential that the group proceed not only carefully and rationally but also engage the imagination and emotions. In this section, we look at how the process of developing a grasp of information related to climate change progresses using Ignatian discernment in a face-to-face group, such as a business unit, small business, or a family, school, church, or neighborhood.

First Step: Reason. The first step in the Ignatian discernment process is to use reason, to state the issue clearly: Is global warming or climate change occurring? If so, does it seem likely that it is a natural occurrence or something that is happening in response to human activity?

It is crucial to gather and to examine the information that is available to determine whether or not global climate change is indeed occurring.[26] The group members individually and collectively examine and then reflect together on some of the readily available material on global climate change. Another way to begin is to view together and discuss the award-winning documentary, *An Inconvenient Truth*, in which Al Gore clearly and succinctly presents complex scientific data that confirm the earth's rising temperatures and shows the effect of greenhouse gas emissions on the earth's temperature. The film also shows some of the effects that this process has had worldwide.[27] Gore states that global warming is a moral and ethical issue, and so demands our attention.

Materials on global climate change are now increasingly found in the popular press. For example, the *New York Times* described the recent reports by the United Nations' Intergovernmental Panel on Climate Change (IPCC), in which droughts were expected in "southern Europe and the Middle East, sub-Saharan Africa, the American Southwest and Mexico, and flooding that could imperil low-lying islands and the crowded river deltas of southern Asia." They noted "that many of the regions facing the greatest risks were among the world's poorest." Although limits on emissions "could lower the long-term risks, vulnerable regions must adjust promptly to shifting weather patterns, climatic and coastal hazards, and rising seas."[28]

For groups that choose to investigate more carefully and in greater detail the scientific data, including probable effects and possible responses, several influential reports of the IPCC and summaries for policy makers are readily available.[29] After gathering the data and weighing the pros and cons as they affect the individuals, the organization, and the larger community, most groups draw their conclusion.

So most human decision-making processes come to a conclusion and stop at this point. Yet, stopping at this point runs the risk of neglecting certain data and not considering valuable, but less popular, points of view. This, in turn, increases the probability of a failed decision. The value of discernment is that it is structured in a way to also encourage the surfacing of less-known information and less "acceptable" positions. Obtaining fuller information, and doing so in a receptive fashion and in prayer, lessens the chance of making an erroneous decision. This is a principal contribution of discernment.

Second Step: Discernment. Discernment builds on the first step described above, but it then shifts to a process that utilizes not only the mind and reason but also the heart, imagination, and prayer. The group uses the earlier rational decision-making process and adds listening, imagination, and prayerful reflection. It is here that what Ignatius called indifference is essential: Within the context of God's love, the members of the decision-making group put aside personal preferences, attachments, and preformed opinions in order to be balanced and open to God's will when making a choice.

The issue is discussed by the individuals in the group with the goal of revealing *all* of the relevant data and points of view. During this process, each individual listens carefully to each of the other persons in the group as everyone presents new information and individual points of view. In this case, questions that the group might pursue are: Is there or is there not substantial evidence that global climate change exists? If so, does it present a problem? What responsibility do we have to the people who are suffering or will suffer from its effects? Is there or is there not evidence that human activity is accelerating it? If yes, what might we as individuals or a group do to mitigate its negative effects?

The group then seeks to arrive at a consensus judgment on the above questions. Recall that those taking part in the discussion are open and accepting of new data and opposing points of view. No one tries to persuade the others that his or her own position is correct. In fact, ideally a person might present data and also the potential consequences that do not support that person's own position. The dialogue proceeds in a prayerful fashion, consciously in the presence of God, until a consensus is reached.

When a consensus judgment is reached, as a confirmation of that judgment the group might then consider the three tests that were earlier suggested by Ignatius: What would you suggest if another person asked for your advice in this matter, keeping in mind that you wish the best for the person and want what is good for the whole community? Imagine that you are on your deathbed, what action would you wish you had taken? Then proceed to make that choice now. Imagine that you are facing God in the last judgment. What action would you wish you had taken? Again, make that choice now.

Group members notice feelings of consolation and desolation. What do such reactions mean to the individual and the group? Is the feeling of consolation coming from God, likely indicating that the decision contributes to the long-term benefit of not only the group but many other people also? If there is an experience of desolation, is it possible to identify the origins of those feelings? Does the desolation stem from a realization that the choice has been made out of selfish reasons or does the sadness or anxiety stem from a realization that the group might have to change or give something up for the greater good?

Let us assume that the group discerns that global climate change is occurring. The group members are then called to engage in a second discernment. What responsibilities do we have to respond to people whose health and safety—even lives—are compromised by its effects, such as drought, fires, flooding, and hurricanes and the consequent destruction and dislocation? If it is agreed that global climate change is caused to a large extent by human activity that generates carbon dioxide pollutants, what responsibilities do we have, individually and collectively, to change our behavior? What actions should we take?

Ignatian Discernment: Possible Actions
to Mitigate Global Climate Change

In this section, we examine how the process of creating an action plan in response to global climate change might develop using Ignatian discernment in a face-to-face group, such as a business unit, small business, or even a family, school, church, or a neighborhood group.

First Step: Reason. Group members review the materials that they examined initially in this particular discernment process. The focus now is to examine actions that the organization might take to alleviate global climate change and respond to its probable effects, such as hurricanes, droughts, and flooding, in various parts of the world.[30] Group members discuss how to lessen the effects of global climate change and put forth specific proposals for personal and organizational change in behavior that would help achieve that end.

As part of this process, they are able to calculate approximately their own contribution to global climate change through carbon dioxide emissions. At the Web site[31] accompanying the documentary *An Inconvenient Truth,* it is estimated that each American generates "about 15,000 pounds of carbon dioxide every year from personal transportation, home energy use and from the energy used to produce all of the products and services we consume." It is possible to assess the number of pounds of carbon dioxide that a family or group generates by using the calculator available at this Web site or at the United States Environmental Protection Agency Web site on climate change.[32]

There are a number of ways that businesses and other organizations, such as churches, schools, and neighborhoods, along with individuals and families, can reduce carbon emissions. Examples range from simple and long-term money-saving options, such as replacing one incandescent light bulb with a compact fluorescent light bulb (saving 150 pounds of carbon dioxide emissions per year), to more complicated and expensive remedies, such as buying or leasing a new hybrid vehicle.

Long-term suggestions include social actions to influence public attitudes and political activity and lobbying to influence legislation. Examples are supporting the campaign of a candidate who backs local or national efforts to reduce carbon dioxide emissions, writing letters to newspapers and magazines, or joining organizations that support the conservation of clean air and water.

Second Step: Discernment. In the discernment process, the group builds upon their rational decision-making process and uses prayerful reflection that involves listening, feeling, imagining, and being aware of the presence of God. Again, indifference is essential as members must put aside their personal preferences, attachments, and opinions in order to be open to understanding what God would want of them in this situation. They interact with respect and a caring attitude for each other as each person presents information and speaks what he believes to be true. Each person listens to the other with an open mind and heart; each teaches and each learns. This conversation takes place in an attitude of prayer with the sense of God's loving presence among the participants.

At this stage, it is important to remain open to the possibilities for action or non action, as brought up by each person, without making any immediate decisions. Each suggestion is considered and the pros and cons for each one are listed out. While doing so, the group considers the following questions: If we take this action, what will be gained? What will be lost? How will others be affected? What do we like? What do we dislike? What are our motives?

Some suggestions can be resolved and acted upon quickly, such as replacing incandescent bulbs with fluorescent bulbs and turning off lights, computers, and televisions when they are not being used. Considering other actions with possible economic and emotional impacts takes a longer time and will involve further study and prayer. For example, disinvesting money from corporations that produce or use only fossil fuels and instead investing in companies that are developing alternate forms of energy such as wind and solar power requires careful consideration. Purchasing more energy efficient appliances, leasing a hybrid automobile, or updating heating and air-conditioning systems are actions that require financial commitment and meeting the individual and collective needs of the group members.

In addition to the three scenarios suggested by Ignatius, the organization or group members can engage the imagination using other scenarios. For example, owners of small businesses engaging in discernment about actions that they might take to reduce global climate change could imagine the business twenty-five or fifty years from now. Where in the world would they choose to locate? How would temperature change affect their suppliers, products, services, and customers? What decisions will they wish they had made now? A family should imagine the plight of their future members, great-grandchildren, and great-great-grandchildren. How might global climate changes affect their lives in the future? What do they want to do now for their future offspring? Or they could imagine a family like theirs in the southern or eastern coast of the United States or in a river delta in Bangladesh and likely to lose their home and perhaps their lives because of hurricanes or flooding. What decisions can they make now to act justly to support such a family?

Paying attention to feelings and physical sensations is part of discernment. As noted earlier, feelings of consolation or desolation are indications of the rightness of a decision. Enacting collective decisions often does not happen overnight. It is a longer process that the group may focus on in an ongoing way, by meeting regularly to evaluate the consolations and desolations that they have experienced as a result of the decisions that they have made.

Summary and Conclusion

Ignatian discernment is a powerful, time-tested, but little-used tool for making major decisions. It can be used by either an individual or a group. When Ignatian spiritual discernment is used carefully, it generally brings to light information and attitudes that would not get considered in purely rational decision making processes, since in the former the imagination is engaged and emotions are considered in the awareness of God's presence. Ignatian discernment provides a wide spectrum of data and positions and lessens the possibility of failed decisions.

Ignatian discernment is most helpful for arriving at decisions that are of vital importance for the individual or the group. It requires time and patience, both of which are in short supply among contemporary managers. Ignatian discernment necessitates the setting aside of personal preferences and biases. It also requires openness to the position of others and a careful consideration of the information that they provide.

Finally, Ignatian discernment urges people to be aware of the feelings of consolation and desolation, both during decision making and after the decision has been made, and to determine the source of those feelings. It also provides several tests of the decision that enable the decision makers to check the validity of the conclusion with the long-term common good and the will of God.

Notes

1. Harvey, F. 2007. Progress on climate change. *Financial Times*, June 11, 16.
2. *Intergovernmental Panel on Climate Change* (IPCC) Working Group III. 2007. Mitigation of climate change. June. http://www.ipcc.ch/.
   Intergovernmental Panel on Climate Change (IPCC) Working Group II. 2007. Impacts, adaptation, and vulnerability. April. http://www.ipcc.ch/.
   Intergovernmental Panel on Climate Change (IPCC) Working Group I. 2007. The physical science basis. February. http://www.ipcc.ch/.
3. Delbecq, A., Liebert, E., Mostyn, J., Nutt, P.C., and Walter, G. 2004. Discernment and strategic decision making: Reflections for a spirituality of organizational leadership. In Moses L. Pava (ed.), *Spiritual intelligence at work: Meaning metaphor and morals. Research in ethical issues in organizations.* 5: 139–174.
4. Lowney, C. 2003. *Heroic leadership: Best practices from a 450-year-old company that changed the world.* Chicago: Loyola Press.
5. Moberg, D.J. and Calkins, M. 2001. Reflection in business ethics: Insights from *St. Ignatius' spiritual exercises. Journal of Business Ethics*, 33(3): 257–70.
6. Gallagher, J.A. and Goodstein, J. 2002. Fulfilling institutional responsibilities in health care: Organizational ethics and the role of mission discernment. *Business Ethics Quarterly*, 12(4): 433–450.
7. Zukowski, A.A. 2005. Discernment in a multi-dimensional world. *Momentum* (November/December): 60–62.
8. Brackley, D. 2004. *The call to discernment in troubled times: New perspectives in the transformative wisdom of Ignatius of Loyola.* New York: Crossroads Publishing.
9. Gallagher, O.M.V. and Timothy, M. 2005. *The discernment of spirits: An Ignatian guide for everyday living.* New York: Crossroad Publishing.
10. Lonsdale, D. 1993. *Listening to the music of the spirit: The art of discernment.* Notre Dame, Indiana: Ave Maria Press.
11. Moberg, D.J. and Calkins, M. 2001.
12. Gallagher, J.A. and Goodstein, J. 2002.
13. Zukowski, A.A. 2005.
14. Gallagher, O.M.V. and Timothy, M. 2005.
15. Toner, S.J. and Jules, J. 1971. A method for communal discernment of God's will. Seminar on Jesuit Spirituality, St. Louis. 3(4).
16. Delbecq, A. et al. 2004.
17. Ganss, S.J. and George E. 1992. *The spiritual exercises of St. Ignatius.* St. Louis: Institute of Jesuit sources. [#53]. The numbers in brackets are from the text of *The spiritual exercises of St. Ignatius.*
18. Brackley, D. 2004.
19. Cavanagh, G. 2006. *American business values: A global perspective.* Upper Saddle River, NJ: Prentice Hall.
20. Nutt, P.C. 2002. *Why decisions fail: The blunders and traps that lead to decision debacles.* San Francisco: Barrett-Koehler.
21. Delbecq, A. et al. 2004.
22. Brackley, D. 2004.

23. Gallagher, O.M.V. and Timothy, M. 2005.

24. Delbecq, A. et al. 2004.

25. Gunther, M. 2001. God and business: Bringing spirituality into the workplace. *Fortune*, July 9: 59–80.

26. Sorkin, L. 2006. Climate change impacts rise. In Starke, L. (ed.), *Vital signs 2006–2007*. New York: W.W. Norton.

27. http://www.climatecrisis.net/takeaction/

28. Kanter, J. and Revkin, A.C. 2007. Scientists detail climate changes, poles to tropics. *New York Times,* April 7. www.nytimes.com.

29. *Intergovernmental Panel on Climate Change* (IPCC) Working Group.

30. Kanter, J. and Revkin, A.C. 2007.

31. http://www.climatecrisis.net/takeaction/

32. http://epa.gov/climatechange/emissions/ind_calculator.html.

Practical Compassion: Toward a Critical Spiritual Foundation for Corporate Responsibility

MARJOLEIN LIPS-WIERSMA AND VENKATARAMAN NILAKANT

Introduction

In the past two decades neoliberalism as an ideology has had far-reaching consequences on how business organizations view their obligations to different stakeholders. Critiques of neoclassical economic theory, which is the basis of neoliberalism, hold that a series of a priori moral principles lay at its heart (McMurthy;[1] Hodgson[2]). In other words, neoclassical economic theory is a construct based on a set of values and assumptions about human conduct. In this chapter, we introduce an alternative set of values and assumptions for managing people and organizations. We introduce practical compassion, a concept that all religions have in common, to engage with the tensions between organizational ideals (as increasingly captured in purpose statements) and the socioeconomic reality in which such organizations find themselves.

We argue that neoliberalism has resulted in a range of management practices and outcomes that are contrary to practical compassion. Examples are erosion of job security, dehumanization of management practice, increased inequality, commodification, and environmental degradation. In recent years, there have been calls for corporate social responsibility (CSR) to mitigate the negative consequences of economic theories of organization. We argue, however, that CSR does not go far enough in addressing the core issues of self-interest versus concern for others that lie at the heart of neoliberalism and the undesirable outcomes described above.

We argue that a critical workplace spirituality (WPS), which engages with the shortcomings of assumptions underpinning neoliberalism, acknowledges the holistic and complex nature of organizational interactions, and engages with organizational goals that transcend self-interest as well as the tensions that arise out of such ideals, can potentially offer an important theoretical and practical alternative.

The chapter is organized as follows: we briefly discuss the effects of neoliberalism on management practice, including CSR practice. Next we discuss the literature on workplace spirituality and describe the conditions under which it can offer a viable alternative. We introduce an alternative set of values and assumptions to that of neoliberal doctrine, named "Practical Compassion," a concept that the original writings of all religious traditions have espoused. We explore four pathways—of "character," "oneness," "human development," and "legacy"—and show how conscious decisions with regard to each of these shape practical compassion and illustrate these with practical examples. We conclude with suggestions for future research and action.

Neoliberalism and Its Discontents

In recent years, a taken-for-granted assumption has pervaded managerial discourse. The assumption is that the primary task of a business organization is to enhance shareholder value. This assumption is part of a larger framework that has become more prominent since the 1980s. This framework, which has been referred to as neoliberalism,[3] is in part due to a radical shift in the underlying institutional logic of business corporations, with the earlier era of managerial capitalism giving way to investor capitalism.[4] Although neoliberalism as an ideology originated in the United States and the United Kingdom, in recent years its policies and practices have rapidly spread to other parts of the world, leading to a convergence toward the U.S. model of capitalism.[5] Drawing from social theories of utilitarianism, libertarianism, and Rawlsian theory of justice, neoliberalism views individual freedom as the indicator and goal of human progress. It draws on two of the components of utilitarianism—consequentialism and welfarism—to argue that all choices must be evaluated by their outcomes and outcomes must enhance individual utilities or personal well-being.[6] It draws on libertarianism and the Rawlsian theory of justice to accord priority to individual liberty.[7] However, it goes beyond Rawls' moderate formulations to assert that personal liberties, including property rights, should take precedence over all other goals.[8] Taken together, neoliberalism "proposes that human well-being can best be advanced by liberating individual entrepreneurial freedoms and skills within an institutional framework characterized by strong private property rights, free markets, and free trade."[9] These individual utilities and personal well-being are best served by pursuing self-interest and hence the ultimate goal of human action from a neoliberal perspective is to pursue self-interest. It is assumed that people either pursue only their own interests with no regard for others' interests or consider others' interests as a means to achieve a personal end.[10] In terms of practical economic strategies and policies, neoliberalism advocates deregulation, privatization, and withdrawal of the state from economic and social activities.

Opponents of neoliberalism have noted its dysfunctional consequences in terms of increased inequality, commodification, environmental degradation, and the substitution of market exchange for human ethics.[11] In the following sections, we briefly discuss its impact on business education and research, internal organizational management, and external social relations.

Impact of Neoliberalism on Business School Education and Research

It has been argued that the dominance of the neoliberal perspective in business schools has discouraged examination of broader social questions in relation to both research and teaching.[12,13,14] As Ghoshal[15] argues, "by propagating ideologically inspired amoral theories, business schools have actively freed their students from any sense of moral responsibility." In relation to business research, Margolis and Walsh[16] found that issues that transcend narrow interests of profit, such as human welfare (which included such constructs as health, satisfaction, justice, social responsibility, and environmental stewardship), were examined in only 19 percent of all articles and 85 percent of these focused their analysis on individual-level phenomena, such as job satisfaction. Less than 2 percent of the outcomes were conceptualized at societal level. On the basis of this research, the authors conclude that it appears that both social objectives and societal issues have had a tenuous standing in organization and management research. Ghoshal,[17] in an eloquent critique of the effects of neoclassical economic theories on management research and teaching, argues that these economic theories are pretences for knowledge, ideologies masquerading as science and devoid of any morality or ethics. More importantly, as Ghoshal observes, adoption of these false ideas dehumanizes managerial practice.

Internal Consequences of Neoliberalism

Within organizations, neoliberal pursuit of self-interest coupled with property rights has led to the adoption of a single goal to guide and monitor managerial behavior. This is the goal of maximizing shareholder value.[18] One of the consequences of this is to treat an organization not as a social institution but as a nexus of contracts.[19] Within this paradigm, employees are seen as costs, which in turn leads organizations to downsize and restructure in order to enhance shareholder value. Job losses have been justified on the grounds that they were necessary to make the organizations more competitive, even though no consistent evidence was found that downsizing led to improved financial performance.[20,21]

Neoliberalism has led to highly competitive organizations, climates and reward structures that support self-interest, loose networks as a result of constant restructuring, and a high turnover of CEOs (increasingly appointed from outside the firm rather than promoted from within) who are primarily judged on short-term results. There is ample evidence that this organizational context impacts on moral decision making. Moral decision making is negatively correlated with organizational settings that promote high competition,[22] organizational climates that support self-interest,[23] and organizations with loose social networks.[24] It is positively correlated with exemplary ethical leadership.[25] Despite these findings, the dominance of neoliberalism has tended to suppress explicit inquiry into ethical and moral aspects of business. As Bird and Waters[26] found, managers demonstrate a reluctance to describe their actions in moral terms, even when they are acting for moral reasons. "They talk as if their actions were guided exclusively by organizational interests, practicality, and economic good sense even when in practice they honour morally defined standards, codified in law, professional convictions, and social mores."[27]

Social and Environmental Consequences
of Neoliberalism

Sennett[28] identifies a number of negative consequences of neoliberal policies on society that resulted in short-term employment structures, rapid redundancies of both new and old skills, collapse of company loyalty, and the uncertain social world of those moving from job to job. Sennett argues that, as a result of such patterns, we are in danger of losing our ability to place ourselves in a narrative and to see continuity in our lives. Loss of coherence, Sennett argues, leads to loss of character, breakdown in moral behavior, and loss of community.

A major criticism of neoliberal policies is that they have resulted in increasing inequality around the world by creating a "winner-take-all" society.[29,30] While "corporate America has increased its share of national income from 7% in mid-2001 to 13% this year…the real weekly wage of a typical American worker in the middle of the income distribution has fallen by 4% since the start of the recovery in 2001."[31] The share of America's top 1 percent earners in total income has gone up from 8 percent in 1980 to 16 percent in 2006.

The strong materialistic approach of neoliberal policies has also led to rampant consumerism. Hamilton and Denniss[32] borrow the term affluenza, first used by de Graaf in the United States, to refer to a painful, contagious, socially transmitted condition of overload, debt, anxiety, and waste resulting from the dogged pursuit of more.[33] These pressures lead to psychological disorders, alienation, and distress, causing people to self-medicate with mood-altering drugs and excessive alcohol consumption.[34]

Finally, there is increasing evidence that the drive for ongoing growth that is core to neoliberalism is not environmentally sustainable.[35]

CSR Perspective

CSR, which emerged as a reaction to neoliberalism, seeks to alleviate some of its dysfunctional features by paying attention to social goals. The CSR literature portrays attention to social goals as a win–win situation for corporations. The majority of conceptual and empirical CSR papers strive to establish a relationship between CSR initiatives and profitability.[36] However, the literature has relatively underemphasized situations involving trade-offs or zero-sum games between social obligations and profits.[37] Even though the relationship between CSR and corporate financial performance (CFP) is not straight forward,[38] firms tend to justify CSR initiatives in terms of profitability rather than ethical conduct. As the CEO of GE remarked, "We are investing in environmentally cleaner technology because we believe it will increase our revenue, our value and our profits...Not because it is trendy or moral, but because it will accelerate our growth and make us more competitive."[39]

Margolis and Walsh[40] suggest that there are a range of consequences of studying CSR within the neoliberalist framework. First, it may reinforce rather than relieve the tensions surrounding corporate responses to social misery as it confirms the economic neoliberal model and accepts its assumptions. As a result, ethical dilemmas between normative and instrumental claims are not addressed and moral muteness continues to be prevalent. In the case of Shell, for example, profit regularly seems to have won over principles.[41]

Singer[42,43] claims that most ethical strategies do little to overcome the limitations of markets and capitalism. He argues that in current neoliberal society, business organizations oppose a strong role for unions, corporate offerings are positioned in ways that create superficial desires and sustain economic externalities, and corporations form pressure groups to maintain patent rights, lower corporate taxes, and stop carbon emission taxes. For instance, the Competitive Enterprise Institute, which describes itself as a "nonprofit public policy organization dedicated to advancing the principles of free enterprise and limited government," has an advertisement campaign that claims that carbon dioxide emissions are good for sustaining life.[44] Hence, as Singer[45] claims, corporations currently are often working against a redistribution of wealth and against environmental recovery. According to him, the negative effects of neoliberalism cannot be mitigated unless we engage with the limitations of the neoliberalist system itself. This involves paying attention to dualities, tensions, and contradictions of firms that try to do good within such a system.

To summarize, CSR perspectives that are confined within a neoliberal ideology ignore the tensions, contradictions, and dilemmas that arise as managers try to satisfy multiple stakeholders. This is because the adoption of CSR within an economic framework results in reframing the organization's responsibility from pure self-interest to "enlightened" self-interest, which essentially translates into "we will do good in order to do well" or "we will do good as long as we do well." We argue that the perspectives that question the underlying values and assumptions in neoliberal economics are needed because (1) there will always be substantial cases of ethical and responsible behavior not leading to increased financial performance;[46] (2) ethical and responsible behavior are found to be driven as much by value-priorities as they are by financial incentives (Margolis and Walsh;[47] Graafland and van de Ven;[48] Tetlock[49]); and (3) if we cynically dismiss higher collective aspirations there is little hope of moral progress.[50,51]

In the next section we assess whether, at present, WPS provides an alternative perspective that questions the underlying values and assumptions in neoliberal theory.

Workplace Spirituality: An Alternative to Neoliberalism or More of the Same?

Critics of the workplace spirituality perspective would argue that it is another form of neoliberalism in that it aims at capturing the hearts and souls of individuals for financial gain. The driving question for most of the WPS studies has been "How does spirituality affect organizational performance?"[52]

There are many examples of WPS articles that aim to show that corporate attention to the human spirit is perfectly consistent with maximizing wealth.[53,54,55] We use the article of Jurkiewicz and Giacalone[56] as an example of this type of theorizing because it is well-argued and comprehensively anchored in extant literature. Jurkiewicz and Giacalone position WPS as a reactive response to the social and business upheaval that has resulted in alienated employees (thus, as a response to the negative side effects of neoliberalism). Employees, it is argued, seek to reconnect to (1) themselves through personal growth as a result of work; (2) others through a more genuine sense of community at work; and (3) some purpose beyond their own self-interest. Jurkiewicz and Giacalone then argue that given that these employee concerns may be viewed (presumably by the academic and management powers that be) to have little demonstrable impact on the bottom line, they have not been given priority in other management theories. They create a "demand" for WPS theory by demonstrating its relevance to profit rather than questioning the assumptions underlying its exclusive focus on shareholder value. In their paper, Jurkiewicz and Giacalone also aim to provide WPS with more credibility by identifying spirituality as a component of organizational culture. They quote a significant body of literature that has found that culture has strong ties to economic performance, is likely to influence per capita real output produced in an economy, and contributes to the level of per capita material wealth. Next, they identify a series of spiritual values and postulate that the degree of WPS evident in a culture is indicated by the positive expression of these values.

It could therefore be argued that workplace spirituality is not providing any, let alone an adequate, alternative for neoliberalism. However, when we study the spiritual values (and language) that Jurkiewicz and Giacalone (and many others in the WPS field) employ, we arrive at a slightly different picture. These are such values as benevolence, generativity, integrity, humanism, and satisfaction. These are not instrumental values, but desirable end states in themselves. However, Jurkiewicz and Giacalone, along with others in the WPS literature, do not really engage in a debate as to whether these values are compatible with hyper competition, loose networks, and temporary employment contracts.

We suggest that for workplace spirituality to make a contribution to management theory, and in particular management theory that contributes to human and ecological well-being, distinctions need to be made between economic freedom and spiritual freedom. Such distinctions inevitably lead to a reassessment of the fundamental purpose of business organizations. In addition, distinctions need to be made between individualized spirituality as consciousness-informing choices (i.e., the choice to behave benevolently) and a spirituality that holistically engages complex organizational systems. Finally, distinctions need to be made between a spirituality that advocates an (often utopian) ideal versus a spirituality that is a process of engaging with the reality in which it finds itself.

Economic and Spiritual Freedoms:
The Case for Practical Compassion

Despite its shortcomings, questions of underlying values and assumptions are also increasingly being raised within WPS. Benefiel,[57] asks "if spirituality is ultimately about nonmaterialistic concerns, is it appropriate to focus on the material gains to be reaped by integrating spirituality into organizational life?" Mitroff and Denton[58] write, "Spirituality may well be the ultimate competitive advantage. However, herein lies a fundamental paradox; those who practice spirituality in order to achieve better corporate results undermine both its practice and its ultimate benefits." Steingard[59] observes that "... current attempts to situate spirituality within management transmogrify the freshness, depth, and transformative potential of spirituality into yet another vehicle to more efficiently produce the materialist ends of business demands."

In other words, for WPS to become a force for social change, it needs to question the neoliberal values and assumptions, particularly the exclusive focus on self-interest, and pay attention to that which assists projects of emancipation and sustainability such as distributive justice and social activism.

Sen[60] distinguishes between two types of behavior in terms of concern for others. When our self-interest is served by concern for others, we are acting with "sympathy," or enlightened self-interest. However, when we decide to ignore our self-interest in order to help others, we are acting with "commitment."[61] The notion of commitment is distinct from enlightened self-interest because it involves making *sacrifices* in order to pursue values such as social justice or protecting the environment.[62]

A spiritual perspective would argue that our spiritual duty is to use our free will to help and not harm others and to further their ends. There is response born in this encounter: it is limitless, it is my responsibility, and it shapes and defines the nature of my *freedom*. My response is not contingent on who the "Other" is, and is not reciprocal.[63] Ultimate spiritual freedom is based on the extent to which we can transcend our self-interest and is thus clearly distinguished from economic freedom, which is based, at its best, on enlightened self-interest.

We agree with rational choice theorists and the neoliberal perspective that individuals seek to maximize their welfare. However, we differ from the neoliberal perspective by arguing that economic well-being is not synonymous with individual welfare. We argue that human beings, irrespective of their ethnicity, race, gender, or sexual/ political preferences, have two universal needs—the desire for happiness and the need for meaning. All economic activities and varieties of human conduct are merely expressions of these two fundamental desires.

Religions and wisdom traditions of the world can also be seen as an attempt to provide solutions to this elusive quest for meaning and happiness. Between 900 and 200 BCE, the so-called axial age, philosophers and sages from different regions of the world arrived at the same solution to reconcile these two needs.[64] Thus people like Buddha, Socrates, Plato, Confucius, Jeremiah, Ezekiel, the mystics of the Upanishads, Mencius, and Euripides in the initial period, as well as Muhammad and Jesus later on, reframed divinity as deep respect and reverence for others, giving rise to the golden rule—treat others as you would want to be treated yourself. Their view of a spiritual life was one based on the acknowledgment of divinity in oneself and others. However, in order to arrive at this state, which they saw as the perfect union of meaning and happiness (bliss), individuals had to transcend their egoism and selfishness and particularly petty desires, cruelty, envy, greed, pride, and hatred.

According to the axial age philosophers and sages, the realization of divinity with and in others is a challenging task, requiring one to undergo suffering and pain. The suffering and pain is associated with letting go of one's ego and selfishness and is comparable to cleansing oneself. The axial age philosophers and sages emphasized that the most effective way to achieve this was through compassion—the humane quality of understanding the sufferings of others and wanting to do something about it. We have termed it as practical compassion because it entails the quest for transcendence while engaging with the realities of day-to-day living.

Practical compassion is both a spiritual quest and a practical activity in that it does not advocate the abandonment of self-interest for exclusive pursuit of altruism, which can be dysfunctional without a moral basis.[65] The golden rule, as Ciulla argues, "provides the bridge between altruism and self interest."[66] Practical compassion, like the golden rule, acknowledges the limits of self-interest and recognizes that there are times when individuals and organizations are required to act against their self-interest for the common good.

Thus transcending self-interest is not just a nice thing to do as long as it does not conflict with other desired outcomes such as pleasure and material wealth. It is also not a prerequisite for spiritual living; it is in fact the very definition of spiritual living itself. In determining the highest purpose of an organization, we ask "What is the ultimate reason for existence of your organization? What is your vision of the future that you are contributing to?" Such a purpose would be arrived at as a consequence of consultation among all members of the organization. Such a purpose moves the organization from answering "Why do we exist?" to answering "Why should we exist?" and serves as the moral foundation of the organization. For human beings to transcend ego and engage in practical compassion, we argue, an organization needs to have a purpose beyond profit, as this enables humanity to collectively rise above self-interest.

Adopting the highest purpose as the core purpose of an organization implies establishing an objective as important as the viability of the firm itself. From a spiritual perspective the firm, regardless of its financial success, would not be viewed as viable without a true commitment to the highest purpose.[67] Purpose statements that commit the organization to the common good are progressively more in place in a wide range of business organizations. The following organizations that we use as examples to illustrate our ideas have the following purpose statements:

- Seventh Generation: to lead and inspire other organizations to foster positive environmental change, make the world a better place, contribute to a society whose guiding principles include sustainability, justice, and compassion for all living creatures and contribute to the restoration of the earth.
- Scott Bader: Scott Bader's purpose statement includes such principles as "environmental care," "equality of opportunity," and "human dignity."
- Interface Carpets: To be the first company that, by its deeds, shows the entire industrial world what sustainability is in all its dimensions: People, process, product, place, and profits (by 2020) and in doing so we will become restorative through the power of influence.
- Reell Precision Manufacturing: We are passionately committed to both serve the common good and contribute to our customers' competitive advantage by developing and providing torque control products of exceptional value.

From a spiritual perspective, organizations can be viewed as instruments to achieve practical compassion. While financial viability is an important goal for an organization, from a spiritual perspective, it is the means to achieve the organization's highest purpose, which is to provide an arena for its members to pursue transcendent goals while they engage with organizational tasks. We believe that the workplace spirituality literature can make a distinctive contribution to mainstream organization studies if it focuses on the highest purpose of organizations, which provides the means for individuals to engage in practical compassion.

The unique contribution of the WPS literature lies in the facilitation of a shift from self-interest through enlightened self-interest to practical compassion, where organizations are willing to forego their

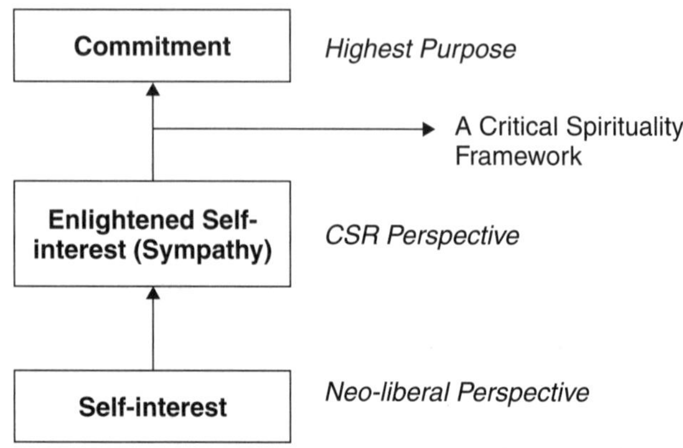

Figure 4.1   The Movement toward Practical Compassion

self-interest in order to commit to goals that will benefit humanity as
a whole (see figure 4.1).

Holistic Responsibility

Workplace spirituality theory and practice can contribute to the extent
that it enhances understanding of the holistic and complex nature of
stakeholder management, rather than simplifying spirituality to individualized consciousness–informing choices.

Hope and vision, developing virtues, and commitment to goals
that benefit humanity as a whole are neither achieved in isolation
of other stakeholders nor through a surefire set of steps or tools.
As Mitroff, commenting on future possibilities for spiritual business
practices, suggests[68] "a systemic approach is a sine qua non condition for any kind of sustainable change to take place." From a spiritual perspective, such approaches would be holistic in the sense that
these would balance a variety of practices as well as the needs of
the various stakeholders. While commitment to goals that benefit
humanity will lie at the foundation of organizations developing on
a spiritual basis, an organization that focuses on leaving a legacy
without ensuring the mental, emotional, and spiritual welfare of its
own employees does not live up to its spiritual purpose. Similarly,
an organization that only focuses on reflective spiritual practices,
such as mindfulness, but does not pay attention to the needs of the

world, does not fully live up to its spiritual purpose either. These issues of complexity, in which an organization attends to a range of stakeholders and management practices simultaneously, are founded on the notion of adequation.[69] This is a philosophical (Plato) as well as theological (Thomas Aquinas) principle that posits that a system, such as an organization, must contain the same level of complexity internally as that expressed in its external environment. It is in engaging with this complexity that compassion becomes sustainable and hence practical.

Practical Compassion

To become a force for social change, we argue, WPS needs to work with and give meaning to the tensions that arise from acting in accordance with a purpose beyond profit in a neoliberal business climate. Spirituality has a rich tradition of engaging with the struggle of living with imperfect selves in an imperfect world (e.g., Evans[70]), and bringing this knowledge into extant management theory and practice could well be one of its most significant contributions.

The Benedictine monk, Anselm Grün, writes about the importance of combining "spirituality from above" and "spirituality from below." Spirituality from above emerges from the human desire to ever improve, rise to greater heights, and achieve nearness to God. This type of spirituality is very important; it provides us with ideals, hope, purpose, and inspiration; in other words, it provides the individual and collective strength to rise above ourselves. If, as Singer[71] argues, "these higher collective aspirations are routinely or cynically dismissed, there is little hope of general moral progress. Yet the latter is needed, both as an end in itself and as a means to sustain the prerequisites for the effective operation of markets and hence enterprise success." However, with a spirituality that focuses on our higher collective aspirations alone, we may lose the connection between ideal and reality, feel hopeless or inadequate, or disengage as a result of cynicism and burnout. So, while it is a distinct strength of workplace spirituality theory to engage with spiritual ideals, this may become its weakness when it ignores the less than ideal social and economic environment in which organizations need to operate.

In view of the above, we conceptualize spirituality as the effort to pursue an ideal of a higher purpose within the practical constraints of everyday organizational life and the context in which this takes place.

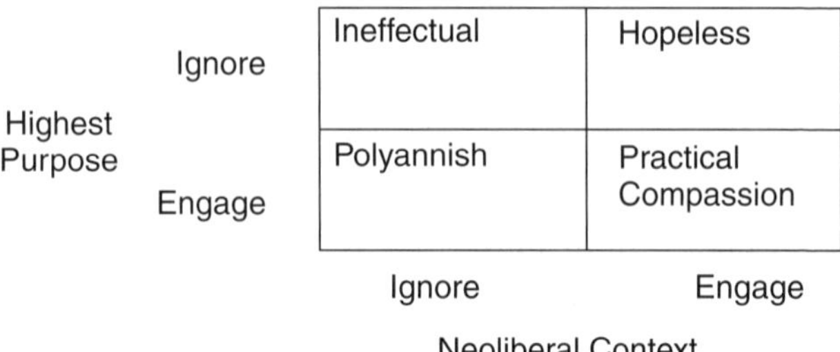

Figure 4.2　Practical Compassion

A spirituality that engages with nonmaterial purposes of organizations without engaging with the constraints put on current business organizations through neoliberalism can become Pollyanish. On the other hand, spirituality that engages with these constraints without exploring the spiritual ideal is without aspirations and without hope. Hence, commitment is achieved through simultaneously engaging with their commitment to their highest purpose and the challenges or constraints to this ideal. Figure 4.2 illustrates this quest for the highest purpose within the context set by neoliberalism.

Pathways for Practical Compassion

There are a number of ways in which organizations can pursue their highest purpose of engaging in practical compassion. We suggest four pathways for engaging in practical compassion. We refer to these as (1) Character; (2) Human Development; (3) Oneness; and (4) Legacy. The extent of compassion in each of these pathways is determined by how the organization responds when its ideals hit practical reality. We suggest that such a response is on a continuum between "increased commitment to the higher purpose" (that is a lasting intrinsic commitment to spiritual principle) and "anticipatory adaptation" (that is change and adaptation of practices in anticipation of a material reward). We propose that in engaging in these tensions, and making conscious choices in response to them, the organization is likely to become more closely committed to its highest purpose beyond profit. If it ignores them, it is more likely to translate neoliberal assumptions into a range of self-interested managerial practices. We illustrate these pathways with four examples.

Character

Organizational values can be on a continuum in which they serve self-interest (what we call "image") and serve other-interest (what we call "virtue"). The pathway of character is one where the organization distinguishes between image and virtue and, over time, moves further toward virtue. Image is driven by two assumptions, first that the organization has a set of values to enhance corporate image[72] and, second, that such a set of values is to be manipulated to increase employee productivity. Character of an organization describes "what is" and "what should be" rather than what "appears to be"[73] even when not expedient.

Seventh Generation, a manufacturer of personal-care products and household products, for example, found that its baby wipes still had a trace of chlorine in them. This was not immediately harmful to the image of the company, as they did not advertise that their products were chlorine-free and they were still by far the best in the market. However, it was felt that this was not consistent with the character of the company, as "it bugged us that we were not able to make a fast and hard commitment to ourselves as to how long we would be willing to accept this undisclosed inauthenticity and continue to collectively rationalize that it was okay to do so." Working with the supplier, Seventh Generation eventually found a solution to this problem, but only after facilitating many discussions about the company's purpose and ongoing dialogue about moral issues (i.e., should we do a self-critique on our Web site? what if our competitors have a field day with this?).[74] Seventh Generation could have chosen to concentrate on the image side of this (potential) issue, or have consciously or unconsciously decided not to do anything, given that there was no image problem. However, on the continuum between image and virtue, they decided to engage with the way they were living up to their commitment. This practice of shifting the organization an inch further along the character pathway reminds managers and employees to see the moral significance of each decision, to maintain coherence of all members around purpose, and push technological development and cooperation with suppliers, thus, in this case enhancing commitment to its higher purpose.

Human Development

Empowerment can be on a continuum in which it serves self-interest (what we call "controlled freedom") and serves other-interest (what we call "true liberty"). The pathway of human development is one where the organization distinguishes between controlled freedom and true liberty and, over time, moves further toward true liberty. Controlled freedom is characterized by empowering organizational members to achieve organizational goals. True liberty, on the other hand, entails focus on the capabilities of people to do and be what they value.[75]

Human development takes place in an environment where management and employees experience true liberty. In controlling freedom, employees are only empowered and grown to the extent that this meets the flexibility and creativity demands of the market, and thus "however well-meaning the intentions of empowerment programs, they will always be constrained by managerial/executive prerogatives and notions of inclusivity—who is, and who is not, to 'be' empowered and in what form."[76] True liberty is more complex.

Scott Bader, which is a manufacturer of specialty resins, polymers, and composites shows "a tussle between ideal and reality, between vision and business demands."[77] Employees partake in major strategic decisions and are encouraged to take part in all activities of the company, its management, and its social responsibilities, so "whether you are a fitter or an accountant, you are equal when it comes to fulfilling these wider functions."[78] People in this company were found to be "real individuals" "the grumpy engineer who is fed up with a recent change, the angry fitter who wants greater adherence to the principles and no outsourcing, the manager who says clearly that this is no Utopia and that divisions exist." As Scott Bader has expanded, and experienced more tensions between its own commitment and the neoliberal environment in which it is operating, it has in some ways almost automatically reverted to more "controlled freedom" with external management recruitment, more managerial layers and formalized structures leading to more of a "them" and "us" feeling.[79] However, at the same time, in the ongoing response to its commitment to the common good, "true liberty" is pursued through increased efforts in workers' education, in the hope of not only kindling their enthusiasm for participation, but also developing the capacity to participate in an increasingly complex business world. In addition, British commonwealth members of SB started to express the need for creating similar provisions for workers in overseas companies, and social principles were harmonized across subsidiaries. This has led to many cocreative conversations in which principles were revised and citizenship experienced at a more inclusive systems level. Scott Bader has stuck to its principles for over half a century, partly as a result of its ongoing efforts toward human development.[80]

Oneness

Stakeholder management can be on a continuum in which it serves self-interest (what we call "exclusion") and serves other-interest (what we call "inclusion"). The pathway of oneness involves distinguishing between inclusion and exclusion and, over time, moving toward inclusion. An organization that is exclusive will primarily see stakeholder management as a communication exercise in which it keeps stakeholders informed and soothes possible concerns. An inclusive organization works from the premises of interdependence and oneness and uses such consultation to articulate and develop moral principles and purpose in the organization[81] and embeds this understanding in core strategies on an ongoing basis.

Oticon Corporation, Denmark, is in the business of producing hearing aids. Its original purpose statement was situated quite strongly in the neoliberal environment in which they operated. They simply wanted to be "the best." In asking themselves whether they were indeed serving the common good, they decided to listen very carefully to their clients. They became aware that they were too oriented toward what they were technically able to accomplish, whereas their clients wanted smaller hearing aids with a more comfortable sound. In becoming more inclusive, they changed their purpose statement from "making the most powerful hearing aids" to "making hearing aids that best serve the human needs of hearing—impaired people."[82]

The first principle of Reell Precision Manufacturing (RPM), which is in the business of producing high-design hinges, clutches, and springs reads "We recognise that profitability is necessary to continue the business, realize our full potential and fulfil our responsibilities to shareholders, but our commitments to coworkers and customers come before short-term profits." The first principle has often been tested, for example, during the 2001 downturn when Reell was faced with serious losses. As the new CEO states, "…The way we went through this together and the dialogue we had around how to deal with the 30 percent drop in revenues was a very collaborative process. The wisdom didn't come from any one place. Seeing the power of all that collectivity and seeing the good result was very confirming." Reell asks how they could ensure the survival of the company and at the same time stay true to their human agenda which, among other goals, makes the security and growth of employees the highest priority of the company. Reell leaders decided not to lay off anyone. First they minimized profits to zero. When that was not enough, they asked everyone to take a pay-cut, but rather than deciding on an across-the-board pay-cut, they did a graduated pay-cut. Thus, the CEOs took a 17 percent pay-cut while most hourly workers took a 7 percent pay-cut and those who earned less than $11.40 took no pay-cut at all. The president described the coworkers' response: "When we called everyone together and explained the situation we faced, and then announced our graduated pay-cuts, there were tears in people's eyes. They thanked us from the bottom of their hearts." Executive pay within Reell was modest to begin with. The CEO received no more than six times the lowest pay of any employee who has been there for five years, and just ten times the lowest starting pay, in stark contrast to the eighty to one hundred times ratios not uncommon in U.S. companies today (Case documented in "Soul at Work" by Benefiel[83]).

Reel has found that where it has been inclusive of its employees, committed to dialogue, discernment, and reverence, the opportunities and threats coming its way have led to deeper transformation and became opportunities to reflect more clearly on itself and learn how to become more inclusive of all stakeholders, including its employees.

Legacy

Corporate responsibility can be on a continuum in which it serves self-interest (what we call "doing the minimum to primarily address business needs") and serve other-interest (what we call "doing the maximum to serve the needs of humanity and the planet" and leave a legacy). The pathway of legacy is one where the organization distinguishes between doing the minimum and maximum and, over time, moves further toward leaving a positive legacy to all humanity and the planet. Minimalist approaches are usually focused on waste management and technological advances that also meet costs savings (usually in production), whereas the pathway of legacy requires the organization to consistently reflect on how the sum of what it hands down truly benefits the next generations.

Reading Hawken's *The Ecology of Commerce*[84] led Ray Anderson, owner of Interface Carpets, to see his accomplishments in an entirely new light. From the point of view espoused by Hawken, Anderson's life was not the simple story of innovation, growth, prosperity, and progress he always thought it was. Interface Carpets, while being a financial success story, had, in Anderson's words, "abysmally failed to conduct its operations in a way that could be sustained into the future." Anderson felt that while Interface was not breaking any environmental laws, it was breaking an unspoken moral contract with the members of the next generation and generations after that. Interface carpets did not only look at technological resolutions, it introduced a comprehensive waste-management program. While the way it did this is in tension with the current neoliberal social and economic environment, Interface Carpets kept looking at what more it could do and as a result reinvented itself from being a product provider to a service provider through its carpet leasing program. Interface is well on the way to internalizing all externalities,[85] and it has consistently expanded its purpose statement to continue to expand its own commitment to the legacy of restorative practice.

Conclusion and Suggestions for Future Research

In this chapter, we have offered an alternative to the neoliberal perspective that dominates research and practice in management. Even though perspectives such as CSR and WPS have attempted to move beyond self-interest, they primarily aim to mitigate the internal and external consequences of neoliberal policies while accommodating the assumptions and values of the neoliberal perspective. We propose that a shift from self-interest through enlightened self-interest to commitment results in different organizational practices. We contend that such practices already exist and that they deserve further study. For WPS to become a force for social change, further study requires a systemic approach, which elicits descriptive data, is sensitive to the journeys that organizations take, and is inclusive of the dilemmas and contradictions that are inevitable in the search for a common good in a neoliberal business environment.

Notes

1. McMurthy, J. 2003. The life-blind structure of the neoclassical paradigm: A critique of Bernard Hodgon's *Economics as moral science. Journal of Business Ethics*, 44(4): 377–389.
2. Hodgson, B. 2001. *Economics as a moral science.* Berlin: Springer-Verlag.
3. Chomsky, N. 1998. *Profit over people: Neoliberalism and global order.* New York: Seven Stories Press.
4. Useem, M. 1996. *Investor capitalism: How money managers are changing the face of corporate America.* New York : Basic Books.
5. Whitman, M.N. 2003. American capitalism and global convergence: After the bubble. Discussion Paper no. 540. Presented at Research Seminar in International Economics, Gerald R. Ford School of Public Policy, University of Michigan, Ann Arbor, Michigan.
6. Sen, A. 1999. *Development as freedom.* New York: Alfred A. Knopf.
7. Rawls, J. 1971. *A theory of justice.* Cambridge, MA: Harvard University Press.
8. Nozick, R. 1974. *Anarchy, state, and utopia.* New York: Basic Books.
9. Harvey, David. 2005. *A brief history of neoliberalism.* New York: Oxford University Press.
10. Rocha, H.O. and Ghoshal, S. 2006. Beyond self-interest revisited. *Journal of Management Studies*, 43(3): 585–619.
11. Harvey, D. 2005.
12. Stern, R.N. and Barley, S.R. 1996. Organizations and social systems: Organizational theory's neglected mandate. *Administrative Science Quarterly*, 41(1): 146–163.
13. Pfeffer, J. and Fong, C.T. 2004. The business school "business": Some lessons from the US experience. *Journal of Management Studies*, 41(8): 1501–1520.
14. Humphries, M. and Suzette, D. 2005. Introducing critical theory to the management classroom: An exercise building on Jermier's "Life of Mike." *Journal of Management Education*, 29(1): 169–195.
15. Ghoshal, S. 2005. Bad management theories are destroying good management practices. *Academy of Management Learning & Education*, (1): 75–91.
16. Margolis, J.D. and Walsh, J.P. 2003. Misery loves companies: Rethinking social initiatives by business. *Administrative Science Quarterly* (June 2003): 286–305.
17. Ghoshal, S. 2005.
18. Useem, M. 1996.
19. Jensen, M. and Meckling, W. 1976. Theory of the firm, managerial behavior, agency costs and ownership structure. *Journal of Financial Economics*, (3): 305–360.
20. Cascio, W.F. 2005. Strategies for responsible restructuring. *Academy of Management Executive*, 19(4): 39–50; 44–45.
21. Stearns, L.B. 1994. Book review of executive defence: Shareholder power and corporate reorganization. *Administrative Science quarterly*, 39 (1): 174–176.
22. Butterfield, K.D., Trevino, L.K., and Weaver, G.R. 2000. Moral awareness in business organizations: Influences of issue-related and social context factors. *Human Relations*, 53(7): 981–1018.
23. Trevino, L.K., Butterfield, K.D., and McCabe, D.L. 1998. The ethical context in organizations, influences on employee attitudes and behaviors. *Business Ethics Quarterly*, 8(3): 447–477.

24. Brass, D.J., Butterfield, K.B., and Skaggs B.C. 1998. Relationships and ethical behavior: A social network perspective. *Academy of Management Review*, 1(23): 14–31.

25. Trevino, L.K. and Brown, M.E. 2004. Managing to be ethical: Debunking five business ethics myths. *Academy of Management Executive*, 2(18): 69–83.

26. Bird, F.B. and Waters, J.A. 1989. The moral muteness of managers. *California Management Review*, 32 (1): 73–88.

27. Ibid.

28. Sennett, R. 1998. *The corrosion of character: The personal consequences of work in the new capitalism*. New York: W.W. Norton.

29. Stiglitz, J.E. 2002. *Globalization and its discontents*. New York: W.W. Norton.

30. Frank, R.H. and Cook, P.J. 1995. *The winner-take-all society*. New York: Free Press.

31. *Economist*. 2006. The new titans: A survey of the world economy. September 16.

32. Hamilton, C. and Denniss, D. 2005. *Affluenza: When too much is never enough*. Crows Nest, NSW: Allen & Unwin.

33. De Graaf, J., Wann, D., Naylor, T. H., Horsey, D., and Simon, S. 2002. *Affluenza: The all-consuming epidemic*. San Francisco: Berrett-Koehler.

34. Hamilton, C. and Denniss, D. 2005. 179–180.

35. Balland, J.M., Bardhan, P., and Bowles, S. eds. 2007. *Inequality, cooperation and environmental sustainability*. Princeton: Princeton University Press.

36. Margolis, J.D. and Walsh, J.P. 2003.

37. Haigh, M. and Jones M.T. 2006. The drivers of corporate social responsibility: A critical review. *Business Review*, 5(2): 245–251.

38. Vogel, D. 2005. *The market for virtue: The potential and limits of corporate social responsibility*. CA: Brookings Institution Press.

39. *Economist*, 2005. Business and climate change: Feeling the heat. May 12.

40. Margolis, J.D. and Walsh, J.P. 2003.

41. Taylor, B. 2006. Shell shocked: Why do good companies do bad things? *Corporate Governance*, 14(3): 181–192.

42. Singer, A.E. 2002. Global business and the dialectic: Towards an ecological understanding. *Human Systems Management*, 20(1): 22–43.

43. Singer, A.E. 2003. Enterprise action for the common good: Market limitations as strategic problems. *Journal of Enterprising Culture*, 11(1): 69–88.

44. http://www.cei.org/pages/co2.cfm

45. Singer, A.E. 2002.

46. Vogel, D. 2005.

47. Margolis, J.D. and Walsh, J.P. 2003.

48. Graafland, J. and van der Ven, B. 2006. Strategic and moral motivation for corporate social responsibility. *Journal of Corporate Citizenship* (Summer 2006): 111–123.

49. Tetlock, P.E. 2000. Cognitive biases and organizational correctives: Do both disease and cure depend on the politics of the beholder? *Administrative Science Quarterly*, 45: 239–329.

50. Singer, A.E. 2002.

51. Singer, A.E. 2003.

52. Benefiel, M. 2003. Irreconcilable foes? The discourse of spirituality and the discourse of organizational science. *Organization*, 10(2): 383–391.

53. Tischler, L., Biberman, J., and Mckeage, R. 2002. Linking emotional intelligence, spirituality and workplace performance: Definitions, models and ideas for research. *Journal of Managerial Psychology*, 17(3): 203–219.

54. Garcia-Zamor, J.C. 2003. Workplace spirituality and organizational performance. *Public Administration Review*, 63(3): 355–363.

55. Duchon, D. and Ashmos, D. 2005. Nurturing the spirit at work: Impact on work unit performance. *Leadership Quarterly*, 16(5): 807–824.

56. Jurkiewicz, C.L. and Giacalone, R.A. 2004. A values framework for measuring the impact of workplace spirituality on organizational performance. *Journal of Business Ethics*, 49(2): 129–142.

57. Benefiel, M. 2003.

58. Mitroff, I.I. and Denton, E.A. 1999. *A spiritual audit of corporate America. A hard look at spirituality, religion and values.* San Francisco: Jossey-Bass Publishers. xviii.

59. Steingard, D. 2005. Spiritually informed management theory. *Journal of Management Inquiry*, (14)3: 227–242.

60. Sen, A. 1999.

61. Ibid.

62. Ibid.

63. Colier, J. and Estaban, R. 1999. Governance in the participative organization: Freedom, creativity and ethics. *Journal of Business Ethics*, 21(2/3): 173–188.

64. Armstrong, K. 2006. *The great transformation: The beginning of our religious traditions.* New York: Alfred A. Knopf.

65. Ciulla, J.B. 2006. The heart of leadership. In Maak, T. and Pless, N.M. (eds.), *Responsible leadership.* Routledgs: New York. 17–32.

66. Ibid.

67. Lips-Wiersma, M.S.   Forthcoming. Workplace spirituality, towards what purpose? In Barry, D. and Hansen, H. (eds.), *The Sage handbook of new and emerging approaches to management and organization studies.* London: Sage.

68. Pauchant, T.C. (ed). 2003. *Ethics and spirituality at work, hopes and pitfalls of the search of meaning in organizations.* Wesport, CT: Quorum.

69. Ibid.

70. Evans, D. 1979. *Struggle and fulfilment.* London: Collins Publishers.

71. Singer, A.E. 2003.

72. Pruzan, P. 2001. Corporate reputation: Image and identity. *Corporate Reputation Review*, (4): 1: 50–64.

73. Ibid.

74. Hollender, J. and Fenichell, S. 2004. *What matters most, how a small group of pioneers is teaching social responsibility to big business, and why big business is listening.* New York: Basic Books.

75. Sen, A. 1999.

76. Fineman, S. 2006. On being positive: Concerns and counterpoints. *Academy of Management Review*, 31(2): 270–291.

77. Lamont, G. 2002. *The spirited business, success stories of soul friendly companies.* London: Hodder and Stoughton.

78. Ibid.

79. Oakeshott, R. 2001. *Inspiration and reality.* Norwich: Micheal Russell.

80. Brown, S.M. 2005. Expanding ethical business: Taking locality around the world, http://systemicbusiness.org/pubs/2005_ISSS_066_Brown.pdf.

81. Conley, J.M. and Williams, C.A. 2005. Engage, embed and embellish. UNC legal studies research paper, No 05-16.

82. Lips-Wiersma, M.S. 2006. Purpose beyond profit: Towards a spiritual foundation for corporate responsibility. Paris: European Bahai Business Forum.

83. Benefiel, M. 2005. Soul at work, spiritual leadership in organizations: Seabury Books

84. Hawken, P. 1994. *Ecology of commerce.* New York: HarperCollins.

85. Jackson, I.A. and Nelson, J. 2004. Profit with principles: Seven strategies for delivering value with values. New York: Currency-Doubleday.

CHAPTER FIVE

Spirituality in Health Care Organizations

Peter C. Olden

Introduction

Spirituality has become part of business and many business organizations, and this development includes American health care and health care organizations (HCOs). At the industry level, health care is including more spirituality because the biomedical scientific model has loosened to accept more nonmedical humanistic values and practices. This has occurred because many patients want spirituality in health care, and research has supported its effectiveness. The Institute for the Future[1] reported that spiritual factors promote health, recovery from illness, and general well-being, noting "the consistency and robustness of studies involving the role of spirituality in health care." Human dramas and events occur in HCOs and raise deeply spiritual questions about birth, life, suffering, renewal, and death.[2] Integrating spirituality in HCOs has sometimes fundamentally affected an organization's mission, goals, products/services, structure, jobs, production processes, culture, and performance measures. Perhaps more than in most businesses, these organizational features and elements change when a health care business decides to embrace spirituality.

This chapter explains spirituality in health care and HCOs that provide spiritual health care. The focus is on American health care; it is understood that other countries and their HCOs consider spirituality in their own ways with similarities and differences. The chapter next defines spirituality for health care and then reports on some of the relevant literature. A brief history of this topic is presented, followed by current practices of spirituality in health care and HCOs. Suggested future directions conclude the chapter. This chapter is important for health care practitioners, scholars, and patients because spirituality is bringing about changes in American health care, how it is provided, and how HCOs are managed and designed.

What Is Spirituality?

Spirituality is difficult to define, perhaps because it is so personal and individual. Roots of the word refer to breath and inspiration; Wilt and Smucker,[3] who draw on centuries of debate and discussion, define it as "recognition or experience of a dimension of life that is invisible, and both within us yet beyond our material world, providing a sense of connectedness and interrelatedness with the universe." One of many other definitions is, "what it is to be human, to search for a sense of meaning, purpose, and moral guidance for relating with self, others, and ultimate reality."[4] Spirituality is a philosophy of one's life and values that comes from culture, education, and personal experience; it can be unifying and bring meaning to one's life and is the essence of who someone is.[5] Spirituality may be further understood by identifying its domains, which could include experiences, functions, development, content, and expressions of spirituality.[6] After reviewing spirituality literature, Young and Koopsen[7] listed these interrelated key elements of spirituality in health care as follows:

- Relationships of oneself, other people, and a higher power or unifying force (perhaps a religious God, life principle, nature, music, art, or source of comfort).
- Meaning or purpose in life, based on searching.
- Hope, based on possibilities and powers beyond oneself and the present.
- Connectedness and harmony with other people, one's God, nature, environment, or universe.
- Beliefs, based on feelings of faith and confidence in something.
- Expressions of spirituality through activities, rituals, hobbies, reflections.

Spirituality is generally viewed as a broader concept than religion and thus can be intrinsic in everyone. "Spirituality implies an inner search for meaning or fulfillment that may be undertaken by anyone, regardless of religion" assert Graber and Johnson.[8] They think that the term "spirituality" has been used more than "religion" because it is nondenominational, nonhierarchical, and nonecclesiastical, and thus rises above differences in ideology and theology among various faiths, religions, and beliefs. Spirituality overcomes differences among religions and theologies by not being tied to any one particular religion or theology[9] And because spirituality does not generally have the formal structured ceremonial aspects of religion, it is more available to all people including those who express their spirituality without formal institutionalized practices.[10] Many people are not religious yet have spiritual beliefs and practices that influence their lives. This distinction is important for health care businesses because it enables practitioners to view spirituality as universal and provide spiritual care to all people (not just religious people).

(The Return of) Spirituality in Health Care

Spirituality and religion have been associated with health, life, and death for all of recorded history.[11] In ancient societies and cultures, illness was considered to be mostly a spiritual problem, and healers called on the Gods. Christianity was greatly concerned with sacred care of the sick and dying, and medieval Christians based health care on religion and church dogma. During the Middle Ages, both Western and Eastern medicine assumed that humans were closely interconnected with nature, natural forces, other species, and the larger world and universe. When the United States was being settled and getting formed, religious groups founded hospitals, religious missionaries undertook health missions, and religious leaders inspired followers to serve the sick.

However, during the nineteenth and twentieth centuries, a medical model became dominant based on a scientific, reductionistic, mechanistic approach. Scientists, researchers, and universities expanded their roles in medicine, new technology divided the body into discrete parts and medicine into specialties, and then medical care no longer treated the body as a whole.[12] Even death was "medicalized" and often viewed as a medical failure; thus, physicians used increasingly desperate technological efforts to save patients from death. While medicine became more mechanistic and scientific, it also became a big business with more organizational structures, bureaucracies, research and technology, colleges, financing, economic power, professional culture, and social prestige. Like other types of organizations, HCOs came to be viewed metaphorically as machines designed for rational decisions and efficiency.[13] Medical research and education valued rational thought, empirical analysis, scientific methods, and reductionistic approaches to the human body and illnesses. Funding, payment, and economics increasingly drove the business. Bureaucracy dehumanized health organizations and professional culture discouraged emotions and spirituality. Writers and practitioners debated then (and still do) whether health care is a business or social calling.

During most of the twentieth century, the rise of the scientific mechanistic impersonal biomedical model over the earlier spiritual natural personal holistic approach left many HCOs with much less spirituality. But toward the end of century, people were uncomfortable with this approach to their life, health, illness, and death. Some people considered this approach harmful.[14] People with health problems (sometimes facing death) were closed off from their spirituality right when they most needed it for understanding their purpose in life, faith in something beyond oneself, hope, love, and forgiveness.[15] Patients facing death often need answers to questions about life, values, God, what happens after death, suffering and pain, personal guilt and forgiveness.[16] Patients wanted their spiritual needs to be fulfilled along with their health care.

Gradually there began a shift back toward more humanistic spiritual health care. A contributing factor within the health care business was the hospice movement, because hospice care had always used a spiritual holistic approach. Hospice care (for dying patients) spiritually viewed dying as part of a journey and a step toward the ultimate destiny. There are health care rituals and activities associated with death and dying, and Cobb[17] believes that these enact meaning, significance, and sacredness to the process and event of dying and death. The American hospice movement began in the 1980s, and as it grew it helped expand spiritual practices in the health care business. Besides hospice, a growing interest in holistic health care, which is concerned with the whole person rather than just the unhealthy part of the person, also promoted spirituality in health care.

Forces outside the health industry also led people to seek a more holistic and spiritual approach to health care. Bright[18] explains how powerful sociopolitical movements including consumerism, ecology/environmentalism, civil rights, and women's rights were influential. And in the business world, employees realized that they spent much of their time and lives at work, so they sought more opportunities to bring personal values and practices into business and include work in their quest for spiritual growth.[19]

Literature and Research

There is a growing body of scholarly literature, popular press, and online pages about spirituality and health, health care, and HCOs. The number of studies has increased rapidly in recent years. While only about 100 scientific papers on religion and medicine were published during 1980–1982, more than 1100 were published during 2000–2002.[20] A meta-analysis by McCullough and others[21] found more than 1000 studies on religious involvement and health, with contributions from multiple disciplines including psychology, medicine, sociology, theology, and other health disciplines. Web searches performed by the author on July 3, 2007 on Yahoo found more than forty-seven million URLs for "spirituality and health"; more than twenty-three million for "spirituality and health care," and more than three million for "spirituality and health care organizations."

In the United States, surveys show that there is both interest in spirituality and belief that it enhances health. More than 90 percent of the population prays and more than 70 percent think God answers prayers to heal incurable illness;[22] 75 percent of hospital inpatients want physicians to consider their spiritual needs.[23] For many dying people, being at peace with God is more important than anything else, except easing physical pain.[24] Spirituality is especially important in older people's ability to cope with aging,[25] with chronic illness,[26] and face mortality.[27] Wilt and Smucker[28] believe people are most likely to experience the spiritual when there are events of great joy (e.g., a birth) or great sadness (e.g., a death).

Spirituality can be viewed as a healthy practice, like eating nutritious foods, exercising, and avoiding tobacco. Sickness, disease, and illness provide opportunity for spiritual growth, and spirituality can provide hope, strength, purpose, emotional and social support, and ability to cope. In addition, it can help the body by biochemically decreasing stress and tension[29] and increasing healthy behaviors. Spiritual care can help patients and others grow and revise their understanding of illness, disability, loss, suffering, and death. This occurs by exploring one's life, purpose, hope, beliefs, and power beyond oneself; by achieving more self-awareness and connectedness to others; and by revising one's values, purpose, and place in the world.[30] O'Brien's[31] interviews with nurses in various nursing specialties convey the importance of spirituality in health care and how much patients want and benefit from it.

In their review of the literature, Graber and Johnson[32] reported scientific studies linking religious beliefs with how people experience heart attacks, pregnancy, depression, cancer, children's diseases, and AIDS. They also cited studies that found religious beliefs affected people's advanced directives and planning for terminal illnesses. Koenig and others [33] critically reviewed more than 1200 empirical studies on the relation of religion or spirituality with health (mental and physical). They concluded "medical patients have religious and spiritual needs that are intimately related to their physical health conditions, and that religious and spiritual beliefs and practices can often be important for emotional healing." Culliford[34] added that their review showed a 60–80 percent relation between religion or spirituality and better health in studies of heart diseases, cerebral vascular diseases, cancer, disability, depression, personality disorders, pain, and other health problems.

While research supports a spirituality-health relationship, it does not have full consensus because of several reasons. First, there are questions regarding the value and interpretation of studies, and even questions of whether empirical research and the scientific method are applicable to spirituality. It has been hard to conceptualize, operationalize, and measure spirituality due to diverse subjective views of what it is. Outcomes of spirituality have been hard to evaluate and integrate into clinical practice.[35] A review by Sloan and others[36] found many studies had methodological flaws, such as lack of control for possible confounding variables and fuzzy measurement of variables (e.g., how is "being spiritual" measured?). The research has not been strong enough to draw strong conclusions and "prescriptions" for cure and care. O'Mathuna[37] illustrates this well: "If we discover that those who attend church less often are less healthy, should church attendance be prescribed? If so, which church, which denomination, which religion?"

Second, despite empirical literature, "controversy remains regarding whether, to what extent, and in what ways religion and spirituality…helps or harms patients' health."[38] Those writers found that many physicians believe spirituality and religion affect general health but not actual medical outcomes. In a study of 1144 physicians (who varied in location, specialty, age, gender, ethnicity, religion, and religiosity), 85 percent believed spirituality could help patients by (1) preventing health problems; (2) enabling them to cope with illness and suffering; or (3) promoting a positive outlook.[39] But, approximately a third of the physicians believed spirituality could harm patients by causing guilt and anxiety or by causing patients to avoid necessary medical treatment. And Baetz and others[40] examined the relationship of spiritual/religious involvement and depressive symptoms by measuring religious attendance, self-perceptions of spirituality and religiousness, and religious importance, and linking them to depressive symptoms. After controlling for demographic, social, and health variables, religious attendance was associated with less depression, but importance of spiritual values and perceived spirituality/religiousness were associated with more depression. Seemingly conflicting results leave health providers less sure about integrating spirituality with health care.

Current Spiritual Practice in Health Care Organizations

Spirituality in health care and HCOs is advocated by the World Health Organization, Association of Professional Chaplains, American Nurses Association, and other professional groups, and it is a mandatory requirement of the Joint Commission on Accreditation of Healthcare Organizations (JCAHO). It has been implemented in many types of HCOs and health care settings, including those for wellness, primary care, acute care, rehabilitation, mental health, long-term care, and substance abuse. Spiritual health care is also provided in non-health organizations such as homes, businesses, prisons, schools, churches, social agencies, and others. These settings vary greatly with respect to people, funds, resources, and patient care time, which affect how much spiritual care is provided and how it is provided. Spirituality in HCOs can affect multiple participants including patients, clients, clinical care providers, nonclinical workers, and spiritual care givers from outside the HCOs, such as pastors and family members.[41] While all these are important, this chapter focuses on spirituality for patients/clients.

Spiritual Assessment, Care, and Activities

As a first step, health care providers should identify a client's spirituality to understand the client, make informed decisions about spiritual care, and reduce suffering.[42] This may be done with a spiritual assessment, which JCAHO requires for home care, hospital care, and long-term care. An assessment discerns a client's denomination or faith, spiritual goals, important spiritual beliefs, how spirituality affects the person's life, and sources and practices for spiritual support. This can be learned using a spiritual assessment scale like the Spiritual Assessment Guide[43] or FICA assessment.[44] Ideally, this would be done on the first day; in reality it often is done later because of the patient's condition, clinical work with the patient, and other factors. Results of spiritual assessment are used to help make the health services effective, appropriate, and culturally sensitive for patients' spiritual needs. If a more in-depth assessment is needed, such as for the aged or those facing death, Hodge[45] suggests four guiding principles: client's self-determination, cultural competency and respect, importance of spirituality in a client's life, and how a client's spirituality affects health service provision (positively or negatively).

In HCOs, a growing range of spiritual practices are offered as spiritual care to heal (not merely cure) patients and clients. Common spiritual care services are prayer, chanting, story telling, meditation, and reflection, plus wellness practices like massage, aromatherapy, and yoga. Newer modalities include energy movement, therapeutic touch, and guided imagery.[46] Music therapy can relax the body, calm and focus the spirit, enhance inner awareness, and nurture positive emotions while decreasing anxiety and depression. Art therapy helps patients express themselves, feel emotions, improve self-awareness, and resolve issues such as conflict, illness, loss, and death. Dance/movement therapy, humor/laughter therapy, and animal/pet therapy are becoming more common for spiritual care. Some of these are covered by health insurers, but lack of widespread insurance coverage reduces the use of these therapies for spirituality in health care.

Spiritual Care Practitioners

Who are the people practicing spiritual care in HCOs? Currently, a wide range of professional and nonprofessional people practice it; they may be governmentally licensed, professionally certified, or not credentialed. Some have extensive training and education in spiritual care and some have little. Young and Koopsen[47] refer to nurses, social workers, and physicians as spiritual care generalists who provide various types of care including spiritual care, whereas chaplains, clergy, parish nurses, and folk healers are spiritual care specialists who have special training to provide spiritual care. Along with them, friends and family often help provide spiritual care and support. Even simple acts by a housekeeper may help meet a patient's spiritual needs.

Unlike nursing care, medical care, and other types of health care, spiritual care in HCOs is not clearly defined, delineated, and sanctioned with standards and responsibilities. Professions like nursing, pharmacy, physical therapy, and medicine control who may practice in these fields, based in part on education and licensure. That is not so for spiritual care. "The issue of professional practice in spiritual care discloses wider debates in health care concerning the nature of orthodox practice, the grounds for therapeutic interventions and the moral nature of care. Educational and professional standards, competence and accountability are all part of these debates."[48] Thus, there is much variation in practice, guidelines, and care. This is changing due to competency standards and certification for pastoral care, such as by the Association of Professional Chaplains; while these are not required now, it seems likely that more HCOs in the future will expect certification.

Sulmasy[49] explains three possible models for how workers provide spiritual care with clinical care. In the doctor-priest model, health care professionals also exclusively provide the spiritual care, resulting in a somewhat shamanistic approach, which he does not advocate. The parallel track model, which he thinks is most common, has health workers doing their work and spiritual workers doing their work separately from each other. He recommends the collaborative model in which health care and spiritual care workers all collaborate to provide holistic care. This collaborative approach is fairly simple to design and implement in a small focused HCO such as a hospice (where it is common) but harder to implement in a large multiscope organization such as a hospital or even a nursing home.

Work Design and Organization Design

Managers must design work and organizations for effective spiritual care and services in HCOs. Often, existing jobs and organizations do not fully enable spiritual care, so HCOs must redesign parts of their organizations, work processes, and jobs. Organization theory[50] offers a useful framework for this. Forces in HCOs' external environment (discussed earlier) are driving HCO leaders to modify their broad strategic direction (mission, vision, values, strategy, and goals) to include more spiritual care. To achieve this new strategic direction, organization theory informs leaders that they should assess—and if necessary redesign—the organization's structure, production processes, control systems, culture, power, decision making, and interorganizational relationships. Jobs and work processes should be considered and revised as needed based on principles of organization behavior.[51] Human resource programs, policies, practices, and procedures must be reevaluated and revised based on human resource management principles and methods.[52] Several of the most important of these management interventions are discussed below.

Cobb[53] argues for standards of spiritual care (similar to other types of health care). Currently, providers are developing performance standards and accountabilities for spiritual care in health care. These help avoid disparities and inequities, limit practitioner discretion, and assure minimal levels of quality. Standards help integrate spiritual care with other health care by letting people know what to expect from spiritual services. The standards must not be too rigid, however, because current practice emphasizes that HCOs must recognize and adapt to various ethnic/racial groups whose spirituality differs from each other. Thus, spiritual care standards and practice should be designed so they are pluralistic enough to allow patients to express and practice their own spirituality.[54] Along with standards, the job descriptions, job ratings, job performance evaluations, and performance rewards/disciplines may have to be revised to expand spiritual care in an HCO. Individual jobs must be linked via coordination and communication among jobs and work units in the HCO. Further, an HCO may have to expand its interorganizational linkages with agencies, care providers, and organizations in the community.

Culture is a powerful element of organization design, and an HCO's culture (norms, values, beliefs) will have to change to support its goal of spiritual care. A shift from a bureaucratic and professional medical culture to a more humanistic holistic culture would enable spiritual care to blossom in the HCO. Culture will also have to support change and innovation. All this requires leaders and "idea champions" to be effective change agents and use the change process to lead their HCO to enhance the provision of spiritual care. Along with designing the work and organization, leaders will have to provide the necessary resources including staff, funds, training, appropriate space, and information. This is especially important and, as discussed later, resource scarcity is often a barrier to spirituality in HCOs. Finally, after managers provide appropriate resources, take actions, and implement change, they should then monitor, evaluate, and control performance to assure the HCO actually fulfills the intended mission, vision, values, and goals for spirituality. The structure/process/outcome approach has been used to measure and evaluate spiritual care performance.[55]

Puchalski and McSkimming[56] report a demonstration project of seven hospitals (secular and nonsecular) becoming healing environments with spiritual care. Objectives include helping caregivers (1) understand and own their professional responsibility for attending to spiritual concerns and (2) understand needed organizational values and infrastructure to enable caregivers to give spiritual care. For each hospital, an interdisciplinary team was formed (as part of the organizational design) with representation from medicine, nursing, social work, and pastoral care. Management revised the job descriptions, care plans, and performance evaluations and took other steps to achieve the objectives. Nondirect caregivers were oriented to the spiritual approach to caring and educated on how their work as housekeepers and dietary staff help the hospital become a healing environment for patients' spiritual needs. Gradually, a culture change evolved in these organizations, which promoted a healing environment for patients and staff. Some were concerned about differentiating "spiritual care" from "customer service" and so the chaplain explicitly identified spiritual elements of care. Factors for success were found to be committed leadership and interdisciplinary teamwork; outcomes included higher patient satisfaction, higher staff satisfaction, and lower staff turnover.

Facility Design

Along with redesigning the work and organization, leaders should consider redesigning the physical facility to enhance spiritual care. Designing and creating a healing physical environment is another aspect of providing "best-practice" spiritual care in HCOs. Until the last quarter of the twentieth century, health facilities were often designed more for health providers and for the technical aspects of providing medical care. Thus, they were too institutional, barren, noisy, cold, and uninviting to provide ideal spiritual care.[57] That has now been changing, and HCOs are enhancing spiritual care with better use of architectural and interior designs. Spirituality of the environment in which someone lives—and perhaps is struggling for survival—can strongly affect one's health. Spiritual care is improved by closer connection with nature and the natural world, which includes pleasant natural light, sounds and aromas, clean fresh air, soft calm colors, quietness, comfortable temperature, plants, and scenes of nature.[58] Design of a healing space requires understanding and attention to all the senses by which people experience a space. Facility design is now making it easier for friends and family to be with their loved ones and support their spiritual needs. Buildings and environments are more inviting, comfortable, appealing, and friendly. As with other elements of spiritual care, what people consider a healing environment varies according to ethnicities, ages, and personal characteristics, so flexibility and adaptability of environment design is important.

Barriers to Spirituality in Health Care Organizations

Not all HCOs are able to meet the spiritual care expectations of patients, because of various barriers. Balboni[59] found that more than 70 percent of terminal cancer patients did not feel their spiritual needs were adequately supported by hospitals, hospital chaplains, physicians, and the health care system. Puchalski and McSkimming[60] reported, "medical students say that, although they are learning important values and practices, they find that the organizations in which they will practice—hospitals, nursing homes, outpatient offices, and others—do not reflect the material taught concerning the importance of spirituality to good health."

Barriers to spiritual care arise from organization design, human resource practices, and lack of resources. Ineffective organization design creates barriers discussed earlier, such as poor coordination, lack of time, lack of needed work processes, and nonsupportive culture. These sometimes occur due to external forces that emphasize efficiency and finance more than compassion and empathy.[61] This leads to less staffing, less staff time with patients, and less nonreimbursable work (such as spiritual care). Lack of resources (e.g., time, staff, training funds, private space) impedes spiritual health care. And like other aspects of health care, resource shortages for spiritual care lead to questions of funding, such as: Who pays for the care? How much will be available? and Under what conditions will payment be made? Insurance coverage is often lacking, which is also a barrier.

Some health workers are unaware, unwilling, unable, or unprepared for spirituality in health care. They may be unaware of patients' spiritual needs, or they may consider it outside of their profession, role, or job. Some workers avoid it because they are uncomfortable with the subject or unsure how to answer questions that might arise. Not all practitioners understand and can use the language and concepts of spirituality to integrate it with traditional medicine (Aldridge 2005). To overcome these barriers, continuing education is currently training practitioners with spirituality added to their curricula in order to prepare them for the future. Only 17 of 126 accredited medical schools in 1994 offered courses on spirituality in medicine whereas 84 offered it in 2004.[62] Yet, even with education and training, it is hard for practitioners to keep up. Spiritual ideas, movements, methods, and activities have proliferated and the "burgeoning range of spiritual options and the seemingly endless possibilities for amalgamation, then, are often confusing..."[63] The research literature and evidence has grown, but some of it is questionable and not accepted by all health professionals. In an HCO, some care givers may feel unprofessional if they engage in spiritual aspects with patients or may feel that they are imposing their beliefs on others if they go too far with spirituality so they avoid it.[64]

Another reason care givers avoid spirituality is because they feel patients' spiritual beliefs at times conflict with medical practice or with the beliefs of other people who are involved. Spiritual beliefs of some people (e.g., some adherents of Christian Science or New Age beliefs) lead to avoidance of standard medical care, which jeopardizes people's health,[65] or even contributes to death. Sometimes a patient's spiritual preferences may differ from those of a family member (similar to disagreement about "heroic measures"). And while physicians think that some patients' spirituality restricts medical care to too little, the opposite situation of physicians wanting to administer too much medical care (not knowing when to stop) causes too little spiritual care to be given to some dying people. All these situations deter appropriate spirituality in health care.

Future Directions for Research, Education, and Practice

Herrman[66] reminds us that past innovations in health and medicine have not always been immediately accepted as useful and worthy of widespread adoption; in some cases (e.g., hand washing in the nineteenth century) they were first rejected outright. Spirituality in health care as a professional practice is still emerging, and future developments in research, education, and practice will strengthen it. To guide this process, Cobb[67] calls for (1) an expanded knowledge base for spiritual practice that draws from multiple disciplines; (2) rigorous research to help develop an evidence-based approach to spiritual practice; and (3) further development of the practice of spiritual care through training and education.

Future research can provide the knowledge base for spiritual care. However, research will have to overcome the challenges of studying people of varying cultures and backgrounds when they are facing spiritual moments and issues. Appropriate theoretical frameworks should guide the research with careful definition and measurement of intangible constructs and concepts. Rigorous research design (both qualitative and quantitative) and careful statistical analysis and interpretation must be used to avoid bias, control confounding factors, and strengthen validity and reliability. An important area for research is the sequential relationships among multiple factors related to health. For example, spiritual meditation may lead to a stronger belief in healthy living, which leads to healthier eating, which in turn improves health. Advancing the research will require standard, consistent measures of spirituality and its multiple dimensions, many spiritual actions and interventions, interactions of spirituality with medical care, and the actual outcomes of spirituality.[68] This will be hard work, but it can lead to an evidence base for spiritual care, especially with effective dissemination of results to practitioners, policy makers, other scholars, educators, and other stakeholders.

Along with research evidence, professional codes of conduct and training/education will enhance spirituality in health care. Ethical codes and professional standards of conduct have been developed and will be adopted increasingly in the future (like in other health professions). This outcome would flow from what it means to be a professional care giver, with its associated norms, standards, trust, and accountability. Many patient care professions now include some spirituality content in their educational curricula; that, along with continuing education for current practitioners, will help assure that practitioners are prepared to provide and integrate spiritual care with health care in health care organizations.

Notes

1. Institute for the Future. 2003. *Health and health care 2010.* San Francisco, CA: Jossey-Bass.
2. Young, C. and Koopsen, C. 2005. *Spirituality, health, and healing.* Sunbury, MA: Jones and Bartlett Publishers.
3. Wilt, D.L. and Smucker, C.L. 2001. *Nursing in spirit: The art and science of applying spiritual care.* Washington, DC: American Nurses Publishing.
4. Canda, E.R. and Furman, L.D. 1999. *Spiritual diversity in social work practice.* New York: Free Press.
5. Tu, M. 2006. Illness: An opportunity for spiritual growth. *Journal of Alternative and Complementary Medicine*, 12(10): 1029–1033.
6. Canda, E. and Furman, L.D. 1999.
7. Young, C. and Koopsen, C. 2005.
8. Graber, D.R. and Johnson, J.A. 2001. Spirituality in healthcare organizations. *Journal of Healthcare Management*, 46(1): 39–50.

9. Cobb, M. 2001. *The dying soul: Spiritual care at the end of life.* Philadelphia: Open University Press.

10. Harvey, I.S. and Silverman, M. 2007. Role of spirituality in self-management of chronic illness among older African and whites. *Journal of Cross Cultural Gerontology*, 22: 205–220.

11. Young, C. and Koopsen, C. 2005.

12. Maugans, T. 1996. The spiritual history. *Archives of Family Medicine*, 5(1): 11–16.

13. Graber, D.R. and Johnson, J.A. 2001.

14. Cobb, M. 2001.

15. Wilt, D.L. and Smucker, C.L. 2001.

16. Twycross, R.G. and Lack, S.A. 1990. *Therapeutics in terminal cancer.* Edinburgh: Churchill Livingstone.

17. Cobb, M. 2001.

18. Bright, M.A. 2002. *Holistic health and healing.* Philadelphia, PA: F.A. Davis Company.

19. Graber, D.R. and Johnson, J.A. 2001.

20. Ortolon, K. 2004. God, MD: Medicine rediscovers role of spirituality in health care. *Texas Medicine*, 100(11): 38–42.

21. McCullough, M., Hoyt, W., Larson, D., Koenig, H., and Thoreson, C. 2000. Religious involvement and mortality: A meta-analytical review. *Health Psychology*, 19(3): 211–222.

22. Walker, S.R., Tonigan, J.S., Miller, W.R., Comer, S., and Kalich, L. 1997. Intercessory prayer in the treatment of alcohol abuse and dependence: A pilot investigation. *Alternative Therapies in Health and Medicine*, 3(6): 79–86.

23. Sloan, R.P., Bagiella, E., Vande Creek, L., Hover, M., Casalone, C., Hirsch, T.J., Hasan, Y., Kreger, R., and Poulos, P. 2000. Should physicians prescribe religious activities? *New England Journal of Medicine*, 342(25): 1913–1916.

24. Szabo, L. 2007. Health system struggles with spiritual care. *USA Today*, February 15, D11.

25. Nelson-Becker, H., Najashima, M., and Canda, E.R. 2007. Spiritual assessment in aging: A framework for clinicians. *Journal of Gerontological Social Work*, 48(3/4): 331–347.

26. Mackenzie, E.R., Rajagopal, D.E., Meibohm, M., and Lavizzo-Mourey, R. 2000. Spiritual support and psychological well-being: Older adults' perceptions of the religion and health connection. *Alternative Therapies*, 6(6): 37–45.

27. Herrmann, R.L. 2004. *Sir John Templeton: Supporting scientific research for spiritual discoveries.* Radnor, PA: Templeton Foundation Press.

28. Wilt, D.L. and Smucker, C.L. 2001.

29. Ortolon, K. 2004.

30. Tu, M. 2006.

31. O'Brien, M.E. 1999. *Spirituality in nursing: Standing on holy ground.* Sudbury, MA: Jones & Bartlett.

32. Graber, D.R. and Johnson, J.A. 2001.

33. Koenig, H.G., McCullough, M.E., and Larson, D.B. 2001. *Handbook of religion and health.* New York: Oxford University Press.

34. Culliford, L. 2002. Spirituality and clinical care. *British Medical Journal.* December 21–28: 1434–1435.

35. Tu, M. 2006.

36. Sloan, R. P., Bagiella, E., and Powell, T. 1999. Religion, spirituality, and medicine. *Lancet*, 353: 664–667.

37. O'Mathuna, D.P. 2002. Spirituality and alternative medicine. In Kilner, J.F., Christopher Hook, C., and Uustal, D.B. (eds.), *Cutting-edge bioethics: A Christian exploration of technologies and trends.* Grand Rapids, MI: Wm. B. Eerdmans.

38. Curlin, F.A., Sellergren, S.A., Lantos, J.D., and Chin, M.H. 2007. Physicians' observations and interpretations of the influence of religion and spirituality on health. *Archives of Internal Medicine*, 167: 649–654.

39. Ibid.

40. Baetz M., Griffin, R., Bowen, R., Koenig, H.G., and Marcoux, G. 2004. The association between spiritual/religious involvement and depressive symptoms in the Canadian population. *Journal of Nervous and Mental Disorders*, 192: 818–822.
41. Wolf, E.J. Spiritual leadership: A new model. *Healthcare Executive*, 19(2): 22–25.
42. Young, C. and Koopsen, C. 2005.
43. O'Brien, M.E. 1999.
44. Puchalski, C.M. and McSkimming, S. 2006. Creating healing environments. *Health Progress*, 87(3). http://www.chausa.org/Pub/MainNav/News/HP/Archive/2006/05MayJun/Articles/SpecialSection/HP0605e.htm (last accessed on July 3, 2007).
45. Hodge, D.R. 2006. A template for spiritual assessment: A review of JCAHO requirements and guidelines for implementation. *Social Work*, 51(4): 317–326.
46. Barnum, B.S. 1996. *Spirituality in nursing: From traditional to new age.* New York: Springer Publishing Company.
47. Young, C. and Koopsen, C. 2005.
48. Cobb, M. 2001. 106.
49. Sulmasy, D.P. 2006. *The rebirth of the clinic: An introduction to spirituality in health care.* Washington, DC: Georgetown University Press.
50. Daft, R.L. 2007. *Organization theory and design.* 9th ed. Cincinnati, OH: South-Western College Publishing.
51. Shortell, S.M. and Arnold D. Kaluzny. 2006. *Health care management.* 5th ed. Albany, NY: Delmar.
52. French, W.L. 2007. *Human resources management.* 6th ed. Boston, MA: Houghton Mifflin.
53. Cobb, M. 2001.
54. Aldridge, D. 2005. Spirituality and medicine: Complementary perspectives. *Spirituality and Health International*, 6(2): 71–80.
55. Cobb, M. 2001.
56. Puchalski, C.M. and McSkimming, S. 2006.
57. Young, C. and Koopsen, C. 2005.
58. Ibid.
59. Balboni, T.A., Vanderwerker, L.C., Block, S.D., Paulk, M.E., Lathan, C.S., Peteet, J.R., and Prigerson, H.G. 2007. Religiousness and spiritual support among advanced cancer patients and associations with end-of-life treatment preferences and quality of life. Journal of Clinical Oncology, 25(5): 555–560.
60. Puchalski, C.M. and McSkimming, S. 2006. 30.
61. Sulmasy, D.P. 2006.
62. Fortin, A.H. and Barnett, K.G. 2004. Medical school curricula in spirituality and medicine. *Journal of the American Medical Association*, 291: 2883.
63. Fallot, Roger D. 2007. Spirituality and religion in recovery: Some current issues. *Psychiatric Rehabilitation Journal*, 30(4): 261–270.
64. Szabo, L. 2007.
65. O'Mathuna, D.P. 2002.
66. Herrmann, R.L. 2004.
67. Cobb, M. 2001.
68. Sulmasy, D.P. 2006.

Intentional Intelligence: How the New Mind of Leadership Manifests Success in Business and Life

DAVID STEINGARD

What Is Intentional Intelligence?

All that a man achieves and all that he fails to achieve is the direct result of his own thoughts.—James Allen[1]

Why do human beings achieve or fail to achieve? Who or what is responsible? How much control over outcomes do we actually have? This chapter explores these questions by advancing "intentional intelligence," a conceptual model for understanding how intrapsychic mental states[2] influence human performance. As a working definition, intentional intelligence is defined as the ability of human beings to achieve individual and collective efficacy through mental intention.[3] Ostensibly, human achievement manifests by action; if you want to achieve something, you must do something. Intentional intelligence suggests that "action" is secondary to "thought," that thought is the "prima causa" (first cause) for both action and achievement. Understandably, this is a provocative proposition. Surely action must have an important role in achievement? Are the mind's interior thoughts, beliefs, and emotions really the dominant causal factor in human achievement and failure?

Inclusion of this chapter on intentional intelligence in this book on spirituality in business[4] is warranted for two reasons. First, intentional intelligence helps make the connection between "pure spirituality" and "applied spirituality"; constructs that are fundamental to the ontological and epistemological underpinnings of the spirituality in business field. Schmidt-Wilk et al.[5] make this distinction:

> We use the term *pure spirituality* to refer to a silent, unbounded, timeless inner domain that any individual may experience within his or her own conscious awareness; we use the term *applied spirituality* to refer to the outer domain, the practical applications, and measurable outcomes that automatically arise from an inner experience of pure spirituality. (Italics in the original)

Intentional intelligence bridges the gap between "conscious awareness" and the "practical applications" of how the mind manifests successful or unsuccessful actions in business. While intentional intelligence talks primarily about the machinations of the mind and not "a silent, unbounded, timeless inner domain," the mind, as will be elaborated later, is actually anchored in and supported by a spiritual source. Second, intentional intelligence helps to extend the extant literature on spiritual intelligence that is an important subdiscipline within the field of spirituality in business. Zohar and Marshall[6] describe spiritual intelligence in existential terms: "We are driven, indeed we are defined, by a specifically human longing to find meaning and value in what we do and experience." One is spiritually intelligent if he or she can successfully "find meaning and value" in his or her life. Intentional intelligence, however, is more concerned with how metaphysical phenomena (like the mind and the source of the mind) "manifest into action," rather than how one intrapersonally "reconciles the existential quality of their life."

Research in a variety of disciplines supports mental variables as being both core and causal, preceding both action and results. Daniel Goleman's[7] emotional intelligence finds repeatedly that interior mental states—self-awareness, self-regulation, and motivation—are far greater predictors of success in business than analytical skills and other applied competencies.[8] Education's "Pygmalion effect"[9,10] documents significantly higher academic achievement from students whom teachers expect to perform better, irrespective of the students' tested abilities or past performance. Sports psychology employs positive visualization of performance and victory as a foundation of athletic training.[11] Neurofeedback,[12] where data on brain wave pattern is therapeutically used by patients to alter their brain functioning, has been shown to be effective in treating attention deficit disorder

(ADD). Medicine has discovered the "placebo effect"[13]—patients' belief that they are receiving medication when only inactive ingredients are actually administered—to be efficacious in mitigating pain.[14] Theoretical and experimental physics offer rigorous accounts of the power of the mind to influence physical reality.[15,16,17] Biology examines the causal role of consciousness in living organisms and systems.[18,19,20] Psychiatrist Viktor Frankl[21] employed the power of his mind to dramatically transform his Nazi death camp experience to one of peace and spiritual contentment.[22] Meditation, a technique to quiet and to focus the mind, is linked to a variety of psychological and physiological health benefits,[23] such as stress reduction and decrease in mortality rate[24] and increase in functional capacity for people with congestive heart failure.[25] Appreciative inquiry,[26] appreciative intelligence,[27] and positive organizational scholarship[28] utilize positive mental images of the future to create substantive changes to organizational strategies, structures, and systems. Positive psychology[29] suggests that positive emotions like hope, love, and forgiveness can lead to better individual health and organizational results. Leadership studies demonstrate how consistent focus on core thoughts—like Gandhi's emphasis on truth and nonviolence—lead to massive, unpredictable geopolitical transformations of nation-states.[30]

In addition, management educators' focus on "Being" moments and "being classes" results from states of mind rather than pedagogical techniques; that is, "being" produces more learning than "doing."[31] Hypnosis, a therapeutic technique that increases a person's receptivity for positive suggestions, evidences beneficial effects in a variety of medical treatments involving allergies, dermatology, anesthesia, neurology, healing, obesity, and others.[32] Professional sales representatives' performance significantly increases by using "positive mental attitude" in building client relationships and closing sales.[33,34]

All of these examples demonstrate the primacy of mind as the *prima causa* of action, and ultimately, of results. To be clear, this is not to say that action, in and of itself, is unimportant; obviously, what one does has a significant impact on the outcome on one's life. Missing here is the idea that human achievement, or lack thereof, is fundamentally related to the thoughts about the situation, that is, one's internal disposition is the primary cause of his or her circumstances in life.[35] Moreover, it is not just the thoughts, but how deeply the thoughts are anchored and actualized in a person, both consciously and unconsciously, that controls action. Socialization, education, media, culture, religion, and other messaging influences powerfully shape thoughts, yet their mechanisms and effects are difficult to ascertain. The theory and application of intentional intelligence allows us to understand what is at the root of the causal chain for human performance, the realm of thought.

How does intentional intelligence relate to the variety of existing intelligences like multiple intelligences,[36] emotional intelligence,[37] social intelligence,[38] appreciative intelligence,[39] and spiritual intelligence?[40,41] In examining this plethora of intelligences, there is one dimension that is implied, but not developed. These intelligences suggest that mastery of their principles allows for a better life—to be and do more. They do not, however, fully articulate or operationalize the underlying dynamics of how these intelligences engender efficacy: "the ability to produce a desired or intended result."[42] Efficacy in intentional intelligence is expanded somewhat and defined twofold: (1) the ability to think about something and achieve it and (2) the positive, existentially validating state of being that comes with achievement. "Meaningful results" capture this two-part integration. How are all of these intelligences employed toward efficacy? How does the engagement of emotional, aesthetic, spiritual, and such other intelligence foster human achievement? One can have a variety of these intelligences but still not really understand the process of human achievement. Intentional intelligence adds to these intelligences the knowledge of how human beings utilize their wide range of faculties to achieve results and avoid failure.

Given the preceding definition of intentional intelligence, its roots in a variety of disciplines, and its contextualization, vis-à-vis, other constructs of intelligence, a more formalized conceptualization can now be offered.

Conceptual Model of Intentional Intelligence

The basic structures and dynamics of intentional intelligence are depicted in the model depicted in figure 6.1.

To begin, let's examine the underlying assumptions of the model on two dimensions: (1) ontologically, or according to the nature of reality and (2) epistemologically, or according to how knowledge and action function in this reality. Because these foundations of the model are so intertwined, they are considered together.

Overall, the model maps the flow of ideation into action in the human experience. The metaphysical transformation threshold[43] divides internal, intrapsychic reality from external, obdurate reality—mind from

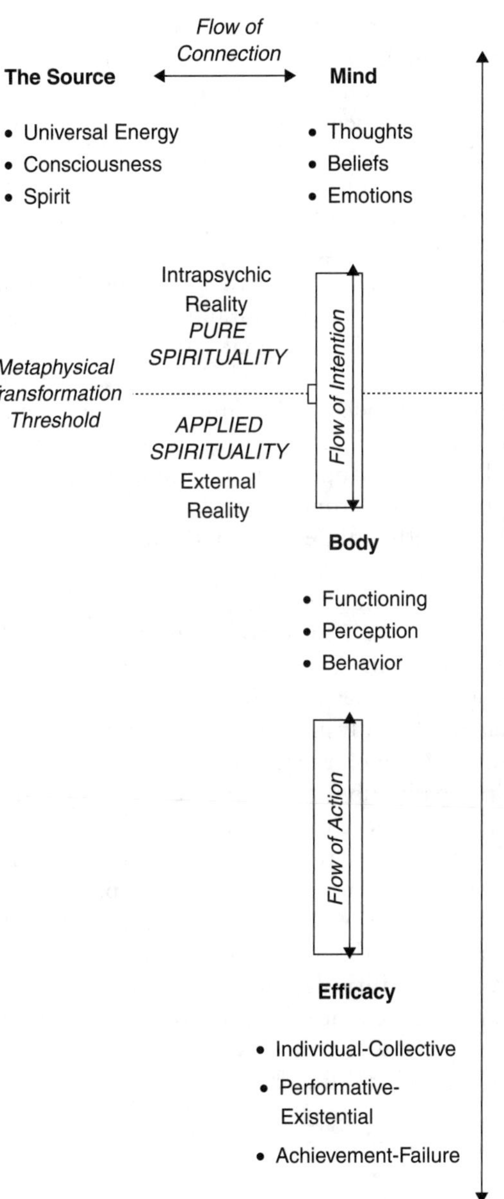

Figure 6.1   Model of Intentional Intelligence

body. Metaphysical means "transcending physical matter or the laws of nature."[44] This distinction is important because intentional intelligence addresses both the mind as nonmaterial and its ability to foster efficacy unrelated to conventional processes of cause and effect endemic to the physical universe's "laws of nature." Intentional intelligence introduces a deeper understanding of cause and effect by operationalizing metaphysical dynamics in what are ultimately practical terms. In terms of spirituality, phenomena above the threshold are considered as "pure spirituality" and those below as "applied spirituality."[45] Relating this model to the Wilber's[46] AQAL (all quadrants, all levels) model of integral philosophy and human development asserts that the realm of the subjective mind and that of the objective physical world are two facets of one phenomenon—two sides of the same coin. For example, meditation can produce internal feelings of peace, connectedness, and joy that directly correlate with changes to respiration, blood pressure, heart rate, and other physiological functioning.[47] Many philosophical and spiritual traditions altogether dispense with the dichotomy of mind and body, employing terms like "bodymind."[48]

New developments in neuroscience suggest that the "stuff of the brain can change in response to the whisper of the mind"[49]; mental thoughts affect physical brain structures and functioning. Empirically, sophisticated brain imaging techniques (e.g., MRI, EEG, PET scan) demonstrate these correlations.[50] Advances in science have made what was once seemingly invisible much more visible. Therefore, the boundary between what is internally subjective and exteriorly objective becomes less of a dividing line and more of a gateway.

Mind is actually a product of the Source or what Lynne McTaggart[51] calls "The Field": the interconnected and all encompassing—from matter to spirit—bedrock of reality. This connection allows us to simultaneously view the mind as both a phenomenon of the individual as well as being connected to an infinite, all-permeating realm of universal energy, consciousness, source, or spirit—elemental conception of reality. Willis Harman[52] provides a three-level metaphysical framework for how ideations of the mind and the physical realm relate:

1. M-1 is labeled "Materialistic Monism" where "Matter gives rise to Mind."
2. M-2 introduces the idea of mind as having its own identity and characteristics—the "Dualism" of "Matter plus Mind."
3. The nondualistic M-3 Metaphysic is a by-product of transcending the mind–body dualism.

Intentional intelligence operates in an "M-3 Metaphysic" where the "Mind" is the primary causal driver—*prima causa*—"Consciousness is Causal." However, as we will see more fully in the discussion of "downward causation" in the following section, this dominant one-way influence is supplemented with "upward causation."[53] There is a logical flow to how human beings manifest their intentions in this causal chain. First, the mind connects with the Source—a combination of inspiration,[54] presence,[55,56] and interconnectedness.[57] Thoughts, beliefs, and emotions combine in the "Mind" and manifest as the flow of intention. Intention causes the body to function, to perceive, and to behave in particular ways. Outward expressions of the body, through speech and physical actions, commence the flow of behavior that ultimately leads to some type of outcome. Outcomes are conceived in terms of efficacy that can be assessed on three dimensions. First, efficacy is conceived to be a product of the individual or collective (sometimes both). Second, as discussed above, efficacy can be existentially fulfilling (internal) or performance-oriented (external); ideally, an integrative admixture of "meaningful results" is sought. Third, efficacy has a very measurable— both qualitatively and quantitatively—characteristic: did the intended thought achieve or fail in its manifestation?

Underlying the dynamics of how intentional intelligence flows through this system is the philosophical concept of "downward causation":

Downward causation can be defined as a converse of the reductionist principle above: the behavior of the parts (down) is determined by the behavior of the whole (up), so determination moves downward instead of upward. The difference is that determination is not complete.[58]

By "*not* complete," Heylighen offers that elements down the causal chain—in the model body and efficacy—can have substantive effects on higher elements like those in the model mind and the Source. The two-headed downward mutual causation arrow in figure 6.1 suggests that "determination" is primarily driven by the mind, but "upward causation" is also possible. For example, the flow of intention can work downward as well. Mental illness, brain structure and functioning irregularities, pharmaceuticals, food, and other physiological influences can generate information that alters the subjective experience of the mind. Similarly, experience with efficacy—the experience of success or failure—can communicate back to the body and mind certain expectations about how manifesting desires work. For example, the familiar adage "success breeds success" indicates how achievement can cause future achievement. Clearly, other people and the physical environment affect behavior and the associated thoughts, feelings, and beliefs underlying them. In light of the selfsameness of the mind and the Source, it is reasonable to speculate a mutually constitutive relationship here as well, although the exact nature of this may be difficult to discover.

With downward causation there is another corollary of observational generativity;[59] the idea that thoughts shape perception, cause action, and ultimately structure reality. As applied to the model, the mental picture (perception) as expressed from mind and body leads to behavior. Flow of action manifests on the physical level; humans are active participants in the establishment and functioning of the universe. Essentially, mind and body do not stand apart from the world, simply observing and describing what is "out there." Instead, human beings choose to generate a particular reality based on the intentions of the mind—what is "in here." The potential to understand how the process of efficacy works and improve upon it, to become more intentionally intelligent, is one of the promises of intentional intelligence.

Seven Abilities of Intentional Intelligence

Based on the model detailed above, we can begin to translate the fundamental flows of intentional intelligence into some abilities of the human experience. Essentially, figure 6.1 models how the "process" of intentional intelligence works in principle, while the following seven abilities specify the particular "content" of mind and consciousness necessary for one to be intentionally intelligent. The purpose here is to apply the model's abstract, theoretical principles to the context of human ideation and behavior. A person needs to be cognizant of and to manage themselves on the following abilities in order to be intentionally intelligent:

1. Intentional Mindfulness: The ability to amplify life-affirming beliefs and to ameliorate self-limiting thoughts.
2. Intentional Causation: The ability to see oneself as the primary cause of life's circumstances and to take responsibility for what one creates.
3. Intentional Presence: The ability to be aware of psychological and physiological states, both internally and of others.
4. Intentional Focus: The ability to feel passionately about what one wants and to visualize its materialization into the future.

5. Intentional Trans-Connectedness: The ability to transcend one's ego and experience life as interconnected to a larger force, source, consciousness, or energy in the universe.
6. Intentional Creativity: The ability to produce innovative, paradigm-breaking ideas.
7. Intentional Appreciation: The ability to value positivity, happiness, and vitality.

Basically, for each ability we find a continuum from what is intentionally intelligent to what is intentionally unintelligent. For example, one who displays a high degree of interior mindfulness is more likely to be intentionally intelligent; one who does not have a purposeful focus is less likely to be. It is worth reiterating that intentional intelligence's goal of efficacy, both existential and performative, will result when these abilities are positively engaged.

Although offered here preliminarily, these abilities are the foundation of what is necessary to operationalize intentional intelligence as an applied discipline of human performance. From these dimensions, intentional intelligence can be distilled into three key aspects: (1) it is a definable set of skills; (2) it has measurable inputs and outputs; and (3) it can be developed through education and practice. The next section will take a more in-depth look at how intentional intelligence fulfills the requirements of a basic intelligence as outlined by Gardner.[60]

Is Intentional Intelligence a
Legitimate Form of Intelligence?

Coupling the conceptual model with the proposed seven abilities, we are now ready to think about intentional intelligence in the context of a legitimate intelligence. First, this is important because if it can be established as an intelligence, then intentional intelligence will be able to complement other intelligences and widen their knowledge bases. Second, methodologies that have proven to work in other intelligences (e.g., inventories, pedagogy) can be adapted to intentional intelligence. Third, by establishing intentional intelligence on the same ground as the other intelligences, intentional intelligence adds to the conversation about intelligences. Fourth, since intentional intelligence overlaps with other intelligences, it may be helpful in furthering the understanding of them.

What exactly is "an intelligence"? Gardner's[61] seminal work on multiple intelligences lays the groundwork and legitimizes a variety of human ways of knowing—musical intelligence, bodily kinesthetic intelligence, logical-mathematical intelligence, linguistic intelligence, spatial intelligence, interpersonal intelligence, and intrapersonal intelligence. Prior to his work, mainstream psychology viewed intelligence singularly as the "ability to answer items on tests of intelligence."[62] Operationally, this one-dimensional view makes intelligence simply a function of a test score—a higher score means one is more intelligent, a lower score less intelligent. Paper and pencil tests of IQ rely primarily on rational, logical, and intellectual cognitive capacities. Conventional conceptions of intelligence correlate with raw intellect and its employment to solve problems—a "brainiac" stereotype, if you will. However, success on intelligence tests only "implies" a connection to some native capacity of being human, most notably to a biophysically superior brain.

Gardner's[63] multiple intelligences theory broadens the possibilities for intelligence:

> An intelligence is a computational capacity—a capacity to process a certain kind of information—that originates in human biology and human psychology....An intelligence entails the ability to solve problems or fashion products that are of consequence in a particular cultural setting or community. The problem-solving skill allows one to approach a situation in which a goal is to be obtained and to locate the appropriate route to that goal.

Unpacking this passage, we can articulate four fundamental requirements of an intelligence:[64]

1. Computational: An intelligence operationalizes the ability to process information, with information being widely defined as a realm of experience fundamental to the human condition.
2. Empirical: Computation of an intelligence must manifest in both biological and psychological domains, what Gardner calls "biopsychological."[65]
3. Operational: An intelligence is invoked to solve a problem or express something meaningful—it can have metaphysical, practical, existential, ethical, and aesthetic aspects.
4. Teleological: Intelligences help human beings fulfill some greater goal at a material-functional level or spiritual-meaning level.

Given Gardner's conception of an intelligence and my distillation of the four fundamental requirements for it, we now have a framework to establish what makes for a valid intelligence and the development of intentional intelligence. I have added an additional requirement discussed in Gardner's work but not made explicit in the quote above: developmental (defined below).

Intentional intelligence is computational because it processes information in the form of intentional thought, the basic unit of analysis. The ability to have intention and its manifestation is endemic to the human condition—for survival, for joy, for efficacy. Intentional intelligence is operational, implying that it can be applied; the seven aforementioned skills are employed to turn thoughts into reality. It can be empirically measured. Like emotional intelligence,[66] intentional intelligence can be evaluated through psychological inventories, 360-degree assessments, and physiological correlations between mind and body. And, most conspicuously, intentional intelligence's ultimate goal of efficacy can be measured, both intrinsically and extrinsically. One's level of expertise in intentional intelligence is simply a product of how efficiently and effectively the desires in one's mind come into fruition. Teleologically, intentional intelligence is a basic ingredient of a life well lived from a humanistic and moral approach—efficacy is endemic to the human condition. Finally, it is key to understand that intentional intelligence is a skill that can be improved upon—it is developmental.

This section has demonstrated how intentional intelligence can be formulated as a proper intelligence. Given this possibility, we can now look at what could be the future implications for intentional intelligence—where to next?

Future Implications for Intentional Intelligence

In this chapter I have introduced the idea of intentional intelligence through examples, a conceptual model, and a preliminary competency typology. I have also evaluated its viability vis-à-vis the existing models of intelligence. Although assembled from a variety of interdisciplinary theories and applied research, intentional intelligence adds unique value to the conversation about human performance. Specifically, intentional intelligence both formulates and begins to answer the question: "What role does the mind have in terms of human performance?" By shifting the focus of human performance from the visible, behavioral realm to the invisible, mental realm, intentional intelligence opens up exciting possibilities for exponentially increasing the efficacy of human beings, both existentially and perfomatively. Indeed, this is a provocative proposition—to suggest that an entire realm of untapped potential for human performance improvement is available seems radical.

Yet, if we look at the preliminary findings and model presented in this chapter, we will find that the seeds are there. This is not to say that conventional efforts to understand what makes human performance excel are outmoded, but merely that they need to be complemented and deepened. By way of analogy, we can look at the quantity of energy released from burning wood versus splitting an atom (nuclear fission). Burn a log of wood and you get fire, split practically invisible atoms, and you get a nuclear explosion. More power with less matter; likewise, improved results with more mind and less physicality, more thinking and less doing.

We hear popularized phrases like, "you create your own reality," "you are 100 percent responsible for your reality," "mind over matter," and "your thoughts create your life." While this "mind makes world" causality may be oversimplified, this chapter has shown that the mind does have a profound influence on the results one produces in life. Are there limits to what the mind can manifest? This is an important question. Our present construction of human causation and efficacy, based in a mechanistic-physicalistic paradigm, may limit what is possible for human beings to achieve. Intentional intelligence broadens the scope of possibility for human achievement because it operates from a different "metaphysical foundation,"[67] with metaphysics being defined as "transcending physical laws or the laws of nature."[68] The very nature of our metaphysical assumptions has enormous influence on what we think is attainable for the human condition. We look to innovation and solutions from within the box of human performance constrained by a mechanistic-physicalist worldview. Continuing with the earlier analogy, we try to think of a variety of ways we can use fire to get things done. At some point, there is only so much you can do with fire; however, by going deeper and utilizing the ultimate power of the mind through intentional intelligence—splitting the atom—we go outside of the box, allowing an unimaginable amount of power to be unleashed. Einstein suggested that we need a different level of thinking—what we might call another metaphysical level of consciousness—to experience a breakthrough in human potential: "The significant problems we have cannot be solved at the same level of thinking with which we created them."[69]

With further development, intentional intelligence can offer a viable body of knowledge and practice to solve problems at a different level of thinking. Given the plethora of exigent social and environmental issues in today's world, intentional intelligence may prove to be very valuable in envisioning and implementing alternative pathways for human evolution. Locating the genesis of human creativity and transformation in the perhaps infinite power of the mind could spark monumental changes to the well-being of people and the planet.

In fact, many of the great advances of humanity have come from the realm of thought unchained to current realities—thinking "outside the box." Given below is a fascinating assembly of quotations proving this point:[70]

> "Heavier-than-air flying machines are impossible."—Lord Kelvin, president, Royal Society, England, 1895.

> "There is no reason anyone would want a computer in their home."—Ken Olson, president, chairman and founder of Digital Equipment Corp., 1977.

> "The concept is interesting and well-formed, but in order to earn better than a 'C,' the idea must be feasible."—A Yale University management professor in response to Fred Smith's paper proposing reliable overnight delivery service [c. 1962]. (Smith went on to found Federal Express Corp.)

> "There is not the slightest indication that nuclear energy will ever be obtainable. It would mean that the atom would have to be shattered at will."—Albert Einstein, 1932.

All of these quotations demonstrate how the primacy of thought is both a limiter and enabler of human achievement. For each of these negating proclamations, somebody sourced an idea from outside the current paradigm and produced astonishing results (e.g., airplanes, personal computers). Intentional intelligence promises to understand and improve the process of how new thoughts engender new worlds. This is vital to the fulfillment of the basic human needs for both performative and existential efficacy.

If intentional intelligence is to become viable, it will have to synthesize much of the extant research around the casual chain of mind-body-efficacy detailed in the conceptual model. As shown throughout this chapter, there are important components of the model already in existence, but they have yet to be fully integrated. This is the goal of intentional intelligence.

What are the practical next steps for intentional intelligence? First, metrics and testing of intentional intelligence's seven abilities need to be developed. Second, the relationship of these abilities to the conceptual model needs to be elaborated, especially concerning the integration of research in fields where the primacy of mind is figural. Third, individuals, groups, and organizations possessing high degrees of intentional intelligence need to be researched; their qualitative stories will help reveal underlying dynamics. Fourth, once adequate measurements are discovered and stories of high-performing people documented, learning models for improving intentional intelligence need to be created. Fifth, given all of this accumulated data about intentional intelligence, a fuller assessment of its contribution to performative and existential efficacy should be made.

Ultimately, the success of intentional intelligence will revolve around answering the question: How does the power of mind help transform the human condition? We end with another fitting quote from Allen[71] about the pathway ahead for intentional intelligence:

Such is the conscious master, and man can only thus become by discovering within himself the laws of thought; which discovery is totally a matter of application, self-analysis, and experience.

Notes

1. Allen, J. 2000. *The wisdom of James Allen: Five books in one: As a man thinketh: The path to prosperity: The mastery of destiny: The way of peace: Entering the kingdom.* San Diego, CA: Laurel Creek Press. 46.

2. Although an important dimension, a psychoanalytic or cognitive treatment of sub/unconscious thoughts is beyond the scope of this chapter. In the main, "thoughts" in this chapter refer to ideations consciously known or generated.

3. See Biberman, J. and Whitty, M.D. 2007. *At work: Spirituality matters.* Scranton: University of Scranton Press, for an excellent survey of the field.

4. For a classic philosophical treatment defining and elaborating intention, see Anscombe, G.E.M. 2000. *Intention.* 2nd ed. Cambridge, MA: Harvard University Press. For a helpful popularized treatment of intention, see Dyer, W.W. 2004. *The power of intention: Learning to co-create your world your way.* Carlsbad, CA: Hay House.

5. Schmidt-Wilk, J., Heaton, D., and Steingard, D.S. 2000. Higher education for higher consciousness: Maharishi University of Management as a model for spirituality in management education. *Journal of Management Education,* 24(5): 581 [580–612].

6. Zohar, D. and Marshall, I. 2001. *SQ: Connecting with our spiritual intelligence.* New York: Bloomsbury. 4.

7. Goleman, D. 2005. *Emotional intelligence.* New York: Bantam Books.

8. Goleman, D. 1998. What makes a leader? *Harvard Business Review,* November-December, 93–102.

9. Jussim, L. and Harber, K.D. (2005). Teacher expectations and self-fulfilling prophecies: Knowns and unknowns, resolved and unresolved controversies. *Personality and Social Psychology Review,* 9(2): 131–155.

10. Rosenthal, R. and Jacobson, L. 1992. *Pygmalion in the classroom: Teacher expectation and pupils' intellectual development.* New York: Irvington.

11. Ibid.

12. Hill, R.W. and Castro, E. 2002. *Getting rid of Ritalin: How neurofeedback can successfully treat attention deficit disorder without drugs.* Charlottesville, VA: Hampton Roads.

13. Crum, A. and Langer, E. 2007. Mind-set matters: Exercise and the placebo effect. *Psychological Science*, 18(2): 165–171.

14. Wager, T.D., Scott, D.J., and Zubieta, J.K. 2007. Placebo effects on human {micro}-opioid activity during pain. Proceedings of the National Academy of Sciences United States of America, 104(26): 11056–11061.

15. Stapp, H.P. 2007. *Mindful universe: Quantum mechanics and the participating observer.* New York: Springer.

16. Tiller, W.A. 1997. *Science and human transformation: Subtle energies, intentionality, and consciousness.* Walnut Creek, CA: Pavior Publications.

17. Edelglass, S., Maier, G., Gebert, H., and Davy, J. 1992. *Matter and mind: Imaginative participation in science.* Edinburgh, Great Britain: Floris Books.

18. Lipton, B.H. 2005. *The biology of belief: Unleashing the power of consciousness, matter and miracles.* Santa Rosa, CA: Mountain of Love/Elite Books.

19. Sheldrake, R. 2002. *Seven experiments that could change the world: A do-it-yourself guide to revolutionary science.* 2nd ed. Rochester, Vermont: Park Street Press.

20. Harman, W.W. and Sahtouris, E. 1998. *Biology revisioned.* Berkeley, CA: North Atlantic Books.

21. Frankl, V.E. 1963. *Man's search for meaning: An introduction to Logotherapy.* Boston: Beacon Press.

22. See Pattakos, A. 2004. *Prisoners of our thoughts: Viktor Frankl's principles at work.* San Francisco: Berrett-Koehler, for a fascinating application of Frankl's principles to management.

23. Majumdar, M., Grossman, P., Dietz-Waschkowski, Kersig, S., and Walach, H. 2002. Does mindfulness meditation contribute to health? Outcome evaluation of a German sample. *Journal of Alternative and Complementary Medicine*, 8(6): 719–730; discussion 731–735.

24. Schneider, R.H., Alexander, C.N., Staggers, F., Rainforth, M., Salerno, J.W., Hartz, A., Arndt, S., Barnes, V.A., and Nidich, S.I. 2005. Long-term effects of stress reduction on mortality in persons > or = 55 years of age with systemic hypertension. *American Journal of Cardiology*, 95(9): 1060–1064.

25. Jayadevappa, R., Johnson, J.C., Bloom, B.S., Nidich, S., Desai, S. Chhatre, S., Raziano, D.B., and Schneider, R. 2007. Effectiveness of transcendental meditation on functional capacity and quality of life of African Americans with congestive heart failure: A randomized control study. *Ethnicity and Disease*, 17(1): 72–77.

26. Srivastva, S. and Cooperrider, D.L. 1990. *Appreciative management and leadership: The power of positive thought and action in organizations.* Jossey-Bass Management Series. San Francisco: Jossey-Bass.

27. Thatchenkery, T.J. and Metzker, C. 2006. *Appreciative intelligence: Seeing the mighty oak in the acorn.* San Francisco, CA: Berrett-Koehler.

28. Cameron, K., Dutton, J.E., and Quinn, R.E. 2003. *Positive organizational scholarship: Foundations of a new discipline.* San Francisco, CA: Berrett-Koehler.

29. Seligman, M.E. 2006. *Learned optimism: How to change your mind and your life.* New York: Vintage.

30. Nair, K. 1994. *A higher standard of leadership: Lessons from the life of Gandhi.* San Francisco: Berrett-Koehler.

31. Ramsey, V. and Fitzgibbons, D.E. 2005. Being in the classroom. *Journal of Management Education*, 29(2): 333–356.

32. Stewart, J. 2005. Hypnosis in contemporary medicine. *Mayo Clinic Proceedings*, 80(4): 511–524.

33. Schweingruber, D. 2006. Success through a positive mental attitude: The role of positive thinking in door-to-door sales. *Sociological Quarterly*, 47: 41–68.
34. Maltz, M. and Kennedy, D.S. 1998. *Zero-resistance selling. Paramus*. NJ: Prentice Hall.
35. Banner, D.K. and Gagné, T.E. 1995. *Designing effective organizations: Traditional & transformational views*. Thousand Oaks, CA: Sage Publications.
36. Gardner, H. 2006. *Multiple intelligences: New horizons*. NY: Basic books.
37. Goleman, D. 2005.
38. Goleman, D. 2006. *Social intelligence: The new science of human relationships*. New York: Bantam Books.
39. Thatchenkery, T.J. and Metzker, C. 2006.
40. Pava, M.L. and Patrick P. 2004. *Spiritual intelligence at work: Meaning, metaphor, and morals*. Vol. 5, Research in Ethical Issues in Organizations. London: Elsevier.
41. Zohar, D. and Marshall, I. 2001.
42. Abate, F. and E. Jewell, E. 2001. *The new Oxford American dictionary* (online edition). New York: Oxford University Press.
43. For more elaboration, please see the "metaphysical breakthrough threshold" in Steingard, D.S. 2005. Spiritually informed management theory: Toward profound possibilities for inquiry and transformation. *Journal of Management Inquiry*, 14(3): 227–241.
44. Abate, F. and E. Jewell, E. 2001.
45. Schmidt-Wilk, J., Heaton, D., and Steingard, D.S. 2000.
46. Wilber, K. 2006. *Integral spirituality: A startling new role for religion in the modern and postmodern world*. Boston: Integral Books.
47. Murphy, M., Donovan, S., and Taylor, E. 1997. *The physical and psychological effects of meditation: A review of contemporary research with a comprehensive bibliography, 1931–1996*. 2nd ed. Sausalito, CA: Institute of Noetic Sciences.
48. Bracken, P. and Thomas, P. 2002. Time to move beyond the mind-body split. *British Medical Journal*, 325(7378): 1433–1434.
49. Nobel Laureate neuroscientist Roger Sperry, as quoted in Begley. Begley, S. 2007. *Train your mind, change your brain: How a new science reveals our extraordinary potential to transform ourselves*. New York: Ballantine Books. 136.
50. Newberg, A.B. and Waldman, M.R. 2006. *Why we believe what we believe: Uncovering our biological need for meaning, spirituality, and truth*. New York: Free Press.
51. McTaggart, L. 2003. *The field: The quest for the secret force of the universe*. NY: Harper Paperbacks.
52. Harman, W.W. 1998. *Global mind change: The promise of the 21st century*. San Francisco: Berrett-Koehler. 30.
53. Heylighen, F. September 15, 1995. *Downward causation*. Retrieved July 29, 2007, from Downward causation. http://pespmc1.vub.ac.be/DOWNCAUS.html.
54. Clark, K.E., Clark, M.B., and Albright, R.R. 1990. *Measures of leadership*. West Orange, NJ: Leadership Library of America.
55. Senge, P.M. 2005. *Presence: Exploring profound change in people, organizations, and society*. 1st ed. New York: Doubleday.
56. Tolle, E. 2004. *The power of now: A guide to spiritual enlightenment*. Rev. ed. Novato, CA: Namaste Publications/New World Library.
57. Mitroff, I.I. and Denton, E.A. 1999. A study of spirituality in the workplace. *Sloan Management Review*, 40(Summer): 83–92.
58. Heylighen, F. 1995.
59. Observational generativity derives from "observational theory" in Radin, D.I. 2006. *Entangled minds: Extrasensory experiences in a quantum reality*. New York: Paraview Pocket Books, 215, and the variety of cognitive biases in psychology: for example, experimenters' bias, expectancy effect, observer/subject effects detailed in Jones, R.A. 1977. *Self-fulfilling*

prophecies: Social, psychological, and physiological effects of expectancies. New York: L. Erlbaum Associates/Halsted Press.

60. Gardner, H. 2006.
61. Gardner, H. 2006.
62. Ibid.
63. Ibid. 6.
64. These four requirements are not intended to comprehensively evaluate intentional intelligence as an intelligence outlined by Howard Gardner in *Multiple Intelligences*. In addition to *Multiple Intelligences*, see the following works for more discussions of Gardner's criteria for an intelligence: Gardner, H. 1999. *Intelligence reframed: Multiple intelligences for the 21st century*. New York: Basic Books, especially chapter 4.
65. Gardner, H. 2006.
66. Goleman, D. 2005.
67. Harman, W.W. and Clark, J. 1994. The metaphysical foundations of modern science. Sausalito, CA: Institute of Noetic Sciences.
68. Abate, F. and E. Jewell, E. 2001.
69. Covey, S.R. 2004. *The 8th habit: From effectiveness to greatness*. New York: Free Press.
70. Beaty, B. *Weird science*. Retrieved July 29, 2007, from http://amasci.com/freenrg/laughed.html (last accessed July 29, 2007).
71. Allen, J. 2000. 21.

Spiritual Leadership: State-of-the-Art and Future Directions for Theory, Research, and Practice

LOUIS W. (JODY) FRY

A person's spirit is the vital principle or animating force traditionally believed to be the intangible, life-affirming force in the self and in all human beings.[1] Now people, as part of their spiritual journey, are struggling with what this means for their work.[2] Some are calling this trend "a spiritual awakening in the American workplace."[3] Patricia Aburdene in her recent book *Megatrends 2010*, states that the focus on spirituality in business is becoming so pervasive that it stands as "today's greatest megatrend." She contends that more and more people are making choices in the marketplace as "values-driven consumers" and the power of spirituality is increasingly impacting our personal lives and spreading into organizations to foster a moral transformation in them.

Many question why this interest in spirituality is occurring. Although there are many arguments, one viable reason is that society is seeking spiritual solutions to better respond to tumultuous social and business changes,[4] and that global changes have brought a growing social spiritual consciousness.[5] Indeed, Duchon and Plowman[6] posit that ignoring spirit at work may mean "ignoring a fundamental feature of what it means to be human."

Work is an integral part of our self-concept and greatly affects the quality of our lives both at work and at home. As employees are spending an increasing amount of time at work, they are actively pursuing opportunities for meaningful experiences in the workplace.[7] Indeed, some employees even expect their employers to provide for such a spiritual search.[8] In addition to the number of work hours required to be put in by employees, the unstable work environment, often characterized by downsizing, has increased distrust in organizations. This distrust has made employees see themselves as expendable resources.[9] This diminished view of work has compelled employees to search for deeper meaning and connection in life and, consequently, integrate a spiritual work identity.[10,11]

However, workplace spirituality has been an ambiguous term, although scholars are increasingly bringing clarity to the definition. Ashmos and Duchon defined workplace spirituality in terms of its components: (1) a recognition that employees have an inner life; (2) an assumption that employees desire to find work meaningful; and (3) a commitment by the company to serve as a context or community for spiritual growth. These dimensions have been incorporated into the term spiritual well-being (SWB), which is a "self-perceived state of the degree to which one feels a sense of purpose and direction."[12]

Other scholars suggest that workplace spirituality can be cultivated to produce increased organizational performance. Reder[13] found that spirituality-based organizational cultures were the most productive, and through maximizing productivity they reach dominance in the marketplace. In addition, there is emerging evidence that workplaces that are spiritually healthy perform better.[14,15,16]

In response to this calling for spirituality to be based on definable and measurable aspects of the work environment, Giacalone and Jurkiewicz,[17] in their *Handbook of Workplace Spirituality and Organizational Performance*, define workplace spirituality as

> A framework of organizational values evidenced in the culture that promotes employees' experience of transcendence through the work process, facilitating their sense of being connected in a way that provides feelings of compassion and joy.

This sense of transcendence—of having a calling through one's work or being called (vocationally)—and a need for social connection or membership are seen as necessary for providing the foundation for any theory of workplace spirituality. Workplace spirituality and spiritual leadership must therefore be comprehended within a holistic or system context of interwoven cultural and personal values. Also, to be of benefit to leaders and their organizations, any definition of workplace spirituality must demonstrate its utility by impacting performance, turnover, productivity, and other relevant criteria of effectiveness.[18]

A growing number of companies, such as Chick-Fil-A, Interstate Batteries, Taco Bell, Pizza Hut, and BioGenenex, are using spiritual lessons in their management and leadership strategies.[19,20] As the concept of spirituality in the workplace has gained strength and interest, the Academy of Management created a new special interest group for its members. The Management, Spirituality, and Religion interest group was created in 2000 and is helping to legitimize the study of spirituality in the workplace while simultaneously paving the way for this emerging concept into the leadership arena.[21] More specifically, as the interest in workplace spirituality grows, more research should be directed to understanding spirituality at work and its relation to leadership.[22]

Spiritual Leadership Theory

Spiritual leadership can be viewed as a field within the broader context of workplace spirituality. To date, Fry[23,24] and Fry and Slocum[25] have developed the only theory of spiritual leadership that has been extensively tested and validated in a variety of settings. Studies have been conducted in over 100 organizations, including schools, military units, cities, police, and for profit organizations (sample sizes ranged from 10 to over 1000). These studies, without fail, have confirmed the spiritual leadership causal model and the reliability and validity of its measures. Results so far support a significant positive influence of spiritual leadership on employee life satisfaction, organizational commitment and productivity, and sales growth.[26,27,28,29,30]

Spiritual leadership is a causal leadership theory for organizational transformation designed to create an intrinsically motivated learning organization.[31] Initially, the theory of spiritual leadership[32] was developed using an intrinsic motivation model that incorporates vision, hope/faith, altruistic love, theories of workplace spirituality, and SWB. The purpose of spiritual leadership is to tap into the fundamental needs for the SWB of both leader and follower, through calling and membership, to create vision and value congruence across the individual, empowered team, and organization levels, and, ultimately, to foster higher levels of organizational commitment and productivity. Operationally, spiritual leadership comprises the values, attitudes, and behaviors that are necessary to intrinsically motivate one's self and others so they have a sense of SWB through calling and membership. This entails the following:[33]

1. Creating a vision wherein leaders and followers experience a sense of calling in that life has meaning, purpose, and makes a difference.
2. Establishing a social/organizational culture based on the values of altruistic love whereby leaders and followers have a sense of membership, feel understood and appreciated, and have genuine care, concern, and appreciation for both self and others.

Fry[34] extended spiritual leadership theory by exploring the concept of positive human health, psychological well-being, and life satisfaction through recent developments in workplace spirituality, character ethics, positive psychology, and spiritual leadership. He then argued that these areas provide a consensus on the values, attitudes, and behaviors necessary for positive human health, psychological well-being, life satisfaction, and, ultimately, corporate social responsibility. Ethical well-being is defined as authentically living one's values, attitudes, and behavior from the inside out in creating a principled center congruent with the universal consensus values inherent in spiritual leadership theory.[35,36,37]

Fry proposed that those practicing spiritual leadership at the personal level will score high on life satisfaction in terms of joy, peace and serenity, positive human health, and the Ryff and Singer[38] dimensions of well-being. In other words, they will

1. Experience greater psychological well-being.
2. Have fewer problems related to physical health in terms of allostatic load (cardiovascular disease, cognitive impairment, declines in physical functioning, and mortality).

More specifically, those practicing spiritual leadership and their followers would have a high regard for one's self and one's past life, along with good quality relationships with others. This in turn helps to create the sense that life is purposeful and meaningful, the capacity to effectively manage one's surrounding world, the ability to follow inner convictions, and a sense of continuing growth and self-realization.

More recently, Fry and Matherly[39] and Fry and Slocum[40] argue that one of the greatest challenges facing leaders today is the need to develop new business models that accentuate ethical leadership, employee well-being, sustainability, and social responsibility without sacrificing profitability, revenue growth, and other indicators of financial performance. Increasingly, there is a need for top managers to simultaneously maximize the so-called triple bottom line or "People, Planet, Profit." Research conducted with Interstate Batteries is offered as a case study of a company that may serve as a role model for spiritual leadership. They also present a general process for maximizing the triple bottom line through the development of motivation and leadership required to simultaneously optimize employee well-being, social responsibility, organizational commitment, and financial performance.

Spiritual Leadership as an Emerging Paradigm

It is important that theories meet the four components that provide the necessary and sufficient conditions for the development of any theoretical model.[41,42] They must specify (1) the units or variables of interest to the researcher; (2) congruence as defined by the laws of relationship among units of the model that specify how they are associated; (3) boundaries within which the laws of relationship are expected to operate; and (4) contingency effects that specify system states within which the units of the theory take on characteristic values that are deterministic and have a persistence through time.

However, theory is but a necessary component for a paradigm. Kuhn[43] defined a paradigm as "An entire constellation of beliefs, values, techniques, and so on shared by the members of a given community." In other words, a paradigm is a philosophical and theoretical framework of a scientific school or discipline within which theories, laws, and generalizations and the methods to test them are formulated. Thus, for spiritual leadership to be an emerging paradigm, it must (1) have an identifiable conceptual domain; (2) have a theory that offers hypotheses that are testable through a variety of methodologies; and (3) specify boundary conditions and system states whereby the relationships among the theory's variables may operate differently (e.g., interactive effects due to a moderating variable).

A special issue on spiritual leadership in 2005 in *The Leadership Quarterly* served as a vehicle for moving the field of spiritual leadership, within the broader context of workplace spirituality, toward paradigmatic status.[44] In that issue, Dent, Higgins, and Whariff[45] and Reave[46] reviewed 87 and over 150 scholarly articles, respectively, and offer 8 areas that have implications for establishing the conceptual domain of spiritual leadership and show that there is a clear consistency between spiritual values and practices and leadership effectiveness. Dent et al.[47] use a qualitative narrative analysis to produce emergent categories to identify and validate eight areas of difference and/or distinction in the workplace spirituality literature, which have implications for defining the domain of spiritual leadership theory: (1) definition; (2) connected to religion; (3) marked by epiphany; (4) teachable; (5) individual development; (6) measurable; (7) profitable/productive; and (8) nature of the phenomenon. Reave[48] argues that values that have long been considered spiritual ideals, such as integrity, honesty, and humility, have an effect on leadership success. Similarly, practices traditionally associated with spirituality have been shown to be connected to leadership effectiveness.

From these articles a theme emerges: what is required for workplace spirituality is an "inner life" that nourishes and is nourished by "calling or transcendence of self" within the context of a "community" based on the values of altruistic love. Satisfying these spiritual needs in the workplace positively influences human health and psychological well-being and forms the foundation for the new spiritual leadership paradigm. By tapping into this basic theme through spiritual leadership, spiritual leaders produce the follower trust, intrinsic motivation, and commitment that are necessary to simultaneously optimize human well-being, corporate social responsibility, and organizational performance.

A Revised Theory of Spiritual Leadership

Duchon and Plowman[49] found that work unit performance is positively related to work unit spirituality. In support of spiritual leadership theory,[50,51,52] they discovered that work unit spirituality is associated with the leader's ability to enable the worker's sense of meaningful work (meaning/calling) and community (membership). In addition, they found that workplace spirituality is associated with the leader's ability to personally incorporate as well as enable/support the unit workers' inner life or spiritual practice (e.g., spending time in nature, prayer, meditation, reading inspirational literature, yoga, observing religious traditions, writing in a journal), which is a central activity in all major spiritual and religious traditions.

On the basis of these findings, a revised causal model of spiritual leadership is offered. In figure 7.1, the source of spiritual leadership is an inner life or spiritual practice that, as a fundamental source of

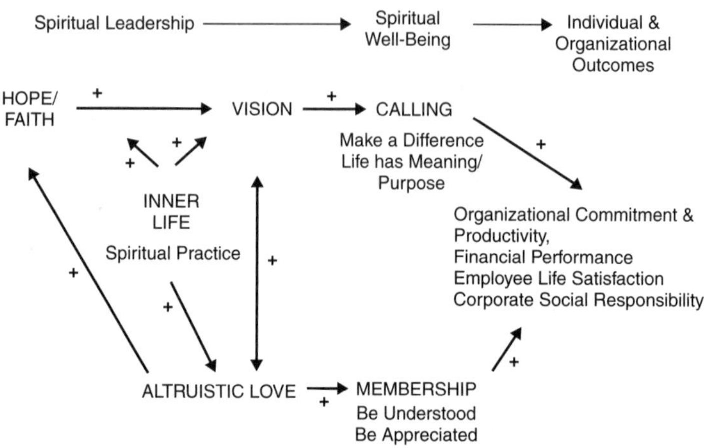

Figure 7.1   Revised Causal Model of Spiritual Leadership

inspiration and insight, positively influences the development of (1) hope/faith in a transcendent vision of service to key stakeholders and (2) the values of altruistic love.

What then are the defining characteristics or qualities of an effective inner life practice? This is clearly an area for future research. To review this topic in detail would require an exploration of the great spiritual and religious traditions as well as current work on presence,[53,54,55] mindfulness,[56,57] and meditation.[58,59,60] This is clearly beyond the scope of this chapter. However, for our purposes we can begin with the notion that employees have spiritual needs (i.e., an inner life) just as they have physical, mental, and emotional needs, and none of these needs are left at the door when one arrives at work. And, at the root of the connection between spirituality and leadership is the recognition that we all have an inner voice that is the ultimate source of wisdom in our most difficult business and personal decisions.[61]

Observing, witnessing, and cultivating this inner voice as it relates to tapping into or drawing upon a higher power[62] is often the purpose of an inner life or spiritual practice. Duchon and Plowman[63] posit that the existence of an inner life is related to two organizational constructs: individual identity and social identity, and that "individual identity is part of a person's self-concept, or inner view of themselves, and the expression of that inner life is in part an expression of social identity." Self-concept theory proposes that a job is more motivating when there is a high level of congruence between the job, its context, and a person's self concept.[64]

Therefore, spiritual leaders who have an inner life or spiritual practice will be more likely to have, or want to develop, the other centered values of altruistic love and a transcendent vision of service to key stakeholders and the hope/faith to "do what it takes" to achieve the vision. To implement spiritual leadership, leaders, through their attitudes and behavior, model the values of altruistic love as they jointly develop a common vision with followers. Subsequently, both leaders and followers gain a sense of membership—that part of SWB that gives one an awareness of being understood and appreciated. This then generates hope/faith and a willingness to "do what it takes" in pursuit of the vision, which in turn produces a sense of calling—that part of SWB that gives one a sense that one's life has meaning, purpose, and makes a difference. Hope/faith adds belief, conviction, trust, and action for performance of the work to achieve the vision. Thus, spiritual leadership theory proposes that hope/faith in the organization's vision keeps followers looking forward to the future and provides the desire and positive expectation that fuels effort through intrinsic motivation.

This intrinsic motivation cycle based on vision (performance), altruistic love (reward), and hope/faith (effort) results in an increase in one's sense of SWB (e.g., calling and membership) and ultimately positive individual and organizational outcomes such as organizational commitment and productivity,[65] employee life satisfaction, and corporate social responsibility,[66] and, given an effective market strategy, financial performance.[67,68,69]

Future Directions for Spiritual
Leadership Research

Research is needed on several fronts on our revised causal theory of spiritual leadership to establish that it is indeed inclusive of other widely accepted leadership theories and extends them, including our initial work, through a valid model that incorporates relevant spiritual, cultural, follower, and organizational effectiveness variables. Of special importance is the need to research the distinction between spirituality and religion.

Spirituality versus Religion. Duchon and Plowman[70] note that a spiritual leader enabling a worker's expression of "inner life" can be problematic if the spiritual leader's enthusiasm or zeal is seen by the worker as coercive. It is important to avoid the negative consequences of a hostile work environment that may result when employers emphasize a particular religion or spiritual practice in the workplace. This can happen, for example, when only the leader's form of inner life expression is accepted and "nonbelievers" (i.e., those preferring a different form) feel marginalized. The spiritual leader's enabling of a worker's inner life has to be undertaken in a work culture based on a norm of individual and collective tolerance and freedom. Organizations are able to avoid these pitfalls through periodic surveys and by allowing openness to spirituality, religion, and transcendence "in full freedom" through adherence to its core values. Robert Ouimet, owner of Tomasso corporation, for example, argues that this "full freedom" approach to work place spirituality is necessary to reconcile productivity and human well-being.[71] Tomasso makes this unambiguous by publicly proclaiming

> All actors in the company's life freely interpret the value of Transcendence in their own way.... Transcendence can mean the Creator; the Higher Power; God Love; God the Father, Son, and Holy Spirit; Allah; Jehovah; Buddha; or any other openings to Transcendence. To this value of Transcendence can be added, for those who so desire and according to their personal choices, different forms of reflection, meditation, and for some silent and personal prayer during work. This is quite possible without stopping work.

A central hypothesis to be tested in future research relates to the distinction between spiritual and religious approaches to workplace spirituality across the individual, group, and organizational levels.[72] A clear distinction between spirituality and religion is offered by the respected Dalai Lama:[73]

> Religion I take to be concerned with faith in the claims of one faith tradition or another, an aspect of which is the acceptance of some form of heaven or nirvana. Connected with this are religious teachings or dogma, ritual prayer, and so on. Spirituality I take to be concerned with those qualities of the human spirit—such as love and compassion, patience tolerance, forgiveness, contentment, a sense of responsibility, a sense of harmony—which brings happiness to both self and others.

Many feel that viewing workplace spirituality through the lens of religious traditions and practice is divisive in that, to the extent that religion views itself as the only path to God and salvation, it excludes those who do not share in the denominational tradition.[74] Furthermore, religious practices often conflict with the social, legal, and ethical foundations of business, law, and public and nonprofit administration.[75] Thus, religion can lead to arrogance that a particular company, faith, or society is better, morally superior, or more worthy than another.[76] Imbuing religion into workplace spirituality can foster zealotry at the expense of organizational goals, offend constituents and customers, and decrease morale and employee well-being.[77] Accentuating the line between religion and spirituality with regard to workplace spirituality is essential in honoring the integrity of both disciplines and is a key area for future research.[78]

Workplace Spirituality. Regarding research on workplace spirituality, Giacalone and Jurkiewicz[79] identify four major weaknesses that must be addressed if this newly emerging paradigm is to achieve acceptance within the scientific community: (1) the lack of an accepted, conceptual definition; (2) inadequate measurement tools; (3) limited theoretical development; and (4) legal concerns. To address these weaknesses and to advance workplace spirituality as a paradigm rooted in science, three critical issues will need to be addressed: (1) levels of conceptual analysis; (2) conceptual distinctions and measurement foci; and (3) clarification of the relationship between criterion variables.[80]

In addition to the key issues mentioned above, research on several fronts is necessary to establish the validity of spiritual leadership theory before it should be widely applied as a model of organizational/ professional development to foster systemic change and transformation. For example, more longitudinal studies are needed to test for changes in key variables over time. Studies are needed that incorporate more objective performance measures from multiple sources (Podsakoff et al.[81]). Other individual outcomes (e.g., joy, peace, and serenity) hypothesized to be affected by spiritual leadership need to be validated for spiritual leadership theory. Finally, the conceptual distinction between spiritual leadership theory variables and other leadership theories, such as authentic leadership, ethical leadership, and servant leadership, needs to be refined.[82,83,84,85]

Spiritual Leadership in Practice

Strategic leaders—through choices about vision, purpose, mission, strategy, and their implementation—are responsible for creating vision and value congruence across all organizational levels, as well as developing effective relationships between the organization and environmental stakeholders.[86] In this regard, two key practices are critical for the practice and implementation of spiritual leadership. First, conduct a periodic assessment of the spiritual leadership causal model to establish a baseline and identify issues for organizational transformation and development interventions. Second, using the results of this assessment, conduct a vision stakeholder analysis to (1) establish and/or reinforce the hope/faith, vision, and cultural values of spiritual leadership as the context for identifying key issues and (2) provide the basis for an organization-wide dialogue concerning the appropriate goals and strategies to address them.

Establishing a Baseline for Intervention. The first step is to gather information through surveys and interviews to establish a baseline for further Organization Development (OD) intervention. It is necessary that top management provides access to critical organizational data and fully supports this effort. All members should be provided with a survey that will measure spiritual leadership. After this, interviews with different members at all levels should be conducted to gain a more detailed insight into what is going on in the organization. Interview questions should likewise include questions that measure the theory's variables to validate findings. Below are the items for the revised theory of spiritual leadership that have seen some initial validation.[87,88]

Vision—describes the organization's journey and why we are taking it; defines who we are and what we do.

1. I understand and am committed to my organization's vision.
2. My organization has a vision statement that brings out the best in me.
3. My organization's vision inspires my best performance.
4. My organization's vision is clear and compelling to me.

Hope/Faith—the assurance of things hoped for, the conviction that the organization's vision/purpose/mission will be fulfilled.

1. I have faith in my organization and I am willing to "do whatever it takes" to ensure that it accomplishes its mission.
2. I demonstrate my faith in my organization and its mission by doing everything I can to help us succeed.

3. I persevere and exert extra effort to help my organization succeed because I have faith in what it stands for.
4. I set challenging goals for my work because I have faith in my organization and want us to succeed.

Altruistic love—a sense of wholeness, harmony, and well-being produced through care, concern, and appreciation for both self and others.

1. The leaders in my organization "walk the walk" as well as "talk the talk."
2. The leaders in my organization are honest and without false pride.
3. My organization is trustworthy and loyal to its employees.
4. The leaders in my organization have the courage to stand up for their people.
5. My organization is kind and considerate toward its workers, and when they are suffering, want to do something about it.

Meaning/Calling—a sense that one's life has meaning and makes a difference.

1. The work I do makes a difference in people's lives.
2. The work I do is meaningful to me.
3. The work I do is very important to me.
4. My job activities are personally meaningful to me.

Membership—a sense that one is understood and appreciated.

1. I feel my organization appreciates me and my work.
2. I feel my organization demonstrates respect for me and my work.
3. I feel I am valued as a person in my job.
4. I feel highly regarded by my leaders.

Inner life—the extent to which one has a spiritual practice.

1. I feel hopeful about life.
2. I consider myself a spiritual person.
3. I care about the spiritual health of my co-workers.
4. I maintain a spiritual practice (e.g., spending time in nature, prayer, meditation, reading inspirational literature, yoga, observing religious traditions, writing in a journal).
5. My spiritual values influence the choices I make.

Organizational commitment—the degree of loyalty or attachment to the organization.

1. I feel like "part of the family" in this organization.
2. I really feel as if my organization's problems are my own.
3. I would be very happy to spend the rest of my career with this organization.
4. I talk about this organization to my friends as a great place to work in.
5. I feel a strong sense of belonging to my organization.

Productivity—efficiency in producing results, benefits, or profits.

1. In my department everyone gives his/her best efforts.
2. In my department work quality is a high priority for all workers.
3. My work group is very productive.
4. My work group is very efficient in getting maximum output from the resources (money, people, equipment, etc.) available.

Satisfaction with life—one's sense of subjective well-being or satisfaction with life as a whole.

1. The conditions of my life are excellent.
2. I am satisfied with my life.
3. In most ways my life is ideal.
4. If I could live my life over, I would change almost nothing.
5. I have gotten the important things I want in life.

Vision/Stakeholder Analysis Process. The next step after the establishment of a baseline using the spiritual leadership survey is to initiate a vision/stakeholder analysis process that produces a vision/purpose/ mission whereby strategic leaders and followers serve the interests of key stakeholders. Research is especially needed on the vision/stakeholder analysis process that creates the energy to drive change throughout the organization.[89,90] The vision/stakeholder analysis process that is central to spiritual leadership is based on appreciative inquiry, which focuses on identifying and addressing key stakeholder issues by discovering what works well, why it works well, and how success can be extended throughout the organization.[91,92] Appreciative inquiry is premised on three basic assumptions. The first critical assumption is that organizations are responsive to positive thought and positive knowledge.

Second, both the image of the future and the process for creating that image produce the energy to drive change throughout the organization. By engaging employees in a dialogue about what works well based on their own experiences, employees recognize that there is much that works reasonably well already and therefore further change is possible. Finally, appreciative inquiry is based on a belief in the power of affirmations; if people can envision what they want, there is a better chance of it happening. This approach is suited to organizations that seek to be collaborative, inclusive, and genuinely caring for both the people within the organization and those they serve. By using an appreciative inquiry approach, organizations can discover, understand, and learn from success, while creating new images for the future.[93,94,95]

The spiritual leadership paradigm also utilizes a stakeholder approach in viewing social organizations as being embedded in layers or levels (individual, group, organizational, societal) with various internal and external constituencies (employees, customers, suppliers, government agencies, etc.), all of whom have a legitimate strategic and moral stake in the organization's performance.[96,97] Each of these stakeholders may have different values and interests as well as different stakeholder relationships with other individuals, groups, and organizations. The vision (what is our journey), purpose (why this journey is important), and mission (what we employees do to fulfill our purpose as we engage in our vision quest) work together to identify key stakeholders. Taken together, the vision/purpose/mission must vividly portray a journey that, when undertaken, will give one a sense of calling, of one's life having meaning and making a difference.

The vision/purpose/mission then forms the basis for the social construction of the organization's culture and the ethical system and values underlying it, which serves as a primary means of communicating, reinforcing, and rewarding appropriate organizational behavior. In spiritual leadership, these values are prescribed and form the foundation for a culture based on altruistic love.[98] To set the stage for initial change efforts, strategic leaders must model these values through their everyday attitudes and behavior throughout the vision/stakeholder analysis process.

The vision is initially created by the strategic leaders for the organization as a whole. All members or representatives of the organization should ultimately be offered the opportunity to participate. The ultimate goal is for all employees to know, believe in, and be fully committed to the vision. The purpose and mission of each department and any branches or subunits within a department are then derived in a linking-pin or cascading process.[99] As this process unfolds, key issues associated with current employee well-being, organizational commitment, corporate social responsibility, and performance are identified. Then a team comprising of members from affected internal and external stakeholders is formed to address these key issues and OD intervention strategies[100] are adopted to apply techniques and technologies for change. These strategies may include traditional interventions such as team building, intergroup development, or total quality management. Else, they may include the introduction of workplace-spirituality-based programs to target issues such as the recovery and development of workaholics and the organizations that nurture them.[101,102]

It is through this process of vision/stakeholder analysis and becoming committed to a vision grounded in service to key stakeholders that employees develop a sense of calling where, through their work, they feel they are making a difference in other people's lives and therefore their life has meaning and purpose. They also develop a sense of membership in being understood, appreciated, and cared for as the organization's key leaders "walk the walk" in cultural values and an ethical system based in altruistic love. The combined experiences of calling and membership are the essence of SWB. The vision/stakeholder analysis process is therefore the key to creating vision and value congruence across the strategic, empowered team and at the individual levels and, ultimately, to foster higher levels of employee well-being, social responsibility, and performance excellence.

Conclusion

Leaders who practice spiritual leadership by drawing on an inner life practice and communicate and model hope/faith, a transcendent vision, and organizational values based in altruistic love will encourage the manifestation of positive performance outcomes for both the individual and the organization. When leaders personify the values, attitudes, and behaviors of altruistic love that result in both the leader and employees feeling understood and appreciated as well as a sense of calling that their job makes a difference, they will tap into the intrinsic motivation cycle that results in high levels of human well-being, corporate social responsibility, and organizational performance.[103,104]

Our revised theory of spiritual leadership in figure 7.1 proposes that spiritual leaders must shape an organization that recognizes the importance of an inner life or spiritual practice that enables both leaders and followers to participate in meaningful work that takes place in the context of community. This inner life practice is the fundamental source for spiritual leaders to draw on and it ultimately produces the follower trust, intrinsic motivation, and commitment that is necessary to simultaneously optimize human well-being, corporate social responsibility, and organizational performance.

Notes

1. Anderson, P. 2000. This place hurts my spirit! *Journal for Quality and Participation*, 23(4): 16–17.
2. Mitroff, I.I. and Denton, E.A. 1999. *A spiritual audit of corporate America: A hard look at spirituality, religion, and values in the workplace.* San Francisco, CA: Jossey-Bass.
3. Garcia-Zamor, J.C. 2003. Workplace spirituality and organizational performance. *Public Administration Review*, 63(3): 355–363.
4. Cash, K.C., Gray, G.R., and Road, S.A. 2000. A framework for accommodating religion and spirituality in the workplace. *Academy of Management Executive*, 14: 124–134.
5. Inglehart, R. 1997. *Modernization and postmodernization: cultural, economic and political change in 43 societies.* Princeton: Princeton University Press.
6. Duchon, D. and Plowman, D.A. 2005. Nurturing the spirit at work: Impact on work unit performance. *Leadership Quarterly's Special Issue on Spiritual Leadership*, 16: 807–833.
7. Neck, C.P. and Milliman, J.F. 1994. Thought self-leadership: Finding spiritual fulfillment in organizational life. *Journal of Managerial Psychology*, 9(6): 9–16, 889–919.
8. Konz, G.N. and Ryan, F.X. 1999. Maintaining an organizational spirituality: No easy task. *Journal of Organizational Change Management*, 12(3): 200–210.
9. Cohen, G. 1996. Toward a spirituality based on justice and ecology. *Social Policy* (Spring): 6–18.
10. Ali, A.J. and Falcone, T. 1995. Work ethic in the USA and Canada. *Journal of Management Development*, 14: 26–33.
11. Noel, M. 2007. United States military academy spiritual leadership: Impact on unit performance. Unpublished manuscript prepared as a final project for a seminar in behavioral science, USMA.
12. Paloutzian, R.F., Emmons, R.A., and Keortge, S.G. 2003. Spiritual well-being, spiritual intelligence, and healthy workplace policy. In R.A. Giacalone and Jurkiewicz, C.L. (eds.), *Handbook of workplace spirituality and organizational performance.* New York: M.E. Sharpe.
13. Reder, M.W. 1982. Chicago economics: permanence and change. *Journal of Economic Literature*, 20: 1–38.
14. Duchon, D. and Plowman, D.A. 2005.
15. Elm, D.R. 2003. Honesty, spirituality, and performance at work. In R.A. Giacalone and Jurkiewicz, C.L. (eds.), *Handbook of workplace spirituality and organizational performance*, New York: M.E. Sharpe.
16. Garcia-Zamor, J.C. 2003.
17. Giacalone, R.A. and Jurkiewicz, C.L. 2003. Toward a science of workplace spirituality. In R.A. Giacalone and Jurkiewicz, C.L. (eds.), *Handbook of workplace spirituality and organizational performance.* New York: M.E. Sharpe. 13.
18. Sass, J.S. 2000. Characterizing organizational spirituality: An organizational communication culture approach. *Communication Studies,* 51: 195–207.
19. Fry, L.W. and Slocum, J. (In press). Maximizing the triple bottom line through a strategic scorecard business model of spiritual leadership. *Organizational Dynamics.*

20. Mitroff, I.I. and Denton, E.A. 1999.

21. Academy of Management. Retrieved November 8, 2006, from Management, Spirituality and Religion Web site http://aom.pace.edu/msr/

22. Noel, M. 2007.

23. Fry, L.W. 2003.

24. Fry, L.W. 2005b. Toward a theory of ethical and spiritual well-being, and corporate social responsibility through spiritual leadership. In Giacalone, R.A., Jurkiewicz, C.L., and Dunn, C. (eds.), *Positive psychology in business ethics and corporate responsibility.* Greenwich, CT: Information Age Publishing, 47–83.

25. Fry, L.W. and Slocum, J. (In press).

26. Fry, L.W. and Matherly, L.L. 2006a. Spiritual leadership and organizational performance. Paper presented at the Academy of Management, Atlanta, Georgia.

27. Fry, L.W., Nisiewicz, M., Vitucci, S., and Cedillo, M. 2007a. Transforming city government through spiritual leadership: Measurement and establishing a baseline. Paper presented at the National Meeting of the Academy of Management, Philadelphia, Pennsylvania.

28. Fry, L.W., Nisiewicz, M., and Vitucci, S. 2007b. Transforming police organizations through spiritual leadership: Measurement and establishing a baseline. Paper presented at the National Meeting of the Academy of Management, Philadelphia, Pennsylvania.

29. Fry, L.W., Vitucci, S., and Cedillo, M. 2005. Spiritual leadership and army transformation: Theory, measurement, and establishing a baseline. *Leadership Quarterly's Special Issue on Spiritual Leadership,* 16: 807–833.

30. Malone, P. and Fry, L.W. 2003. Transforming schools through spiritual leadership: A field experiment. Paper presented at the August meeting of the Academy of Management, Seattle, WA.

31. Fry, L.W. and Whittington, J.L. 2005a. Spiritual leadership as a paradigm for organizational transformation and development. Paper presented at the Academy of Management, Honolulu, Hawaii.

32. Fry, L.W. 2003.

33. Ibid.

34. Ibid.

35 Cashman, K. 1998. *Leadership from the inside out.* Provo, Utah: Executive Excellence Publishing.

36. Covey, S.R. 1991. *Principle-centered leadership.* New York: Fireside/Simon & Schuster.

37. Fry, L.W. 2003.

38. Ryff, C.D. and Singer, B. 2001. From social structure to biology: Integrative science in pursuit of human health and well-being. In Snyder, C.R. and Lopez, S.J. (eds.), *Handbook of positive psychology.* Oxford, New York: Oxford University Press.

39. Fry, L.W. and Matherly, L. 2007. Workplace spirituality, spiritual leadership and performance excellence. In Rogelberg, S.G. (ed.), *Encyclopedia of industrial/organizational psychology.* San Francisco: Sage Publications.

40. Fry, L.W. and Slocum, J. In press.

41. Dubin, R. 1978. *Theory building.* New York: Free Press.

42. Fry, L.W. and Smith, D.A. 1987. Congruence, contingency, and theory building. *Academy of Management Review,* 12(1): 117–132.

43. Kuhn, T.S. 1967. *The structure of scientific revolutions.* Chicago: University of Chicago Press.

44. Fry, L.W. 2005a. Toward a paradigm of spiritual leadership. *Leadership Quarterly,* 16: 619–622.

45. Dent, E., Higgins, M.E., and Wharff, D. 2005. Spirituality and leadership: An empirical review of definitions, distinctions, and embedded assumptions. *Leadership Quarterly,* 16: 625–653.

46. Reave, L. 2005. Spiritual values and practices related to leadership effectiveness. *Leadership Quarterly,* 16: 655–687.

47. Dent, E., Higgins, M.E., and Wharff, D. 2005.

48. Reave, L. 2005.

49. Duchon, D. and Plowman, D.A. 2005.

50. Fry, L.W. 2003.

51. Fry, L.W. 2005a.

52. Fry, L.W. and Slocum, J. (In press).

53. Rodgers, C.R. and Raider-Roth, M. 2006. Presence in teaching. *Teachers and Teaching*, 12(3): 265–287.

54. Tolle, E. 1999. *The power of now.* Novato, CA: Namaste Publishing.

55. Tolle, E. 2005. *A new earth: Awakening to your life's purpose.* New York: Plume.

56. Feldman, G., Hayes, A., Kumar, S., Greeson, J., and Laurenceau. 2007. Mindfullness and emotional regulation: The development and initial validation of the cognitive and affective mindfulness scale-revised (CAMS-R). *Journal of Psychopathological Assessment*, 29: 177–190.

57. Hirst, I.S. 2003. Perspectives on mindfulness. *Journal of Psychiatric and Mental Health Nursing*, 10: 359–366.

58. Kaiser R.B. and Kaplan, R. 2006. The deeper work of executive development: Outgrowing sensitivities. *Academy of Management Learning and Education*, 5(4): 463–483.

59. La Forge, P.G. 2004. Cultivating moral imagination through meditation. *Journal of Business Ethics*, 51: 15–29.

60. Manocha, R. 2001. Researching meditation: Clinical applications in healthcare. *Diversity*, 2(5): 3–10.

61. Levy, R. 2000. My experience as participant in the course on spirituality for executive leadership. *Journal of Management Inquiry*, 9(2): 129–131.

62. Fry, L.W. 2003.

63. Duchon, D. and Plowman, D.A. 2005. 811.

64. Shamir, B. 1991. Meaning, self and motivation in organizations. *Organization Studies*, 12(3): 405–424.

65. Fry, L.W. 2003.

66. Fry, L.W. 2005a.

67. Fry, L.W. and Matherly, L. 2006a.

68. Fry, L.W. and Matherly, L. 2007.

69. Fry, L.W. and Slocum, J. (In press).

70. Duchon, D. and Plowman, D.A. 2005.

71. www.our-project.org

72. Zinnbauer, B.J. and Pargament, K.L. 2005. Religiousness and spirituality. In Paloutzian, R. and Park, C.L. (eds.), *Handbook of the psychology of religion and spirituality.* Newbury Park, CA: Sage Publications.

73. Dalai Lama XIV. 1999. *Ethics for the new millennium.* New York: Putnam. 22.

74. Cavanaugh, G.F. 1999. Spirituality for managers: Context and critique. *Journal of Organizational Change Management*, 12: 186–199.

75. Nadesan, M.H. 1999. The discourse of corporate spiritualism and evangelical capitalism. *Management Communication Quarterly*, 13: 3–42.

76. Nash, L. 1994. *Believers in business.* Nashville: Nelson.

77. Giacalone, R.A. and Jurkiewicz, C.L. 2003.

78. Giacalone, R.A., Jurkiewicz, C.L., and Fry, L.W. 2005. From advocacy to science: The next steps in workplace spirituality research. In Paloutzian, R. and Park, C.L. (eds.), *Handbook of the psychology of religion and spirituality.* Newbury Park, CA: Sage Publications.

79. Garcia-Zamor, J.C. 2003.

80. Giacalone, R.A., Jurkiewicz, C.L., and Fry, L.W. 2005.

81. Podsakoff, P.M., MacKenzie, S.B., Podsakoff. N.P., and Lee. J.Y. 2003. The mismeasure of man(agement) and its implications for leadership research. *The Leadership Quarterly*, 14: 615–656.

82. Fry, L.W. and Matherly, L.L. 2006b. Spiritual leadership as an integrating paradigm for positive leadership development. Paper presented at the International Gallup Leadership Summit, Washington, DC.

83. Fry, L.W., Matherly, L., and Vitucci, S. 2006. Spiritual leadership theory as a source for future theory, research, and recovery for workaholism. In Burke, R. (ed.), *Research companion to workaholism in organizations* (New Horizons in Management Series). Cheltenham, UK ; Northampton, MA: Edward Elgar Publishing. 330–352.

84. Fry, L.W., Matherly, L.L., Whittington, J.L., and Winston, B. 2007. Spiritual leadership as an integrating paradigm for servant leadership. In Singh-Sengupta, S.A. and Fields, D. (eds.), *Integrating spirituality and organizational leadership*. Delhi: Macmillan India Ltd. 70–82.

85. Fry, L.W. and Whittington, J.L. 2005b. In search of authenticity: Spiritual leadership theory as a source for future theory, research, and practice on authentic leadership. *Leadership and Management*, 3: 183–200.

86. Maghroori, R. and Rolland, E. 1997. Strategic leadership: The art of balancing organizational mission with policy, procedures, and external environment. *Journal of Leadership Studies*, 2: 62–81.

87. Fry, L. 2007. A test of the revised spiritual leadership model in a CPA firm. Working paper. Tarleton State University.

88. Noel, M. 2007.

89. Bushe, G.R. 1999. Advances in appreciative inquiry as an organization development intervention. *Organizational Development Journal*, 17(2): 61–68.

90. Johnson, G. and Leavitt, W. 2001. Building on success: Transforming organizations through appreciative inquiry. *Public Personnel Management*, 30(1): 129–136.

91. Fry, L.W. et al. 2007a.

92. Malone, P. and Fry, L.W. 2003.

93. Appreciative inquiry and the quest. 2004. Retrieved May 6, 2007, from the Appreciative Inquiry Web site http://www.appreciative-inquiry.org

94. Johnson, G. and Leavitt, W. 2001.

95. Whitney, D. and Trosten-Bloom. 2003. *The power of appreciative inquiry*. San Francisco: Barrett-Koehler Publishers.

96. Freeman, R.E. 1984. *Strategic management: A stakeholder approach*. Boston: Pitman Publishing.

97. Jones, T.M., Felps, W., and Bigley, G.A. 2007. Ethical theory and stakeholder–related decisions: The role of stakeholder culture. *Academy of Management Review*, 32(1): 137–155.

98. Fry, L.W. 2003.

99. Malone, P. and Fry, L.W. 2003.

100. Brown, D. and Harvey, D. 2006. *An experiential approach to organization development*. 7th ed. New Jersey: Prentice Hall.

101. Fry, L.W., Matherly, L., and Vitucci, S. 2006.

102. Giacalone, R.A. and Jurkiewicz, C.L. 2003.

103. Fry, L.W. 2005a.

104. Fry, L.W. and Matherly, L. 2006a.

CHAPTER EIGHT

Awakening the Leader Within: Behavior Depends on Consciousness

DENNIS HEATON AND
JANE SCHMIDT-WILK

Global business today (Lawler and O'Toole,[1] Hitt,[2] Stead, Stead, and Starik[3]) calls for every worker to set goals, influence other people, and create and implement process innovations that are cognizant of organizational systems, customers, and the natural environment—in effect, it calls for every member of the organization to be a leader. Can we rely on the leadership training and development programs today to cultivate such leaders? Despite society's investment in the multibillion dollar leadership training industry, relatively little research exists on the effectiveness of leadership programs.[4]

This chapter discusses a research-based approach of developing leadership through development of consciousness. Development of consciousness is explained as a holistic transformation of the personality and mental structure that underlies thinking and behavior. The approach of developing consciousness can be seen as more fundamental than leadership training for new conceptual understanding or new behavioral skills, yet it can complement such training. The great need for such an approach was noted by Kegan[5] who argued that the mental demands of modern life require not just "a new set of skills to be 'put in' but a new threshold of consciousness."[6] Even as new forms of organization entail expectations that all organizational members will function with greater personal autonomy as well as more genuine collaboration, Kegan noted that these very behaviors are beyond the capacity of many adults at their current levels of development. The expectation that workers will be self-initiating, self-correcting, and be able to conceive of the whole organization demands not merely skills that can be taught but a qualitative reordering of mental complexity.

Developing personal and collective evolution of consciousness holds promise for catalyzing transformational changes of institutions and societies. Young and Logsdon[7] have explained, "it is clear that the level of consciousness that executive leaders have attained may influence virtually every aspect of their organizations"—including leadership, strategy formulation, organizational culture, ethical culture, and human resource management. They argue that evolution from mental-rational to integral frames of meaning enables leadership to see interdependencies and encompass expanded stakeholder perspectives. Such development can be said to create leaders who "tend less toward their own self-interest,"[8] but can also be understood as serving the interest of an infinitely connected sense of self. Higher stages of development have been associated with spiritually intelligent leadership, characterized by maintaining equanimity, feeling connected to the holistic flow of nature (*Tao*), and behaving with compassion and wisdom, with a decreasing need to control.[9] The following sections explore development of consciousness—from research based on both Western and Eastern psychology—and the significance of such development for the performance of leaders.

Psychological Development Is
Fundamental to Leadership Development

The Range of Adult Development. Psychologists have observed that as individuals develop from childhood to adulthood, there are stagelike shifts in the cognitive, interpersonal, and moral structures through which they make meaning of their lives. Loevinger's[10] construct of ego development refers to the evolution of a person's frame of reference— the deep structure of how the individual understands or makes sense of his or her world and own self. Writing in *Harvard Business Review*, Rooke and Torbert[11] use the term "developmental action logics" for this construct. In his model of psychological growth, Kegan[12] uses the term "orders of consciousness" as a synonym for stages of ego development.

Researchers such as Loevinger,[13] Cook-Greuter,[14,15] Kegan,[16] and Kohlberg[17] have found a wide range of developmental positions among adults and have discovered that only exceptional individuals are found at the highest stages of development. These psychologists have used the term "postconventional" to describe the mature stages at which the individual not only differentiates the self from roles and expectations of authorities but also defines moral values in terms of self-chosen principles.[18] The postconventional range of development has also been described in terms of psychological autonomy and integration, self-actualization, greater access to feelings and intuition, and wisdom.[19]

Loevinger's Washington University Sentence Completion Test (SCT) is a widely used measure to assess stages of ego development.[20] Studies of large samples using the SCT have found that most adults score at the conformist, self-aware, or conscientious stages. Only 8 percent of adults measure at the Individualistic, Autonomous, or Integrated stages, which are considered postconventional; and only 2–3 percent of these are at or above the Autonomous level (Loevinger and Wessler;[21] Cook-Greuter[22]). Referring to Loevinger's instrument as the Leadership Development Profile, Rooke and Torbert[23] report that in their sample of 497 managers, 15 percent scored at or above the Individualistic stage. A quantitative review concluded that adult ego development remains relatively stable throughout adult life and that investigators do not know what experiences promote postconventional development among adults.[24]

Applications of Psychological Development To Leadership. Evidence suggests that each progressive stage of development, with its broader construction of one's identity, one's world, and one's relation with others, unfolds greater capability for effective leadership. Assessments of psychological development in managers have noted leadership styles characteristic of different developmental positions (Kuhnert and Lewis;[25] Rooke and Torbert[26]). For example, Merron, Fisher, and Torbert[27] correlated developmental stages, as measured by the SCT, with performance on an in-basket exercise. Managers at Loevinger's Self-Aware stage, which is the modal stage in adult populations, performed as firefighters; they tended to treat each in-basket item as given and fixed, separate from one another, and requiring quick, unilateral action. Managers at Loevinger's individualistic and autonomous stages exercised more systemic management—they found relationships among items and looked not just at each problem in isolation but at the organizational context, assumptions, and goals underlying them, and moved toward building shared vision through collaborative interaction. Psychological development has also been linked with ethical behavior (Ponemon;[28] Rest;[29]

Trevino and Youngblood,[30]) capability for managing in an international context that involves multiple time frames and contradictory social perspectives,[31] and facilitating organizational change and innovation (Bushe and Gibbs;[32] Hirsch;[33] Rooke and Torbert[34]).

It has been observed that training in new management skills, such as becoming an empowering leader, will not "graft" well when those skills represent a stage of development too much higher than that of the person being trained (Merron, Fisher, and Torbert;[35] Bartunek, Gordon, and Weathersby;[36] Drath[37]). Thus, Fisher, Merron, and Torbert[38] argued that

> Human development would seem to be a central concern of management educators in universities, management trainers in organizations, and organizational development professionals.... Given this view, organizations and schools of management would place as much emphasis on creating learning environments conducive to personal development as on teaching specific knowledge and skills.

Despite growing recognition of the importance of behaviors and cognitive styles associated with more advanced psychological development, behavioral science is still searching for practices that could promote developmental advances in adults. Rooke and Torbert[39] report some individual successes from Action Inquiry as a process for increasing self-awareness and openness to new action logics. This chapter presents a model of how psychological development is accelerated by experiences of transcendence, and how experiences of transcendence promote both psychological development and leadership capabilities (see figure 8.1).

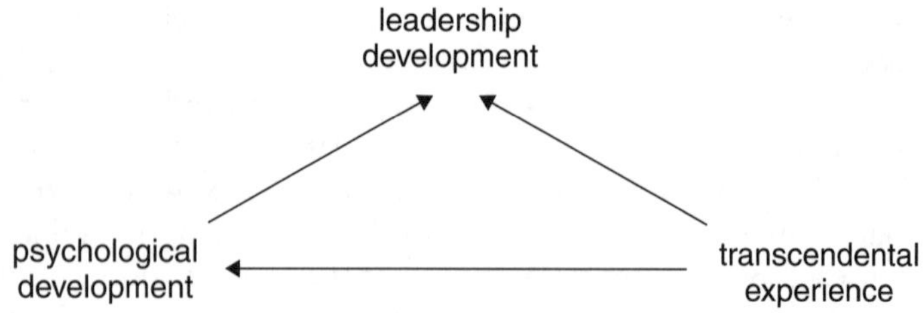

Figure 8.1   Inner Foundations of Developing Leadership

A Theory of Leadership Based
on Development of Consciousness

Transcendence and Leadership. Maslow[40] reported that growth of self-actualization was often stimulated by "peak" or transcendental experiences in which the individual identifies, to some extent, with infinity, universality, or perfection. Such experiences have perennially been noted in spiritual traditions throughout the world[41] and tend to stimulate creative impulses toward transformational change. Thus, spiritual experience has often been significant in the lives of leaders around the world who have left a lasting mark on human progress.

A study of world-class leaders found that they report more frequent experiences of transcendence than do college students.[42] In a recent study in Norway, top-rated managers reported more frequent experiences of transcendence compared to controls, and these experiences were correlated with physiological measures of greater orderliness of brain functioning and higher levels of moral reasoning.[43]

Business people may be conceptually and experientially familiar with such transcendental experiences from diverse systems of thought and meditative practices. Indeed, a variety of models posit that a higher range of human development can be accessed through experiences of transcendence, though these models may differ about the nature and sequence of the highest stages.[44] Likewise, a number of meditation techniques exist, and they differ in important ways (Shear;[45] Fehr;[46] Engel;[47] Orme-Johnson and Walton[48]).

In this chapter we focus on a particular practice—the Transcendental Meditation (TM) technique®—for operationalizing the construct of transcendental experiences. This technique is described as an effortless procedure for experiencing Transcendental Consciousness—a state of quiet self-awareness beyond thought.[49] This technique has been taught in a consistent manner around the world and thus has lent itself to scientific study. In fact, the TM technique has been the most thoroughly researched meditation practice.[50] Of particular interest is the research associating experiences of transcendence through the TM technique with developmental advances, as measured by a variety of instruments with different subject populations.[51] Regarding this research, Wilber[52] has noted as follows:

Moreover, unlike most of the meditation teachers in the country, Alexander and his colleagues have been taking standard tests of the various developmental lines (including Loevinger's ego development, Kohlberg's moral development, tests of capacity for intimacy, altruism, and so on) and applying them to populations of meditators, with extremely significant and telling results. The importance of this line of research is simply incalculable.

Besides the research that associates the TM technique with developmental change, we also chose to focus on this technique for its theory of higher states of consciousness,[53] which psychologists have related to developmental models from Western psychology (Alexander et al.;[54] Alexander, Heaton, and Chandler[55]).

Transcendence and Higher States of Consciousness. Alexander, Heaton, and Chandler[56] posit that experiences of transcendence unlock the natural continuation of psychological development in the direction of higher states of consciousness, as described by Maharishi Mahesh Yogi[57] (see also Dillbeck and Alexander[58]). The first of these higher states is called Transcendental Consciousness—"a state of inner wakefulness with no object of thought or perception, just pure consciousness aware of its own unbounded nature."[59] Maharishi has equated the experience of this pure wakefulness with "pure spirituality."[60]

Alexander, Heaton, and Chandler's[61] integration of Eastern and Western psychology argues that in the absence of such transcendental experience, all that one can know are representational notions about one's self—which is how identity is constructed at conventional stages of development. Self-identity remains framed in terms of socially derived conceptual ideas about one's self. It is necessarily changeable, dependent, and vulnerable; and perception is limited by self-protective bias and emotional variability. As explained by Maharishi: "Since the mind ordinarily remains attuned to the senses, projecting outwards towards the manifested realms of creation, it misses or fails to appreciate its own essential nature, just as the eyes are unable to see themselves."[62]

Through repeated experiences of inner silence alternated with active living, one's identity naturally grows to another higher state of consciousness—Cosmic Consciousness, in which pure consciousness in maintained throughout activity. With this growth, the individual gains an increasingly intrinsic, postconventional sense of personal autonomy and identity. One becomes stable and independent of changing circumstances, which in turn enables one to perceive all phenomena with objectivity and evenness. Maharishi has described Cosmic

Consciousness as a state in which "...union of the mind with the divine intelligence...remains established...bringing into harmony the inner creative silence and the outer activity of life...to act with precision and success."[63] This is a state in which one spontaneously lives the realization described by "perform actions having abandoned attachment and having become balanced in success and failure";[64] action in this higher state of consciousness is "motivated not by selfish individuality but by cosmic purpose."[65]

Alexander, Heaton, and Chandler[66] suggest that the characteristics of Cosmic Consciousness constitute a developmental milestone beyond the stages commonly observed in adults, a stage of "full differentiation of the Self, conservation of the unvarying subject."[67] In a similar vein, Cook-Greuter has presented evidence of a "postobjective" self-view[68] in which one does not identify oneself with any of the changing contents of awareness. Subjects at this unitive or "ego transcendent" range of development, Cook-Greuter[69,70] observes, tend to be oriented toward a higher self and a sense of cosmic purpose.

The following self-report, from Alexander, Heaton, and Chandler,[71] provides an example of growth of Cosmic Consciousness in a subject who scored at the highest level of Loevinger's test of ego development:

That Silence just witnesses the drama of life that my individuality acts in. And because I identify most deeply with the Silence [Self], I don't tend to get caught up in the drama like I used to. So even while my individual ego is involved and dynamic and having ideas and making decisions, the sense of being transcendent to all that lets the whole thing become a sort of spontaneous flow....I'm at ease and comfortable with whoever or whatever's outside."[72]

Evidence of Psychological Development through the TM Technique. Research relating experiences of transcendence through the TM technique with developmental advances has been reviewed in Orme-Johnson.[73] Specific findings include age-dependent cognitive tasks in children (Alexander et al.;[74] Dixon et al.;[75] Warner[76]); moral development in college students;[77] and ego development advances in prison inmates, a population generally considered to be recalcitrant to change (Alexander and Orme-Johnson;[78] Alexander et al;[79] Alexander, Walton, and Goodman[80]). Longitudinal studies employing the personal orientation inventory have consistently found evidence of growth of self-actualization (Alexander, Rainforth, and Gelderloos[81]).

A longitudinal study compared changes in ego development over a ten-year period in graduates from Maharishi University of Management (MUM),[82] where the TM program is incorporated into the college curriculum,[83] to changes in matched samples from three well-known universities offering standard curricula. All tests were scored by an expert rater who was blind to the subjects' group affiliation. In contrast to the control groups, the TM sample showed significant increase in ego development, $t(131) = 5.303$, $p = .0000004$ (two-tailed). The effect size associated with this change was large: $d = .9$. At posttest, 53 percent of the M.U.M. subjects scored at the Individualistic stage or above, with 38 percent scoring at Loevinger's Autonomous and Integrated stages compared to 1percent of controls ($p < .0001$). MUM subjects' results also increased to high posttest levels of intimacy ($p < .01$) and principled moral reasoning ($p < .001$).[84] The proportion of M.U.M. subjects achieving postconventional development in this study is the highest observed in decades of published studies using the Loevinger test. Given the evidence associating postconventional development with greater leadership effectiveness, these findings may have great significance for the development of leadership.

Development of Consciousness Enhances Leadership Capabilities. Studies on the TM program in business settings lend support to the view that development of consciousness enhances leadership capabilities. In an eight-month pretest-posttest control group study in one company, subjects who learned the TM technique improved significantly more than controls in their expression of leadership behaviors, as measured by the Leadership Practices Inventory:[85] encouraging the heart, enabling others to act, modeling the way, challenging the process, and inspiring a shared vision. When interviewed, the meditators also described increased comfort in taking initiative, increased ability to negotiate, increased ability to think clearly, increased energy, and decreased tendency to be affected by stress.[86] Related studies have found that business people practicing this technique report improved health, decreased anxiety, increased productivity, and improved relations (Alexander et al.;[87] Schmidt-Wilk, Alexander, and Swanson;[88] Schmidt-Wilk;[89] Alexander et al.[90]).

A study in Sweden found that managers practicing the TM technique grew in holistic thinking and became much more perceptive of the important issues facing the company, as assessed by a corporate superior.[91] The following interview data from one of the meditating managers clearly indicates a developmental shift in what Loevinger calls "frame of reference":

> My conception of the world has changed, something I did not expect. Things that were solid reference points before aren't as solid anymore and have not been replaced by new solid reference points. In the beginning it meant a certain chaos, but now I have got used to questioning things which everybody takes for granted...I'm less worried at work and I have more distance to it. But I am more engaged than ever.[92]

Research on three European top management teams that introduced the TM technique as a management development program found that this approach, which allows managers to access inner latent capacities, meets criteria described in the literature for effective management and team development programs. Personal benefits reported included increased alertness, wakefulness and clarity of thinking, increased energy, greater resiliency in stressful situations, improvements in physical and mental health, as well as greater effectiveness in the task and role. The managers' reports of spontaneous behavioral changes, indicative of increasing integration of seemingly opposing characteristics, are signs of the balanced maturation characteristic of higher stages of human development. Participants also reported how their new abilities to build trust and acceptance, improve communication, and resolve conflicts in positive ways led to corresponding improvements in interpersonal and team relations.[93]

A case study of one of these top management teams illustrates how this meditation practice promotes psychological development in a specific managerial context. Through their long-term practice of the TM program, members of a Swedish top management team developed essential leadership skills, including self-awareness, comprehension of the viewpoints of others, systemic thinking, innovative problem-solving, and proactive behaviors. Their inner growth enabled them to meet challenges in ways not previously possible for them: to move from a narrow focus on self- and department-protection to a collaborative cross-functional perspective, and then to direct that cross-functional exchange toward fulfilling a common strategic purpose.[94]

Herriott[95] conducted interviews with twenty-one entrepreneurs who were long-term practitioners of the TM and TM-Sidhi programs. These subjects reported subjective states—such as inner fullness, inner silence, and a secure feeling of being anchored to something deeper.

From such responses, Herriott identified a common factor that she termed "unshakability," implying an ability to stay calm inside and unaffected even in the face of chaotic circumstances.

These managerial subjects also described their business performance in terms of growing intuition, holistic perspective, and fortunate coincidences. Intuition was described by interviewees as a hunch or subtle impulse from within, and as a knowingness that does not require intellectual analysis. Another feature of managerial performance reported by Herriott's subjects was good fortune, described in one subject's words as "being in the right place at the right time [in] alignment with the evolutionary flow of the universe."[96] Herriott reported, "Many interviewees noted that synchronicity, in the form of lucky breaks or happy coincidences, played a role in the unfoldment of their career or business."[97] Her subjects reported an association between instances of things "organizing themselves" and feelings of settledness (inner silence, lack of rush or strain).

Subjects also commonly referred to a pervasive sense of being part of a larger wholeness. According to Herriott, her subjects reported "an awareness of a more holistic, all-encompassing level of truth and reality, as a sense of integration of the inner and outer dimensions of life."[98] As a consequence of feeling a deep sense of connectedness, entrepreneurs adopted "more universal values: going beyond individual interests to the wider interests of employees, community, or environment as a whole."[99]

Herriott's qualitative data concerning values orientations is consistent with an investigation of moral development and higher states of consciousness by Nidich, Nidich, and Alexander,[100] who reported that higher scores on EEG (brain wave) coherence, an indicator of Transcendental Consciousness, correlated with higher scores on a measure of Kohlberg's seventh, cosmic stage of moral development. This stage is said to entail an appreciation of an inherent order within the universe and a connection between oneself and this cosmic order.[101] Nidich, Nidich, and Alexander[102] explain that transcendental experience is instrumental in fostering a shift to a cosmic moral perspective that takes the perspective of a single fundamental wholeness rather than of one distinct individual.

The findings of these studies indicate that the results reported in the psychology literature are also applicable to leaders in business settings. Experiences of transcendence reduce stress and improve job performance; they also promote development of higher states of consciousness and have practical implications for leaders and business.

Continuing Research at Maharishi
University of Management

In this chapter, we have briefly summarized research on psychological development and shown that psychological development underlies leadership development. Using Alexander, Heaton, and Chandler's[103] model, we have presented research indicating that experiences of transcendence promote both psychological and leadership development. We therefore conclude that to develop leaders for today's global business, methods for tapping the inner spiritual source of human consciousness must be integrated into leadership training and development programs as a complement to existing cognitive, affective, and behavioral approaches to leadership development.

Our research in the PhD program in Management at Maharishi University of Management aims to advance management theory and practice through the development of consciousness. We are exploring how systematic cultivation of transcendent states of awareness, by accelerating psychological development, can supplement cognitive and behavioral training approaches to enhance the effectiveness of leadership development programs. Measures of developmental outcomes are incorporated in assessment research with both undergraduate and MBA students. We are building on our earlier research concerning measuring spirituality in organizations[104] to develop physiological, psychological, and behavioral profiles of the consciousness of leaders for use in selection, placement, and development in organizations.

Leadership is not just a function involving individual development of the leader, but is a field phenomenon that depends on the collective consciousness of leaders and followers.[105] Therefore the unit of analysis for exploring leadership development in relation to the development of consciousness is not only at the level of the individual leader, but also at the levels of teams and business units. While collective consciousness has been researched as a sociological and political phenomenon (Orme-Johnson et al.;[106] Hagelin et al.[107]), more research is called for to explore the phenomenon of leadership in relation to the development of collective consciousness in organizations.

In terms of management theory, we are exploring the dynamics of consciousness underlying organizational practices for environmental sustainability and human fulfillment. Einstein noted: "We cannot solve the problems that come with the world we have made thus far from the same level of consciousness at which we created them."[108] A corollary is that developing higher consciousness provides a foundation for resolving and preventing problems—a new consciousness creates a different world. It is our observation that a fundamental shift in consciousness is taking place, through which new, more spiritual principles and practices of management are arising to express greater values of wholeness and positivity in organizations.

Notes

1. Lawler, E. and J.O'Toole. 2007. *The new American workplace*. Rpt. ed. New York: Palgrave Macmillan.
2. Hitt, M.A. 1998. Twenty-first-century organizations: Business firms, business schools and the academy. *Academy of Management Review*, 23: 218–224.
3. Stead, E., Stead, J., and Starik, M. 2003. *Sustainable strategic management*. Armond, NY: M.E. Sharpe.
4. Yukl, G. 2006. *Leadership in organizations*. 6th ed. Upper Saddle River, NJ: Prentice Hall.
5. Kegan, R. 1994. *In over our heads: The mental demands of modern life*. Cambridge, MA: Harvard University Press.
6. Ibid. 165.
7. Young, J.E. and Logsdon, J.M. 2006. Integral sensemaking for executives. *Journal of Management, Spirituality and Religion*, 2: 67–103.
8. Ibid. 88.
9. Wigglesworth, C. 2006. Why spiritual intelligence is essential to mature leadership. *Integral Leadership Review*, 6(3). http://www.integralleadershipreview.com/archives/2006_08/2006_08_wigglesworth.html (Last accessed July 21, 2007).
10. Loevinger, J. 1976. *Ego development: Conceptions and theories*. San Francisco: Jossey-Bass.
11. Rooke, D. and W.R. Torbert. 2005. Seven transformations of leadership. *Harvard Business Review*, April 83(4): 1–11. Rpt.
12. Kegan, R. 1994.
13. Loevinger, J. 1976.
14. Cook-Greuter, S.R. 2000. Mature ego development: A gateway to ego transcendence? *Journal of Adult Development*, 7: 227–240.
15. Cook-Greuter, S. 2002. A detailed description of the development of nine action logics in the leadership development framework: Adapted from ego development theory. http://www.cook-greuter.com. (Last accessed July 27, 2007).
16. Kegan, R. 1994.
17. Kohlberg, L. 1969. Stage and sequence: The cognitive developmental approach to socialization. In Goslin, D.A. (ed.), *Handbook of socialization theory and research*. New York: Rand McNally.
18. Colby, A. and L. Kohlberg. 1987. *The measurement of moral judgment*. New York: Cambridge University Press.
19. Chandler, H.M., Alexander, C.N., and Heaton, D.P. 2005. Transcendental meditation and postconventional self development: A 10-year longitudinal study. *Journal of Social Behavior and Personality*, 17: 93–121.
20. Hy, L.X. and Loevinger, J. 1996. *Measuring ego development*. Mahwah, NJ: Lawrence Erlbaum Associates.
21. Loevinger, J. and Wessler, R. 1970. *Measuring ego development 1: Construction and use of a sentence completion test*. San Francisco: Jossey-Bass. N = 1640.

22. Cook-Greuter, S.R. 1990. Maps for living: Ego development theory from symbiosis to conscious universal embeddedness. In Commons, M.L., Armon, C., Kohlberg, L., Richards, F.A., Grotzer, T.A., and Sinnott, J.D. (eds.), *Adult development: Models and methods in the study of adolescent and adult thought.* 2nd ed. 79–104. New York: Praeger. 1996.

23. Rooke, D. and Torbert, W.R. 2005.

24. Cohn, L.D. 1998. Age trends in personality development: A quantitative review. In Westenberg, P.M., Blasi, A., and Cohn, L.D. (eds.), *Personality development: Theoretical, empirical, and clinical investigations of Loevinger's conception of ego development.* Mahwah, NJ: Lawrence Erlbaum Associates. 133–143.

25. Kuhnert, K.W. and P. Lewis. 1987. Transactional and transformational leadership: A constructive/developmental analysis. *Academy of Management Review*, 12: 648–657.

26. Rooke, D. and Torbert, W.R. 2005.S.

27. Merron, K., Fisher, D., and Torbert, W.R. 1987. Meaning making and management action. *Group and Organization Studies*, 12: 274–286.

28. Ponemon, L.A. 1992. Auditor underreporting of time and moral reasoning: An experimental lab study. *Contemporary Accounting Research*, 9: 171–189.

29. Rest, J.R. 1986. *Moral development: Advances in research and theory.* New York: Praeger Publishers.

30. Trevino, L.K. and Youngblood, S.A. 1990. Bad apples in bad barrels: A causal analysis of ethical decision-making behavior. *Journal of Applied Psychology*, 75: 378–385.

31. Weathersby, R. 1992. Developing a global perspective: A crucial changing of our minds. *Journal of Management Education*, 16: 10–27.

32. Bushe, G. and Gibbs, B. 1990. Predicting organization development consulting competence from the Myers-Briggs Type indicator and stage of ego development. *Journal of Applied Behavioral Science*, 26: 337–357.

33. Hirsch, J.A. 1988. Toward a cognitive-developmental theory of strategy formulation among practicing physicians. *Dissertation Abstracts International*, 49-08A, 2302.

34. Rooke, D. and Torbert, W.R.. 1998. Organizational transformation as a function of CEO's developmental stage. *Organization Development Journal*, 16: 11–28.

35. Merron, K., Fisher, D., and Torbert, W.R. 1987.

36. Bartunek, J.M., Gordon, J.R., and Weathersby, R.P. 1983. Developing "complicated" understanding in administrators. *Academy of Management Review*, 8: 273–284.

37. Drath, W.H. 1990. Managerial strengths and weaknesses as functions of the development of personal meaning. *Journal of Applied Behavioral Science*, 26: 483–499.

38. Fisher, D., Merron, K., and Torbert, W. 1987. Human development and managerial effectiveness. *Group &Organization Studies*, 2: 257–273.

39. Rooke, D. and Torbert, W.R. 2005.

40. Maslow, A. 1976. *Farther reaches of human nature.* New York: Viking Press.

41. Huxley, A. 1945. *The perennial philosophy.* New York: Harper and Row.

42. Harung, H.S., Heaton, D.P., and Alexander, C.N. 1995. A unified theory of leadership: Experiences of higher states of consciousness in world-class leaders. *Leadership and Organizational Development Journal*, 16: 44–59.

43. Travis, F., Harung, H.S., and Blank, W. In review. Higher development and excellence in leadership: Toward a brain measure of managerial capacity.

44. Miller, M.E. and Cook-Greuter, S.R. 1994. *Transcendence and mature thought in adulthood: The further reaches of adult development.* Lanham, MD: Rowman & Littlefield.

45. Shear, J. 2006. *The experience of meditation: Experts introduce the major traditions.* St. Paul, MN: Paragon House.

46. Fehr, T. 2002. The role of simplicity (effortlessness) as a prerequisite for the experience of pure consciousness—the nondual state of Oneness: "Turiya," "Samadhi" in meditation. Journal for Meditation and Meditation Research, 1: 47–99.

47. Engel, K. 2001. Meditative experience and different paths: Data based analyses. Journal for Meditation and Meditation Research, 1: 35–53.

48. Orme-Johnson, D.W. and Walton, K.G. 1998. All approaches to preventing and reversing the effects of stress are not the same. *American Journal of Health Promotion*, 12: 297–299.

49. Roth, R. 1987. *Transcendental meditation*. New York: Donald I. Fine.

50. Murphy, M. and Donovan, S. 1996. *The physical and psychological effects of meditation: A review of contemporary research with a comprehensive bibliography 1931–1996*. 2nd ed. Sausalito, CA: Institute of Noetic Sciences.

51. Orme-Johnson, D.W. 2000. An overview of Charles Alexander's contribution to psychology: Developing higher states of consciousness in the individual and society. *Journal of Adult Development*, 7: 199–216.

52. Wilber, K. 1997. *The eye of spirit: An integral vision for a world gone slightly mad*. Boston: Shambhala Publications. 232–233.

53. Maharishi Mahesh Yogi. 1969. *On the Bhagavad-Gita: A new translation and commentary*. Harmondsnorth, Middlesex, England: Penguin.

54. Alexander, C.N., Davies, J.L., Dixon, C., Dillbeck, M.C., Druker, S.M., Oetzel, R., Muehlman, J.M., and Orme-Johnson, D.W. 1990. Growth of higher stages of consciousness: Maharishi's vedic psychology of human development. In Alexander, C.N. and Langer, E.J. (eds.), *Higher stages of human development: Perspectives on adult growth*. New York: Oxford University Press. 286–341.

55. Alexander, C.N., D.P. Heaton, and H.M. Chandler. 1994. Advanced human development in the vedic psychology of Maharishi Mahesh Yogi: Theory and research. In Miller, M.E. and Cook-Greuter, S.R. (eds.), *Transcendence and mature thought in adulthood: The further reaches of adult development*. Lanham, MD: Rowman & Littlefield. 39–70.

56. Ibid.

57. Maharishi Mahesh Yogi. 1969.

58. Dillbeck, M.C. and Alexander, C.N. 1989. Higher states of consciousness: Maharishi Mahesh Yogi's physiology of human development. *Journal of Mind and Behavior*, 10: 307–334.

59. Maharishi Mahesh Yogi. 1976. *Creating an ideal society: A global undertaking*. West Germany: MERU Press. 123.

60. Maharishi Mahesh Yogi. 1995. *Maharishi University of Management: Wholeness on the move*. Vlodrop, Holland: Maharishi Vedic University Press. 271 fn.

61. Alexander, C.N., Heaton, D.P., and Chandler, H.M. 1994.

62. Maharishi Mahesh Yogi. 1966. *The science of being and art of living*. Los Angeles: International SRM. 30.

63. Maharishi Mahesh Yogi. 1969. 135–136.

64. Ibid. 135.

65. Ibid. 209.

66. Alexander, C.N., Heaton, D.P., and Chandler, H.M. 1994.

67. Ibid. 53.

68. Cook-Greuter, S.R. 1994. Rare forms of self-understanding in mature adults. In Miller, M.E. and Cook-Greuter, S.R. (eds.), *Transcendence and mature thought in adulthood: The further reaches of adult development*. Lanham, MD: Rowman & Littlefield. 119–147.

69. Cook-Greuter, S.R. 2000.

70. Cook-Greuter, S.R. 2002.

71. Alexander, C.N., Heaton, D.P., and Chandler, H.M. 1994.

72. Ibid. 63.

73. Orme-Johnson, D.W. 2000.

74. Alexander, C.N., Kurth, S.C., Travis, F.T., and Alexander, V.K. 2005. Effect of practice of Maharishi *Word of wisdom* technique on children's cognitive stage development: Acquisition and consolidation of conservation. *Journal of Social Behavior and Personality*, 17: 21–46.

75. Dixon, C., Dillbeck, M.C., Travis, F., Msemaje, H.I., Clayborne, B.M., Dillbeck, S.L., and Alexander, C.N. 2005. Accelerating cognitive and self-development: Longitudinal studies with preschool and elementary school children. *Journal of Social Behavior and Personality*, 17: 65–92.

76. Warner, T.Q. 2005. Awareness and cognition: The role of awareness training in child development. *Journal of Social Behavior and Personality*, 17: 47–64.

77. Chandler, H.M., Alexander, C.N., and Heaton, D.P. 2005.

78. Alexander, C.N., and Orme-Johnson, D.W. 2003. Walpole study of the transcendental meditation program in maximum security prisoners II: Longitudinal study of development and psychopathology. *Journal of Offender Rehabilitation*, 36: 127–160.

79. Alexander, C.N., Rainforth, M.V., Frank, P.R., Grant, J.D., von Stade, C., and Walton, K.G. 2003. Walpole study of the transcendental meditation program in maximum security prisoners III: Reduced recidivism. *Journal of Offender Rehabilitation*, 36: 161–180.

80. Alexander, C.N., Walton, K.G., and Goodman, R.S. 2003. Walpole study of the Transcendental meditation program in maximum security prisoners I: Cross-sectional differences in development and psychopathology. *Journal of Offender Rehabilitation*, 36: 97–125.

81. Alexander, C.N., Rainforth, M.V., and Gelderloos, P. 1991. Transcendental meditation, self-actualization, and psychological health: A conceptual overview and statistical meta-analysis. *Journal of Social Behavior and Personality*, 6: 189–247.

82. Formally Maharishi International University.

83. Schmidt-Wilk, J., Heaton, D.P., and Steingard, D. 2000. Higher education for higher consciousness: Maharishi University of Management as a model for spirituality in management education. *Journal of Management Education*, 25: 580–611.

84. Chandler, H.M., Alexander, C.N., and Heaton, D.P. 2005.

85. Kouzes, J.M., Posner, B.Z., and Peters, T. 1996. *The leadership challenge*. 2nd ed. San Francisco: Jossey-Bass.

86. McCollum, B. 1999. Leadership development and self development: An empirical study. *Career Development International*, 4: 149–155.

87. Alexander, C.N., Swanson, G.C., Rainforth, M.V., Carlisle, T.W., Todd, C.C., and Oates, R. 1993. Effects of the transcendental meditation program on stress-reduction, health, and employee development: A prospective study in two occupational settings. *Anxiety, Stress, and Coping*, 6: 245–262.

88. Schmidt-Wilk, J., Alexander, C.N., and Swanson, G.S. 1996. Developing consciousness in organizations: The transcendental meditation program in business. *Journal of Business and Psychology*, 10: 429–444.

89. Schmidt-Wilk, J. 2000. Consciousness-based management development: Case studies of international top management teams. Journal of Transnational Management Development 5: 61–85.

90. Alexander, C.N., DeArmond, D.L., Heaton, D.P., Stevens, M.M., and J. Schmidt-Wilk. 2004. Does spiritual practice reduce managerial stress? A prospective study of the Transcendental meditation program in business. Paper presented at the Academy of Management, MSR Division, on August 9 in New Orleans, LA.

91. Gustavsson, B. 1992. *The transcendent organization*. PhD diss., University of Stockholm.

92. Loevinger, J. 1976. 320.

93. Schmidt-Wilk, J. 2000.

94. Schmidt-Wilk, J. 2003. TQM and the transcendental meditation program in a Swedish top management team. TQM Magazine, 15: 219–229.

95. Herriott, E. 1999. Elements of entrepreneurial success: An exploratory study of the links between inner competencies, inner development, and success. PhD. diss., Maharishi University of Management, Fairfield, IA.

96. Ibid. 164–165.
97. Ibid. 165.
98. Ibid. 168.
99. Ibid. 172.
100. Nidich, S.I., Nidich, R.J., and Alexander, C.N. 2000. Moral development and higher states of consciousness. *Journal of Adult Development* 7: 217–225.
101. Kohlberg, L. and Ryncarz, R. 1990. Beyond justice reasoning: Moral development and consideration of a seventh stage. In Alexander, C.N. and Langer, E.J. (eds.), *Higher stages of human development: Perspectives on adult growth.* 191–207. New York: Oxford University Press.
102. Nidich, S.I., Nidich, R.J., and Alexander, C.N. 2000.
103. Alexander, C.N., Heaton, D.P., and Chandler, H.M. 1994.
104. Heaton, D.P., Schmidt-Wilk, J., and Travis, F. 2004. Constructs, methods, and measures for researching spirituality in organizations. *Journal of Organizational Change Management,* 17: 62–82.
105. Blank, W. 1995. *The nine natural laws of leadership.* New York: Amacon.
106. Orme-Johnson, D.W., Alexander, C.N., Davies, J.L., Chandler, H.M., and Larimore, W.E. 1988. International peace project in the Middle East: The effects of the Maharishi Technology of the Unified Field. *Journal of Conflict Resolution,* 32: 776–812.
107. Hagelin, J.S., Rainforth, M.V., Orme-Johnson, D.W., Cavanaugh, K.L., Alexander, C.N., Shatkin, S.F., Davies, J.L., Hughes, A.O., and Ross, E. 1999. Effects of group practice of the Transcendental Meditation program on preventing violent crime in Washington DC: results of the National Demonstration Project, June–July, 1993. *Social Indicators Research,* 47: 153–201.
108. Cooperrider, D.L. and Khalsa, G.S. 1997. The organization dimensions of global environmental change. *Organization and Environment,* 10: 331–341.

CHAPTER NINE

Infinite Leadership: The Power of Spirit at Work

MARGARET BENEFIEL AND
KERRY HAMILTON

Action research, long regarded as a stepsister in the academy, has at last begun to attain its own place. Action research has its roots to the work of Kurt Lewin in the 1940s; it grew out of Lewin's concern that academic research remained disconnected from practical action, particularly action that would improve the world. His experiments at the Tavistock Institute included applications to democracy and organizational change.[1] Now action research spans a wide range of inquiry methods, while at the same time retaining a common core of concern for practical knowledge and for contributing "to the increased well-being—economic, political, psychological, spiritual—of human persons and communities, and to a more equitable and sustainable relationship with the wider ecology of the planet of which we are an intrinsic part."[2] Contemporary action research ranges from the tightly structured "action science" of Argyris[3] and Schön,[4] to the more flexible "cooperative inquiry" of Heron and Reason,[5,6] and to the fluid "action inquiry" of William Torbert.[7]

We believe that action research is particularly relevant for Management, Spirituality, and Religion (MSR) research, since much of what motivates MSR scholars is a quest for practical knowledge that contributes to the increased well-being of human persons and communities. Most MSR scholars, like most action researchers, long to do research that contributes directly to a better world. Furthermore, some MSR topics (like the ones in the following examples) lend themselves more naturally to action research than to traditional quantitative or qualitative research methods.

This chapter will demonstrate the use of action research for MSR topics through one form of action research—cooperative inquiry. Cooperative inquiry, we believe, is inherently spiritual. It creates a spiritual context and "way of being" in the following ways:

- Cooperative inquiry is implemented in community—all active subjects are fully involved as members of this active community, and all decisions are community-based decisions. As such, the research design fosters teamwork (community), creates open communication, and displays honesty and trust of the corporate body, one for another.
- Spirituality is part of the intentional interplay between reflection and experience. Individuals reflect and draw upon inner knowing, and then move that inner knowing into community engagement and experience. Research subjects work in an agreed-upon way, thereby experiencing the qualitative outcomes of the new ways of being.
- Primacy is given to transformative inquiries that involve action. Cooperative inquiry requires of the subjects that they be open to transformation in themselves, their community, and the world around them.
- In addition, the whole person is invited into the inquiry—body, mind, and spirit. That is, the full range of human capabilities and sensibilities is available as an instrument of inquiry, lending a holistic view and spiritually qualitative presence to the research and the outcomes of research.

In their definitive chapter "The Practice of Cooperative Inquiry: Research 'With' Rather than 'On' People" in *Handbook of Action Research*,[8] John Heron and Peter Reason outline (1) the elements that must be present in cooperative inquiry and (2) the phases through which a research project on cooperative inquiry proceeds. We will demonstrate the use of MSR action research in two settings: a fourteen-year group intervention in which coauthor Margaret Benefiel participated, and an executive coaching engagement with a service company in which coauthor Kerry Hamilton participated, using Heron and Reason's process as a guide.

Seeing Things Whole and Landry's Bicycles

"Seeing Things Whole,"[9] both a model and a process created by cofounders Dick Broholm and David Specht, seeks to link faith and organizational life. The Seeing Things Whole mission statement outlines the challenge it seeks to address:

> To the extent that religious communities have consciously addressed themselves to organizations, most often they have been prone to our cultural ambivalence of looking at organizations either with the eyes of unquestioning trust and support or, more frequently, the perspective of cynicism and suspicion. The resulting lack of a balanced perspective which integrates both the pastoral and the prophetic significantly weakens the capacity of religious congregations to thoughtfully engage organizations and those who lead them around the role and purpose and faithful performance of organizations in today's world.[10]

Springing from Christian roots, Seeing Things Whole also seeks to include wisdom from all religious traditions. Its vision includes the following:

> We are drawn by the vision of a world in which organizations measure themselves and are evaluated by others no longer on the basis of the single bottom line, but rather multiple "bottom lines" which represent concerns for the quality of life of those who work within the organization and for the ways in which the organization relates to and impacts the world around it... We believe that [our] insights and learnings... will powerfully inform not only our understanding about organizational life and leadership, but also our understanding of faith and its relevance to today's world.[11]

Seeing Things Whole sponsors regular roundtables in the Boston area and in the Twin Cities in Minnesota, and occasional roundtables in other geographic areas. Comprising representatives of four to five organizations, each roundtable meets several times a year. At each roundtable meeting lasting for three and a half hours, one member organization presents a current challenge it is facing, and the group, guided by a trained facilitator, uses the Seeing Things Whole model and process to help illuminate the challenge.

Landry's Bicycles,[12] a founding member of Seeing Things Whole's Boston roundtable, has been a focus organization annually for the past fourteen years. Landry's, comprised of seventy-five employees and four retail bicycle shops in the greater Boston area, displays its core values prominently in its stores and on its Web site, also declaring its affiliation with Seeing Things Whole:

> Our core values, which guide everything we do at Landry's Bicycles, include:
>
> a. Treating all our customers as honored guests.
> b. Connecting with the larger realm of bicycling.
> c. Making the world a better place through our work.
> d. Celebrating the quality of our people.
> e. Fostering teamwork, open communication, honesty, and trust.
> f. Taking intelligent risks.
> g. Continuously improving how we do things.
>
> In addition, Landry's is a founding member of Seeing Things Whole, a professional network seeking to understand the intersection of faith and organizational life.[13]

Tom Henry, managing director of Landry's, claims that Seeing Things Whole has served as his "board of trustees" over the years, helping Landry's stay true to its values and mission.

Because of their focus on the intersection of faith and organizational life, the Seeing Things Whole cooperative inquiry process used in conjunction with Landry's Bicycles constitutes MSR action research. How is the Seeing Things Whole method an example of cooperative inquiry? The following section will examine Seeing Things Whole's fourteen years of action research with Landry's Bicycles, from 1993 through 2007, illustrating how the elements and phases of cooperative inquiry are present in the roundtables and in what occurs between successive roundtables.

Elements

Seeing Things Whole coresearchers, a group consisting of a team representing Landry's, the Seeing Things Whole facilitator, and seasoned participants (participants representing other organizations, who have experience with challenges similar to the focus challenge Landry's is bringing) gather at the roundtable to engage in cooperative inquiry. Heron and Reason outline eight elements of cooperative inquiry. All are present in the Seeing Things Whole process, and will be illustrated by Landry's participation in Seeing Things Whole roundtables.[14]

1. *All the active subjects are fully involved as coresearchers in all research decisions.* In the Seeing Things Whole process, the trained facilitator meets prior to the half-day gathering with a team of Landry's "subjects" to plan the intervention. Together, the facilitator and the Landry's team plan the "focus challenge" for the half-day gathering with Seeing Things Whole participants. They also plan together the structure of the gathering. The "focus challenge" directs the attention of the participants. For example, one of the half-day gatherings focused on the challenge Landry's faced in developing leadership from within the ranks as the business grew.

2. *There is intentional interplay between reflection and making sense on one hand, and experience and action on the other.* In the Seeing Things Whole process, the half-day gathering focuses on reflection and making sense. The Landry's team leaves the gathering with a commitment to action and to experimenting with the insights that arose from the gathering. In fact, the last step of the Seeing Things Whole roundtable gathering is to generate options for engaging the challenge, thereby helping Landry's to begin to move from reflection to action. After the gathering focused on developing leadership, for example, the Landry's team went back to the office, designed a leadership training program, and put it into action.

3. *There is explicit attention, through agreed procedures, to the validity of the inquiry and its findings.* The primary procedure is to use inquiry cycles, by moving several times between reflection and action. Since Landry's sits in the center of the roundtable annually, it has experienced twelve cycles of moving between reflection and action.

4. *There is a radical epistemology for a wide-ranging inquiry method that integrates experiential knowing through meeting and encounter; presentational knowing through the use of aesthetic, expressive forms; propositional knowing through words and concepts; and practical know-how.* The Seeing Things Whole roundtable incorporates a wide range of ways of knowing. The typical half-day gathering begins with a

presentation from the Landry's team about their focus challenge, followed by questions from the participants. The group then breaks and returns to focus on a sacred text, meditating and sharing thoughts that arise, consciously keeping the meditation separate from Landry's focus challenge. After another break, the group returns to allow individual participants to reframe Landry's focus challenge through Seeing Things Whole's nine "strategic lenses," with each participant choosing a different lens. Then the Landry's team chooses one or two of the reframed challenges, now posted on the wall, on which to focus for the remainder of the gathering. The group then offers thoughts through the perspective of the reframed challenge, and the Landry's team takes home the ideas. In addition, at various times Seeing Things Whole gatherings have included drama, music, communal spiritual discernment, and small group discussion.

5. *There are, in addition to validity procedures, a range of special skills suited to such all-purpose experiential inquiry, including fine-tuned discrimination in perceiving, acting, and remembering; bracketing off and reframing launching concepts; and emotional competence, including the ability to manage effectively anxiety stirred up by the inquiry process.* Because the Seeing Things Whole roundtables have practiced cooperative inquiry together for many years and because a trained facilitator facilitates them, the participants are skilled at perceiving, acting, and remembering. The facilitator takes careful notes for the Landry's team. The process itself specializes in bracketing off and reframing launching concepts. The facilitator's skill in being a nonanxious presence helps the group live with the anxiety stirred up by the inquiry process.

6. *The inquiry method can be both informative about and transformative of any aspect of the human condition that is accessible to a transparent body-mind.* Over the years, Landry's teams have worked with a wide range of focus challenges, from "shrinkage" in inventory (when employees take items without paying for them) to leadership training, lobbying legislators, recapturing market share from "big box" stores, and making the world a better place through cycling.

7. *Primacy is given to transformative inquiries that involve action.* When the Landry's team chooses a focus challenge for the meeting, they do so with the understanding that they are open to transformation and that they will act on the insights they gain.

8. *The full range of human capacities and sensibilities is available as an instrument of inquiry.* When the Landry's team gathers with the roundtable, the participants are open to a wide range of questions and methods of inquiry.

Phases

Heron and Reason point out that a cooperative inquiry cycles through four phases of reflection and action. Just as the elements of cooperative inquiry are all present in the Seeing Things Whole process, so are the phases.[15]

1. *In Phase 1, a group of coresearchers come together to explore an agreed area of human activity.* In the first part of Phase 1, they agree on the focus of their inquiry and develop together a set of questions or propositions they wish to investigate. Then they plan a method for exploring this focal idea in action through practical experience. In the final part of Phase 1, they devise and agree on a set of procedures for gathering and recording data from this experience: diaries, self-assessment rating scales, audio or video recordings, feedback from colleagues or clients, and so on. In Seeing Things Whole research with Landry's, Phase 1 occurs when the Seeing Things Whole facilitator meets with a Landry's team to prepare for the roundtable. At this meeting, the facilitator and the Landry's team articulate the "focus challenge" and the method for exploring it at the roundtable. They also agree on how they will record data from the roundtable gathering.
2. *In Phase 2, the coresearchers now also become co-subjects; they engage in the actions they have agreed, and observe and record the process and outcomes of their own and each others' action and experience.* Phase 2 occurs at the Seeing Things Whole roundtable gathering, where the Landry's coresearchers also become cosubjects. They engage in exploration of the "focus challenge" in the ways outlined in Element 4 (above).
3. *In Phase 3, the cosubjects become fully immersed in and engaged with their action and experience.* Phase 3 occurs when the Landry's team leaves the Seeing Things Whole roundtable and goes back to practice in daily life the insights gained from the Seeing Things Whole process. For example, Phase 3 occurred when the Landry's team designed a leadership training program as a result of the Seeing

Things Whole roundtable, carried out the program, and recorded data about how it went and what was learned.

4. *In Phase 4, the coresearchers reassemble to share their practical and experiential data, and to consider their original ideas in the light of it.* Phase 4 occurs when a team representing Landry's regathers with Seeing Things Whole roundtable members and reports on what it learned from putting the previous session's insights into practice. A new question is framed and the group wrestles with that new question.

Co-active Coaching in a Service Company

Co-active coaching in this engagement with a service company also exemplifies the elements of Heron and Reason's model of cooperative inquiry. In this setting the executive coach, trained in the co-active coaching model, was approached by the service company with a potential assignment to serve as executive coach to a high performing executive. Heron and Reason note that cooperative inquiry is collaborative action among people of shared concerns and interests.[16] The shared concern of both the service company and the coach was a concern for building upon an energized, heartfelt, and creative company environment, where each team member effectively motivates and collaborates with others—a company environment where employees are fully engaged and spirited. The coach introduced the co-active coaching model[17] to the company and based the engagement on the principles of this model.

The International Coaching Federation (ICF) defines coaching as follows:

> Coaching is partnering with clients in a thought-provoking and creative process that inspires them to maximize their personal and professional potential. Professional coaches provide an ongoing partnership designed to help clients produce fulfilling results in their personal and professional lives. Coaches help people improve their performances and enhance the quality of their lives.[18]

The co-active coaching model (offered through the Coaches Training Institute[19] and recognized by the ICF) utilizes the designed alliance as a critical relationship built between the coach and client.[20] The relationship is designed with the needs of the client solely in mind. It is a relationship built on trust, authenticity, and honesty, a sacred space where a client is free to be his or her whole self. In the co-active model, the alliance continues to be redesigned over the length of the engagement to serve the interests of the client. As such, the coach is involved in creating the design of the engagement with the client, and as in the cooperative inquiry method, codesigns and redesigns over time.

The Engagement

The company is an entrepreneurial service company specializing in creative problem-solving for its broad range of client companies. Along with being known as a highly creative and customer-focused company, the service company has a strong business model and is highly profitable.

The assignment is an example of MSR research dealing with a company environment that was successful financially but had issues that affected the quality of life of its employees because of the style of a senior executive. The senior executive is a highly skilled professional, key to the success of the organization through his result-oriented frame of reference and actions. The concern was that this executive was working from a command and control leadership perspective, a style that was highly directive, exclusive, and controlling of the processes to achieve goals. The style left little room for disagreement, collaboration, creativity, or teamwork. The environment, the company, and the culture were calling for a collaborative, empowering, and inclusive leadership style.

The goal of the engagement was to help the executive/coachee be more persuasive and collaborative, thereby creating a more positive working environment—without diluting the high standards that the success of the company was based on. It was important to do this in an authentic way that would serve the integrity of the executive/coachee.

In this setting, we illustrate the fundamentals of cooperative inquiry and the co-active coaching model. The elements of the Heron and Reason's method are noted here in italics, followed by the corresponding elements of the co-active method.[21]

1. *All the active subjects are fully involved as coresearchers in all research decisions.* In the co-active method, the initial intake session focuses on the goals of the group and the outcomes they desire from

the coaching work. In the service company setting, the primary group, the CEO, and the executive/coachee, all agreed on the goals for engagement with the coach. The executive team was also brought into the discussion for input.

2. *There is intentional interplay between reflection and making sense on one hand, and experience and action on the other.* The co-active coaching method utilizes reflection tools such as visualizations, inquiries, and powerful questions. From an experiential standpoint, the client agrees to action that deepens learning. Continual follow-up to action deepens learning and informs future action decisions.

3. *There is explicit attention, through agreed procedures, to the validity of the inquiry and its findings.* The primary procedure is to use inquiry cycles, moving several times between reflections and action. The procedure used for the coaching relationship alternated between seeking input and reflection on the executive/coachee's impact and action to improve and change his impact. In addition, throughout the six-month engagement, there was a series of measures to support and quantify change. These measures were designed with the primary team, and the design was vetted with the secondary team. All group members participated in the measurement.

4. *There is a radical epistemology for a wide-ranging inquiry method that integrates experiential knowing through meeting and encounter; presentational knowing through the use of aesthetic, expressive form; propositional knowing through words and concepts, and practical know-how.*
   - Experiential knowing: conversation, face-to-face encounter.
   - Presentational knowing: drawing on imagery, metaphor, and meta-view, co-active coaching serves to expand the boundaries of a client and open the way to what is possible through imaginative exercises.
   - Propositional knowing: through the use of language and metaphor.
   - Practical knowing: exhibiting practical learning through identification of action, deepening skills and learning, and trial and feedback.

5. *There are, in addition to validity procedures, a range of special skills suited to such all-purpose experiential inquiry, including fine-tuned discrimination in perceiving, in acting, and in remembering; bracketing off and reframing launching concepts; and emotional competence, including*

the ability to manage effectively anxiety stirred up by the inquiry process. The coach uses a wide range of special skills in the engagement, with emphasis on teaching these skills to both the executive coachee and the executive team. Reframing experience and reviewing and implementing the use of concepts, such as emotional intelligence, identified and de-emotionalized the areas of concentration to provide both a platform for change and a safe space to create that change. In addition, when anxiety and stress surfaced, they were named and used as part of the solution and change process.

6. *The inquiry method can be both informative about and transformative of any aspect of the human condition that is accessible to a transparent body-mind.* The Co-Active method serves true change and transformation by stepping beyond the everyday little agendas and focusing on the big agendas of the client, thereby creating a more fulfilling, balanced, and experiential life.

7. *Primacy is given to transformative inquiries that involve action.* The primary goal of the engagement was to create positive change in impact for the executive coachee and the executive team. The client changed the way of being and doing to the extent that it was noted, validated, and commended. Change remains part of the ongoing ways of being and doing for the executive and the company.

8. *The full range of human capacities and sensibilities is available as an instrument of inquiry.* In every meeting related to the engagement, individuals and teams brought the full range of skills, emotions, and spirits to the gathering, operating as whole beings engaging all human capacities for the greater good of the executive/coachee specifically, and the executive team generally.

Designing the Alliance and the Inquiry

Creating an alliance between a coach and an executive coachee is an important first task. This coach and client worked within the context of confidentiality—everything was confidential unless approved for release by the executive/coachee. In this case, the executive/coachee was very open and sharing, and approved all of the work that was done to be shared within the group. The CEO and the executive team participated in the design of the engagement.

Designing an Alliance

In the co-active model, the designed alliance is fundamental to the health and viability of the relationship and outcome. This designed alliance had the following characteristics:

- It provided safe and courageous space.
- It created the context for the client to experience fulfillment, the choice of balance, and the process of his life.
- It was a relationship that combined all of the players, where the whole was greater than the sum of the parts. Both the coach and the coachee granted power to the relationship, and it was in the relationship that learning was created and action was forwarded.
- It was authentic, honest, and trusting.

The designed alliance creates the context for the work. It defines the way that the coach and client work together. The alliance grants power to the relationship, which in turn adds liveliness and spirit to the coaching, with the ultimate purpose being to create the most powerful and creative life for the client.

In addition, an alliance was designed with the CEO and with the executive team, which upheld the confidentiality of the client and created an environment for an honest interchange of ideas and feedback.

Frequent meetings were fundamental to the coaching relationship and success of the engagement. The coach and the executive/coachee met weekly for one to two hours for six months. The coach met with each member of the partner group three times during the engagement and with the CEO six times during the length of the engagement. Throughout this entire process, the confidentiality of the executive/coachee was honored. And the executive/coachee engaged the CEO and executive team on a regular basis in active feedback and discussion on his interaction and his ways of being.

The goal-setting was done in the primary group with the CEO, the executive, and the coach through experiential knowing (primarily through storytelling). Through the recounting of stories of the company culture, interpersonal successes and conflicts, and important company events, the team identified company values and the strengths embodied in the company culture that created resonance, team/family orientation, and success. The goals for the executive/coachee were a direct product of the identification of what the company values.

Inquiry Skills

Heron and Reason's cooperative inquiry method points to specific inquiry skills that are also present in the co-active coaching method and were utilized in the engagement with the service company. Drawing on this research method and the work of the Coaches Training Institute (CTI) and the co-active model of coaching,[22] the work of this study was designed and conducted.

Being present and open. A fundamental skill of a coach, being present to what is said, verbally as well as nonverbally and through body language, was a key skill used in discerning resonance, embodying empathy, and connecting and attuning with important personal values of the executive/coachee and team. The coach conducted informational interviews with all members of the team in a 360-degree view. The coach gathered information from people surrounding the executive/coachee—boss, peers, and direct reports in all functional disciplines of the company. The interviewing methodology asked open-ended questions about the company culture, the valuable contributions of the executive/coachee, and the impact of the executive/coachee's ways of doing and being on the people and the company. The spirit of the company culture shone through in the number of times the word love was used to express the appreciation that the team had of the executive/coachee. Clearly, a spirit of love is integral to the culture of this company.

Bracketing and reframing (changing perspective). The co-active coaching skill of changing perspectives (or bracketing and reframing) was important to identify different ways to reimagine soft skill behavior and leadership style. The executive/coachee, through practice of reframing the situation, was able to create a leadership "way of being" that encompasses the ability to listen and understand others' ideas. Specific actions were created and tested—a method in which the executive/coachee catches herself or himself in the act of old behavior and choosing an approachable and collaborative "way of being" proved to be a great success in building the muscle for a collaborative leadership style. Reframing and changing perspective created the soft landing pad necessary for hearing the hard truth of needed change and embracing it.

Congruence. The skill of identifying congruence is one of both Heron and Reason's method and the co-active coaching model. A skill of values identification was utilized for identifying both company values and the personal values of the executive/coachee. The areas of congruence or resonance were identified and underlined. Importantly, the areas of dissonance were also identified. One value showed great importance. The executive/coachee identified a strong value of accountability, defined as doing exactly what you were asked or told to do by the specific deadline. In this service-oriented business, often the needs of clients were trumping the internal deadlines of the organization. The identification of the dissonance that was created in the executive/coachee by lapsed internal deadlines created an important perspective shift. The executive/coachee identified the trigger to his command and control behavior as linked directly with missed internal deadlines. His decision to become aware of this behavior in real time, and his choice to react differently and more effectively in negotiating outcomes, created a greater understanding for the entire team in renegotiating internal deadlines and accountability. This has improved interpersonal relationships in the company.

Nonattachment. The engagement focused on creating intention and setting goals for the engagement. That said, creating an environment for testing and action without the attachment to the success of that action is critically important for both models. The coach and the executive/coachee developed and tested many behaviors, some of which proved to be successful. The ability to learn as much as possible from the unsuccessful action accelerated and deepened the learning process and served to create a forward action toward transformation.

Emotional competence. Emotional competence is an area that many businesses are exploring deeply, looking for ways to develop and strengthen emotionally intelligent behavior in their managers and leaders. The executive/coachee and coach designed four emotional intelligence areas for focus as described by Daniel Goleman.

- *Empathy.* Sensing what people are feeling and able to take their perspective, cultivating rapport.
- *Self-awareness.* Knowing the emotions that we are feeling in the moment and using those preferences to guide our decision making.[23]
- *Conflict resolution.* Drawing out different perspectives and finding a common solution that everyone can endorse.
- *Developing others.* Cultivating people's abilities, leveraging their strengths and recognizing weaknesses; giving timely and constructive feedback.[24]

In the case of each of these attributes, the coach and the executive/ coachee codesigned the behaviors and actions that were tested on the team. Impact was noted, and firsthand feedback encouraged and sought to measure the viability of the action for further development. An interesting benefit was the identification in learning and change of behaviors in the other members of the team as a result of the engagement with the executive/coachee. As team members observed the changing behavior and actions of the executive/coachee, they themselves learned different ways of being that were more constructive and in keeping with the company's culture of love and putting people first.

Validity Procedures

As in the case of the Inquiry skills, validity procedures noted by Heron and Reason are also present in the co-active coaching method as noted below.

Research cycling. Cooperative inquiry utilizes the cycling of the following four phases in the inquiry:

1. Agreement on focus.
2. Engaging in the action and noticing the subtleties of experience.
3. Being fully engaged and immersed in their action and experience.
4. Sharing of results.

Once the agreed-upon focus was determined, the cycle was repeated twice, coming back in mid-engagement to measure the outcome and at the end of the engagement to measure the final results. In the co-active coaching method, similar stages are identified in the flow of coaching. Beginning with the designed alliance, emphasis was on action (What do I do?); experiencing ways of being (Who am I?); and determining forward action (What now, what's next?). The last step is a definitive finish including the results and the pluses and minuses.[25] A simple approach to completion includes the questions: "What worked? What didn't work? What would you like to have or see more of?" The co-active coaching method is based on truth-telling, and upholds the fact that there is no negative consequence to truth. The growth and learning that results is the positive consequence.[26]

Authentic collaboration. In the case study, the executive/coachee developed a higher level of self-awareness and was willing to hear honest truth. The company environment and the reaction of the other executives were open and honest. Each member of the team weighed in with a truthful opinion, and each individual opinion was held as important and of equal weight rather than weighted by title or status of the members. The CEO was more concerned with a positive outcome and feedback from the executive team than with his own measures of success. He exhibited the willingness to "walk the talk" of company values of putting people first and treating the team as family.

Challenging consensus collusion. Heron and Reason point to the permission of any inquirer to adopt the role of devil's advocate. In a similar way, the Co-Active model challenges participants to seek the truth underneath the words and to notice when values are being ignored. Intuition,[27] the ability to access an inner knowing, was a skill utilized by the coach and executive/coachee, and trained into the executive team. This led to a deeper discussion of issues and challenges, and a willingness to see beyond and below what was being said (or often e-mailed in this company). It led to more face-to-face discussion as against discusssion via e-mail, because of the understanding and recognition of the deeper level of communication inherent in a more active communication. In addition, specific formal feedback via mini surveys was gathered during the middle of the engagement and at the end of the engagement. This feedback was quantitative, utilizing trend scales to rate change in behavior based on the chosen emotional intelligence attributes. In addition, participants were asked qualitative questions about what more they wanted to see in the "ways of being" of the executive/coachee, a method of feed-forward that lets go of the past and seeks to look to the future for possibility and transformation.[28]

Managing distress. Managing distress took the form of allowing emotional issues to surface and acknowledging the dissonance, as well as pointing to the value that was being violated. Often, once the value was identified, the emotion abated, and humor and fun were utilized to move the team to resonance. The willingness to allow the emotions to surface and be given room to breathe allowed for the meeting of issues head-on, and the movement could progress to a more resonant place of understanding and action.

Reflection and action. Throughout the engagement, the cycle of meeting, creating action, getting feedback, and course-correcting action created a natural circle from reflection and action, and action and reflection, through transformative change. In the case of the executive/coachee, as well as partner group members, much conversation and learning was applied to home and family life. The team took the learning home to their families, where the larger value of the work played out in the whole lives of the participants.

Feedback. Two waves of feedback were directed throughout the engagement: (1) The feedback from the CEO/Executive Team to the executive/coachee and (2) feedback for the coach from the client throughout the engagement and at the end of the engagement. Feedback was verbal and written, as well as qualitative and quantitative. It was designed with the goal of asking specific questions to coax out what was missing and what was needed in the coaching engagement.

The executive/coachee had specific feedback on what the transformation meant to him—"Others are more comfortable challenging and asking me for what they need now. I am noticing that people are asking me directly for what they want. This has been very helpful." When asked what was most surprising in this process, the executive/coachee said, "I make an active decision to slow down now and choose my reaction."

How did the rest of the team view the change? "Well, I always loved him. Now he is listening and more relaxed." "There is continual improvement in a positive direction. The change is very apparent."

Finally, structures are needed to support the transformation. Change happens with a stimulus: the coming together of the group, the coach, the coachee, meetings, conversations, reflection, action, and feedback. All the aspects must be put into place to make the transformation real and ongoing. The coach and executive/coachee discussed a wide range of possible structures to create true transformation. The executive/coachee chose a method of tapping members of the executive team to be his ongoing partners for sustained change.

Conclusion

In the two settings described above, the value of the cooperative inquiry method for MSR research is noted. In the case of SeeingThingsWhole and Landry's Bicycles, the spiritual roots of both organizations were woven into an action-oriented process. Through reflection and contemplation, this has created an ongoing transformation for Landry's

Bicycles for over a decade. In the setting of the service company, the co-active coaching methodology was interwoven with the cooperative inquiry method. This method created change in both a senior executive and an executive team that served to strengthen the company culture. Ultimately, the intervention has created a positive sustained change of family spirit and love in this company. In both cases, cooperative inquiry engaged employees, resulted in positive organizational change, and created knowledge that could be used by the companies in the future.

In addition to the knowledge created that was useful for the two companies involved, cooperative inquiry created knowledge useful for other organizations, beyond the two companies. In the case of Seeing Things Whole and Landry's, Seeing Things Whole has built up a body of knowledge over the years that helps organizations articulate and live by their deepest values. The Seeing Things Whole model of organizational life, balancing identity, purpose, and stewardship through examining an organization through nine strategic lenses, has grown out of cooperative inquiry roundtables with Landry's and other organizations. In addition, Seeing Things Whole researchers have identified enabling forces that help organizations stay on track in living out their deepest values and block out those forces that throw organizations off track. The co-active coaching model also has developed over the years out of the experience of coaches, and continues to be refined as coaches engage in the type of cooperative inquiry described above.

Notes

1. Greenwood, D.J. and Levin, M. 1998. *Introduction to action research: Social research for social change.* Thousand Oaks, CA: Sage Publications.
2. Reason, P. and Bradbury, H. eds. 2001. *Handbook of action research.* London: Sage Publications.
3. Argyris, C., Putnam, R., and Smith, D.M. 1987. *Action science.* San Francisco: Jossey-Bass.
4. Schön, D. 1987. *Educating the reflective practitioner.* San Francisco: Jossey-Bass.
5. Heron, J. and Reason, P. 1997. A participatory inquiry paradigm. *Qualitative Inquiry,* 3(3): 274–294.
6. Heron, J. and Reason, P. 2001. The practice of cooperative inquiry: Research "with" rather than "on" people. In Reason, P. and Bradbury, H. (eds.), *Handbook of action research.* London: Sage Publications. 179–188.
7. Torbert, W.R. 1991. *The power of balance: Transforming self, society, and scientific inquiry.* Newbury Park, CA: Sage Publications.
8. Heron, J. and Reason, P. 2001.
9. www.SeeingThingsWhole.org
10. Seeing things whole. Mission statement, 2001. http://www.seeingthingswhole.org/images/ MissionWithCopyright.pdf (last accessed July 26, 2007).

11. Ibid.

12. Landrys.com

13. Landry's bicycles. Who we are: Landry's core values. http://www.landrys.com/whoweare/default.aspx (last accessed July 27, 2007).

14. Each of the eight elements is listed in italics, in slightly abbreviated form, followed by the example of Landry's engagement in the Seeing Things Whole process.

15. Each of Heron and Reason's phases is listed in italics, in slightly abbreviated form, followed by an outline of how the Seeing Things Whole process as used by Landry's practices that phase.

16. Heron, J. and Reason, P. 2001.

17. Whitworth, L., Kimsey-House, H., and Sandahl, P. 1998. *Co-active coaching: New skills for coaching people towards success in work and life.* Mountain View, CA: Davies-Black Publishing. 3–6.

18. International Coach Federation. What is a coach? http://www.coachfederation.org/ICF/For+Coaching+Clients/What+is+a+Coach/ (last accessed July 28, 2007).

19. Coaches Training Institute. http://www.thecoaches.com (last accessed July 30, 2007).

20. Whitworth, L., Kimsey-House, H., and Sandahl, P. 1998. 13–15.

21. Ibid.

22. Ibid.

23. Goleman, D. 1998. *Working with emotional intelligence.* New York: Bantam Books. 315.

24. Goleman, D., Boyatzis, R.E., and McKee, A. 2004. *Primal leadership: Learning to lead with emotional intelligence.* Boston: Harvard Business School Press. 256.

25. Whitworth, L., Kimsey-House, H., and Sandahl, P. 1998. 160–162.

26. Ibid. 17.

27. Ibid. 49–50.

28. Goldsmith, M. Marshall and linkage, incorporated: Developing ourselves, CIM solutions, Inc., http://www.marshallgoldsmithlibrary.com/cim/Linkage.php (last accessed July 30, 2007).

Critical Theory Approaches to Spirituality in Business

David Boje

This chapter reviews the work of Critical Theory (CT) to assess the orientation of business to spirituality. It has been mistakenly assumed that, given its Marxist heritage, CT is against spirituality. However, in the work of Horkheimer, Adorno, and Fromm of the Frankfurt School of CT, there are instances where they discuss their own religious and spiritual orientations. I would like to suggest some points of convergence between CT and spirituality. In particular, I want to extend the implications of the CT approaches to spirituality in business.

In the past, I have been rather critical of the spirituality in business movement.[1,2,3,4] First, spirituality (and religion) is too often used instrumentally as a way to motivate employees to higher levels of identification and commitment to so-called spiritual leaders and so-called spiritual business to boost performance, lower resistance (e.g., obedience), promote submissiveness, and manipulate servility (e.g., serving the customer and considering him or her as sovereign king). Second, since there are a variety of spiritual and religious practices, there is a difference between the rhetoric of "spiritual business" and the enactment of spiritual practices at work, as well as between espoused religious theory of spirit and what is practiced in the name of business. Third, critical theorists who have focused on the ways spirituality is abused in business may be dismissed by the mainstream as anti-spiritual, or as having no interest at all in developing viable spiritual practices in business.

In this chapter, I summarize the spiritual abuse theory within Christian circles and then discuss the parallel work by several critical theorists, including Horkheimer, Adorno, and Fromm. I suggest some ways in which critical theorists assume the role of a "doubting Thomas," opening up a space for being critical of spiritual abuse in business, but not dismissing spirituality altogether. I call this space a "critical spirituality" approach to ethical leadership and business practices. It is a side of the story that has been forgotten. The contribution this chapter makes is for the first time, it relates spiritual abuse theory to critiques made by several critical theorists, which open a door for ethical spiritual practices.

I contend that the critical theory work began at a particular stage of spiritual leadership and spiritual business discourse in post–World War II when fascism was reaffirming its grip on business practice.

A Brief History of Spirituality

Spirituality and leadership has a long history. In each historical period the relationship had a different emphasis.

Early Discipleship Model. In the first three centuries AD, spirituality and leadership meant selecting leaders from the community who exhibited the following nine gifts of the spirit:[5,6]

1. Faith
2. Knowledge
3. Wisdom
4. Miraculous power
5. Discernment of spirits
6. Healing
7. Prophecy
8. Speaking in tongues
9. Interpretation of tongues

The model of Christ was discipleship, apprenticeship, and mentoring of younger leaders, such as Paul, Timothy, Silas, John, and Mark. Abuse of spiritual gifts for selfish gain or to manipulate compliance was well known. Spiritual abuse was socially discernable when nine fruits of the spirit were not observed: joy, love, peace, longsuffering, kindness, goodness, faithfulness, gentleness, and self-control (Galatians 5:22–23).

Monastic Model. By the time of Emperor Constantine (274–336 AD), spiritual gifts and their fruit ceased to be of great importance to the church. People sought spirituality by retreating into monasteries where celibacy, meditation (e.g., *lectio divina* of St. Benedict), ascetic discipline, and piety were thought to mold spiritual life. St. Augustine (354–430 AD) formalized the monastic model, integrating his skeptical and neoplatonic philosophy with Christian-gnostic practices, and seclusion from the outside world. Some monastic orders developed universities, which was the beginning of scholasticism. Scholasticism, the reconciling of classic philosophy with medieval Christian theology, relies on the method of dialectical reasoning.

Protestant Reformation Model. Martin Luther (1483–1546), Huldrych Zwingi (1484–1531), and John Calvin (1509–1564), building on work by John Wycliffe and Jan Hus, emphasized spirituality critical of Catholic practices, which included selling indulgencies, elevation of saints, instilling fear of purgatory, worship of Virgin Mary, and general widespread church corruption (i.e., buying leader positions such as that of a priest or a bishop). Zwingi differed from Luther and Calvin by going beyond grace in baptism to a covenant of work as necessary for salvation. Another difference is the Eucharist. For Zwingi it is a symbolic, not literal, presentation of the body and blood of Christ. For Calvin, Christ is spiritually present, but not physically (as with Luther). Despite differences, protestant reformation favored the return to Christ-centered piety and an intellectual understanding of spirituality (head and heart). Monasteries were then closed down. A study of scripture (*sola scriptura*) was considered to be the way to educate the clergy. Greek and Hebrew were used in universities.

Seminary Model. In the nineteenth century, seminaries, such as Harvard and Princeton, were founded. The seminaries began to form a separate organizational identity from the universities. It was in the seminaries that a kind of training workshop in the Holy Spirit, as well as in pastoral training, took place.

Holocaust and Fascism. Hitler was baptized as a Catholic in Austria; he was later confirmed as one, was an alter boy, and also attended monastery school. On June 26, 1934, Hitler said, "The National Socialist State professes its allegiance to positive Christianity." Such statements about his Catholic support were likely to have been part of his propaganda to manipulate the public and to counter the criticism that Nazism was an antireligious party.[7] Hitler said, "So it's not opportune to hurl ourselves now into a struggle with the Churches. The best thing is to let Christianity die a natural death" (October 14, 1941). Hitler had Catholics killed and nuns removed from public service. Hitler merged his anti-Semitism with anti-Marxism. Of relevance to this chapter is that the critical theorists of the Frankfurt school were in double jeopardy. Further, Hitler was an advocate of social Darwinism, a philosophy widely critiqued by the Frankfurt School of critical theory. Social Darwinism refers to an idea of natural selection that predates Darwin's text. In particular, Herbert Spencer (1820–1903) held that competition among individuals, organizations, or nations in "survival of the fittest" is said to be the driver of social evolution. Spencer's[8] book was released two years before Darwin's *Origin of Species*. Spencer equated survival of the fittest with progress as a matter of predestination, whereas for Darwin, evolution is spurred by random variation.

Civil Rights Model. In 1960s education moved beyond the Ivy League universities and seminaries and onto the picket lines of the civil rights movement. Spirituality was the basis to sustain people in the struggle for social justice.

Modernity Model. The last fifty years of modernity has stressed a CEO approach to spiritual leadership, where the spiritual leader is a transformational, not a transactional, leader. It is in the last fifty years of modernity that the managerial paradigm has taken root, where spirituality is subordinated to profit and hierarchy. Transformative leadership was confused with leading a spiritual life in the previous periods: Early Discipleship (gifts of the spirit); Monastic life (discipline and meditation); Reformation (intellect and heart); Seminary (Holy Spirit workshop); Civil Rights (social justice).

Next, we examine spiritual abuse.

Spiritual Abuse

There is ample writing on spiritual abuse occurring in churches and organizations, especially in those with top-down authoritarian structures.[9,10,11,12,13,14,15,16,17] Spiritual abuse is defined as a misuse of the power of position, manipulative charisma, and authoritarian structures to enslave followers to pursue a leader's self-interests (often fraudulent ends) in a culture of exclusivity. The Bible presents two opposing spiritual systems. The first is under the reign of God (bringing life and freedom to people), and the second is false or pseudospiritual practice (bringing bondage and shepherding to people).

There are many biblical examples of spiritual abuse and its correction. The most famous is Christ overturning the tables of the money changers and using his cords as a whip, driving out the people buying and selling doves, cattle, and sheep in the temple (Matthew 21:12–13; Mark 11:15–18; Luke 19:45–47; John 2:13–16). Matthew (21:12–13) says, "Jesus entered the temple area and drove out all who were buy[ing] and selling there. He overturned the tables of the money changers and the benches of those selling doves." In John (2:16), "How dare you turn my Father's house into a market?" In Ezekiel (34:1–10) when God says, "Woe to the shepherds of Israel who only take care of themselves! Should not shepherds take care of the flock?" The charges include leaders' (shepherds) feeding themselves rather than the flock, ignoring the healing of those who were hurt, ruling over them by force and cruelty, and not binding up the hurt, healing the sick, or strengthening the weak. Instead, they were being ruled with harsh brutality. In Matthew 23:1–4, Christ said, "The teachers of the laws and the Pharisees sit in Moses' seat... [But] they do not practice what they preach. They tie up heavy loads and put them on men's shoulders, but they themselves are not willing to lift a finger to move them." Then there is the servant leadership construct developed in Matthew and Mark. In Matthew (23:10–11) the concept of servant leadership is developed as follows: "The greatest among you will be your servant. For whoever exalts himself will be humbled, and whoever humbles himself will be exalted." In short, those who are lording spirituality over others are "hypocrites" and "blind guides!" (Matthew 23:13, 16). In Mark (10:41–45), instead of "lording it over them" the style of the servant leaders was stressed, "For even the Son of Man did not come to be served, but to serve, and to give his life as a ransom for many" (Mark, 10:45). In Acts (7:51–56), Stephen was called before the high priest to defend against (false) charges of speaking against God. Stephen in his testimony said, "You stiff-necked people, with uncircumcised hearts and ears! You are just like your fathers. You always resist the Holy Spirit!" (7:51). For this he was stoned to death. Life by the spirit is summed up in Galatians (5:13–15): "You, my brothers, were called to be free. But do not use your freedom to indulge the sinful nature; rather, serve one another in love. The entire law is summed up in a single command: 'Love your neighbor as yourself.' If you keep on biting and devouring each other, watch out or you will be destroyed by each other." There are certainly many other examples of spiritual abuse.

Table 10.1   Summary Characteristics of Spiritual Abusive Organizations and Leaders

Boje's Summary Dimensions	Ronald Enroth (1994)	Agnes and John Lawless (1995)	David Henke (2005)
1. Authoritarian position or charismatic leader power	Authority and Power	Charisma and Pride	Authoritarian
2. Manipulative control of loyalty by anger and intimidation	Manipulation and Control	Anger and Intimidation; Demanding Loyalty & Honor	
3. Elitism and righteous image maintained by exclusivity and elitism	Elitism and Persecution	Exclusivity	Image Conscious (righteous exclusivity)
4. Lifestyle is unbalanced spiritual practices to claim new revelation	Lifestyle and Experience	New Revelation	Unbalanced spirit practices (to claim unique path to God); Perfectionistic
5. Discipline in enslaving authoritarian structure to suppress criticism	Dissent and Discipline	Enslaving Authoritarian Structure	Suppresses Criticism
6. Greed and fraud, or other immorality		Greed and Fraud; Immorality	

While the authors working on "spiritual abuse" theory focus on abuse by mainline churches and cultic offbeat churches, I think the dimensions are applicable to the spirituality in business movement. There is no reason to assume that spiritual leadership is always positive or used for the greater good. My thesis here is that spiritual abuse can occur in any business organization, reinforcing a top-down, highly authoritarian, and hierarchical structure. Some spiritual leaders are authoritarian, developing spiritually addictive, rather than socially healthy, organizations. They contend the practice is as old as religion itself.

Table 10.1 provides a comparison and summary of spiritual abuse dimensions in Ronald Enroth,[18] Agnes and John Lawless,[19] and David Henke.[20] We can summarize the six main dimensions that cut across studies of abusive spirituality as follows:

1. *Authoritarian position or charismatic leader power.* Abusive leaders (and groups of followers) distort spiritual authority and charisma concepts by arrogating power to certain leaders (usually office holders), overemphasizing authority, and making it inappropriate for

followers to question or challenge leader's decisions in forums of open accountability. Leaders establish an abusive spiritual system as they claim that God himself gave them their leader position and the right to command followers, which goes against (Mathew 22:1–23) passages about servant leadership and woes befalling those who are spiritual hypocrites and blind guides. Such leaders and organizations, claiming God blesses their submission and servanthood, distort moral authority.

2. *Manipulative control of loyalty by anger and intimidation.* The office bearers appropriate spirituality to themselves, making unquestioning submission a condition of loyalty. Abusive spiritual leaders (and groups) use fear, guilt, and threats to produce unquestioning obedience, group conformity, and tests of loyalty. Biblical concepts of leader-disciple relations are distorted by them to emphasize hierarchy, leader decision control, and usurpation of the disciple's right to make choices on spiritual matters or on daily routines (employment, diet, clothing, etc.).

3. *Elitism and righteous image maintained by exclusivity and elitism.* Abusive spiritual leaders (and groups) separate the group from other organizations or institutions, thus diminishing the possibility of criticism and evaluation that would bring reflection and correction. There is paranoia about critics. Critics of the abusive system are labeled "evil people" or as outsiders who are so worldly they would not understand. Evaluations by critics outside their denomination are dismissed as disruptive. Leaders manage their image of righteousness to outsiders, often misrepresenting organization history and covering up or denying the flaws in their character. The result is the secretive nature of the spiritual practices of the group, because their spiritual practices and beliefs cannot stand up to open scrutiny. At the same time, abusive spiritual leaders keep secrets from members while imposing impossible standards on them, and the leaders are held up as superior examples. Failure of followers to live up to or submit to stories of the spiritual leader's standards is a constant reminder of the follower's inferiority.

4. *Lifestyle is unbalanced spiritual practices to claim new revelation.* Abusive spiritual leaders (and groups) foster rigid beliefs and behaviors that require unswerving conformity to leader and group ideals and mores. Instead of grace available unconditionally, in abusive spiritual organizations, grace, salvation, and blessings come through performance. The result is perfectionism, insistence on following

the spiritual rules, and even pride in following them. Over time, perfectionism by performativity can lead to spiritual burnout. Those who fail to perform to standards are labeled weak (apostates) and can be ostracized and abandoned.

5. *Discipline in enslaving authoritarian structure to suppress criticism.* Abusive spiritual leaders (and groups) suppress internal challenges and dissent over leader's decisions by acts of discipline that can include emotional humiliation, physical violence, deprivation, and severe acts of punishment. Dissent is curtailed by claiming that submission to a hierarchy (or chain of command) will be a spiritual "covering" or "umbrella of protection" to those who submit and conform to punishment. The result is that the critic becomes the problem, rather than the issue about the so-called anointed leadership and hierarchy being raised. All criticism is taken as a challenge to leaderly authority or as a sign of unbelief in God. Thinking for oneself, or questioning, is discouraged. Only the leaders think and hand down decisions. The result is that the followers self-discipline their own thoughts for fear of doubting God's leaders.

6. *Greed and fraud, or other immorality.* Absolute power corrupts, and shepherding styles of abusive spirituality are no exception. Spiritual abuse is used to hide and perpetuate fraud and other immorality. This is not a new phenomenon. For example, in the history of the Catholic Church, indulgencies were sold to raise money. In the revival movement of the 1920s, a healing was accompanied by the collection of donations for that ministry. In the present time, TV evangelists put on a spectacle to raise money.

Next, I look at how critical spirituality by several critical theorists anticipates several of the dimensions of spiritual abuse.

Critical Spirituality and Critical Theory

Critical spirituality is defined as the study of how people at work engage the transcendental. I believe critical spirituality makes an important contribution to business practice, theory, and research. For me, critical spiritually is an inquiry into the dark side of managerialism and our late (post)modern global capitalism. Managerialism implies taking the manager's (owner's agent) perspective, while marginalizing implies taking the other stakeholders' perspectives. One way this marginalization takes place is by avoiding direct discourse among the stakeholders, and instead letting managers presume that they speak for everyone else.

There are several uses of the term "critical." The word "critical" refers to Critical Theory (in capitals, to represent early work by the Frankfurt School between 1931 and the decade following World War II); "critical theory" (in lower case is the usual designation for a variety of approaches since then, including "critical postmodern," of which I am a part).

Big CT. Big "Critical Theory" (hereafter CT) refers to work by the Frankfurt School Institute for Social Research, including work by its directors, Max Horkheimer and Theodor Adorno, as well as numerous associates, including Walter Benjamin, Herbert Marcuse, and Erich Fromm. The Frankfurt School was founded in 1923, and Horkheimer became its director in 1931.

Little "ct." Little "ct" refers to critical theory that follows the Frankfurt School. This would include critical postmodern theory. "Critical postmodern," in which I work, is defined as a combination of "critical theory" and "postmodern theory," which moves beyond the supposedly "radical postmodern" positions of Lyotard (incredulity to grand narrative) and Baudrillard (all is simulacra) by recognizing the interplay of grand narratives of modernity with the spectacularity of virtuality and hyper-competitiveness that is the basis of global predatory late modern and postmodern capitalism. The critical postmodern position does not do away with all grand narratives.

Several versions of less critical postmodern theory, such as those of the appreciative postmodernists, embrace the transcendental, spiritual, mysticism, and metaphysical in their various premodern and New Age guises. The critical approaches to postmodern are decidedly more skeptical about the supposed "good" that spirituality can do for the human condition. Other postmodern versions are decidedly rational, such as the versions of postmodern complexity theory focused on emergent processes. In short, there is as much variety in postmodern approaches as there is in religions.

Critical spirituality, the focus of this chapter, is skeptical of the appropriation of spirituality and religion into strategy practices. It is fearful that it is yet one more example of social Darwinism. Social Darwinism is a corporate reading of the transcendental forces of an invisible hand of competition that sorts the rich from the poor. Horkheimer's[21] book *Critique of Instrumental Reason* is mostly about spirituality, with essays on "Theism and Atheism," "The Soul," and "The German Jews." His essays from 1957 to 1967, I will argue, are an attempt to resituate spirituality and business (and the state), rather than for the common conclusion that critical theorists are against their interrelationship. Adorno's later works also seem to me to be about finding a resituation of spirituality in relation to late capitalism. For example, Adorno[22] said, "The great religions have either, like Judaism after the ban on graven images, veiled the redemption of the dead in silence, or preached the resurrection of the flesh." Given its doubting Thomas stance, critical spirituality can find throughout CT (and ct) support for spirit at work, but with caution to its potential for abuse. Before continuing our exploration of the relationship of critical theorists to spirituality, I would like to provide a brief overview of the phases of CT scholarship.[23,24] I do this digression now because part of the confusion in carrying out an inquiry into the relation of spirituality and business in the work of critical theorists is that their position changes. I will argue that it is in the second phase of CT that one finds more support for a relationship between spirituality and business.

Phase 1 of CT. In the early phase of CT, Theodor Wiesengraund Adorno (1903–1969) and Max Horkheimer (1895–1973) were directors of the Frankfurt School Institute for Social Research. Besides Adorno and Horkheimer, Walter Benjamin (1892–1940), Erich Fromm (1890–1980), Henry Gossmann, Arkadij Gurland, Otto Kirchheimer, Leo Lowenthal, Herbert Marcuse (1898–1979), Franz Newmann, Freidrich Pollock, and successor Jurgen Habermas are recognized figures in CT. The Frankfurt School was founded in Frankfurt in 1923, but it was Horkheimer's directorship after 1931 that gave it prominence. Horkheimer and Adorno led the first Phase of CT focused on an empirical and historically grounded interdisciplinary research program to overcome the inadequacies of Hegelian, Marxist, and Kantian theories. With Hitler's holocaust of the Jews, the Frankfurt school's Jewish faculty went into exile, reconstituting the school in Columbia University (NY) from July 1934 to 1943. At the end of this phase, it became clear to some CT writers that the culture industry made even a reformed Kant unable to be the basis of reform.

Phase 2 of CT. Horkheimer and Adorno's (1944/1972) *Dialectic of Enlightenment* is regarded as a turning point in CT, and the marker of its second phase, the aesthetic critique of the culture industry. The Nazi fascism of World War II left them disillusioned that any positive program of empirical interdisciplinary study would curtail it. Clearly their goal of ultimate emancipation from fascism lay elsewhere than in scientific enlightenment. They turned to more Weberian and Nietzchean skepticism to contend with the dark reality of post–World War II. In particular, Phase 2 work indicates a distrust of state and corporate control over culture industry. Adorno[25] ends his series of 1963 lectures by declaring, "There is no ethics...in the administered world." Adorno says he owes Nietzsche "the greatest debt" for his skepticism. After World War II, Horkheimer and Adorno returned to Frankfurt. In Phase II of CT, Horkheimer and Adorno tried to find the German–Jewish intellectual roots.

Phase 3 of CT. Since 1970, Jurgen Habermas has led the third phase of CT into its linguistic turn. I would argue that Habermas has turned the clock back to redeem Phase 1 CT in proposing a linguistic-communicative rationality. Habermas seeks the enlightenment ideal, an emancipatory potential attainable by neo–Kantian moral philosophy applied to social science. This can be seen in Habermas' communicative ethics. More recently, Habermas picks up on Luhmann as well as Parsons in a turn that can only be described as structural functionalist system theory. The result is that whereas Horkheimer, Adorno, and Fromm (as well as Marcuse) were moving away from formal, absolutist, universalistic ethics to one Bakhtin[26,27] calls an ethics of answerability, Habermas is headed in the other direction. Bakhtin[28] defines it as follows, "an answerable act or deed is precisely that act which is performed on the basis of an acknowledgment of my obligative (ought-to-be) uniqueness." For Bakhtin,[29,30] it is our unique standpoint in-the-moment of being, in participation with others, where we have no alibi, since no other person is there to listen or tell, to make a valuation, to act, and to put signature to story. Bakhtin[31] called for "seeking an answerable life"[32] for there is no universal ought, that is, there is no moral ought.[33]

Next, we examine the kinds of critical spirituality; the seeking of an answerable life that various key figures in CT pioneered.

Critical Spirituality According to Critical Theory

The theme of spirituality grew out of the CT group's concerns over the World War II Holocaust, and over the fascism and anti-Semitism in the forms of capitalism after World War II. For example in Horkheimer's essay "The Jews and Europe," he says, "No one can ask the émigrés to hold a mirror up to the world that has produced fascism in the very place in which they are being offered asylum. But those who do not wish to speak of capitalism should be silent about fascism."[34] While Wiggershaus[35] chides Horkheimer and Adorno for not being more radical and revolutionary in resisting fascism, for being too much about theory and not enough about practice, I see the history quite differently.

To me, Horkheimer and Adorno change course from the Phase 1 project of some union of diverse theory disciplines in an empirical science of CT. Rather, like their colleague Benjamin, they realize that the culture industry is leading the masses to support the marriage of fascism and capitalism. They therefore set out to develop tools to deconstruct the culture industry and to show how the Spectacle (in Debord's terms) of consumption has overtaken production processes as a means of social acculturation and control into hierarchical servitude.

In Adorno's[36] *Minima Moralia: Reflections From a Damaged Life,* he remembered the Jewish culture destroyed by World War II fascism and Holocaust. Adorno[37] said in his most quoted, and misunderstood, phrase, "To write poetry after Auschwitz is barbaric." The context of the phrase, its entire sentence, gives us deeper insight.[38] "The critique of culture finds itself confronting the last stage of the dialectic of culture and barbarism: to write poetry after Auschwitz is barbaric—and that fact, that situation devours even the insight and intelligence that speak out about why poetry has become impossible." To write poetic utopia is to effect amnesia about the Holocaust. For this essay, the insight is that for spirituality to gain any right to exist, it must be critical of spiritual abuse and its attempt to ignore the history of spiritual barbarism. "Abstract utopia is all too compatible with the most insidious tendencies of society."[39]

My position is closer to that of Douglas Kellner,[40] who says that rather than advocates for spiritual (or religious) approaches to organization, Horkheimer and Adorno, were ambivalent:

The Frankfurt School had a highly ambivalent relation to Judaism. On one hand, they were part of that Enlightenment tradition that opposed authority, tradition, and all institutions of the past—including religion. They were also, for the most part, secular Jews who did not support any organized religion, or practice religious or cultural Judaism. In this sense, they were in the tradition of Heine, Marx, and Freud for whom Judaism was neither a constitutive feature of their life or work, nor a significant aspect of their self-image and identity.

Ambivalence is one way to look at what I am proposing as critical spirituality. That is, while spiritual practices are appropriated by the state and by business capitalism in order to co-opt the masses, there is opportunity, now and again, to use spirituality as a form of resistance, and as a way to bring about distributive justice by making power aware of the embedded mechanisms of exploitation and oppression.

Next we look more closely at Adorno, Horkheimer, Benjamin, and Fromm's critical spirituality views.

Adorno: Dialectic Spheres

Adorno's oeuvre has frequent reference to the theology of Kierkegaard. Adorno's[41] first major philosophical work, *Kierkegaard: Construction of the Aesthetic,* appeared in bookstores on Feb 27, 1933, the day Hitler revoked freedom of the press. Adorno believes that there is something flawed in Kierkegaard's three spheres of existence:

1. *Aesthetic Sphere.* An immediacy where desire acquires no object (except erotic reflection); it is a naive idealism, such as the emotional freedom of one's first love kept in a diary.
2. *Ethical Sphere.* Desire seeks its object in multifariousness resulting in repentance and obligation, such as in marriage as freedom of necessity.
3. *Religious Sphere.* The synthesis of the preceding two spheres (turning them into stages of desire).

Adorno's reading is Kierkegaard, who is polemic against Hegel, nevertheless posits a dialectic between the first two spheres (the aesthetic and the ethical) that becomes synthesized in the third (the religious).

However, there are several problems. The way Kierkegaard does his dialectic places actuality into a subjectivity that is outside of existence (i.e., outside of history and outside of social and economic questions). In Hegelian dialectic, the three spheres would "articulate their development in time."[42]

Adorno accuses Kierkegaard of a "circular argument," where ethical is not a true antithesis and religious is not a synthesis, there is an "idealist origin of the 'spheres.'" In the three spheres is an "appropriation of grace" into a mythical harmony that relies on astrological categories.[43] As a result, "the totality of the infinite is closed [by Kierkegaard] to contingent human consciousness."[44]

Kierkegaard views humans as living in "mythical deception," which for Adorno puts them at a distance from ontology (historical concretion that is fundamental to dialectics).[45] Kierkegaard's spirituality is necessarily melancholic.[46] We live life that is a riddle looking to scripture that is so cryptic as to be unreadable.[47]

Further, the dialectic of the spheres in Kierkegaard is hierarchical, where the good versus bad is set out in the aesthetic, carries through the ethical, and into the religious. The aesthetic sphere is situated prior to decisiveness. In addition, predestination becomes the foundation of Kierkegaard's dialectic theology.[48] And with reconciliation and repentance in the religious sphere, the dialectic comes to a full stop.[49] The hierarchy of the spheres only grants authority to the aesthetic and religious spheres, making the ethical sphere a kind of transitional stage (in a three-stage model). In sum, for Adorno, "Theological truth crashes down to human level as aesthetic truth and reveals itself to man a sign of hope."[50] The aesthetic sphere transcends the religious while devaluing the ethical (as a passage point). "Thus the system of the spheres finally collapses over the question of concretion, which originally distinguishes from Hegelian systematic universality."[51]

What I think we can learn from Adorno's critique of Kierkegaard is to place spirituality in its social, economic, and historical contingency.

Adorno's[52] book, *Problems in Moral Philosophy,* finds Kant's formalistic ethics to be more critical than Kierkegaard's or even Hegel's "content-based ethics."[53] Ironically, Hegel is the one who engages with the social phenomena, whereas Kant's universalistic ethics do not. On the other hand, Kierkegaard critiques Hegel's dialectic, without addressing Kierkegaard's own "thoroughgoing idealism" in his theological idealism, that is, his "radical philosophy of interiority."[54] The reason for Kant's critical stance is his radical exclusion of everything empirical.[55]

The result is we can posit several types of critical spirituality. Hegel's critical spirituality is realized in the mediation of thesis and antithesis, with Spirit as the "prime mover"[56] in history and political economy. Kierkegaard and Kant each reject the empirical, but in different moves. Kierkegaard relies on sensual desire, and its corruption in the aesthetic to prompt an obligation to ethics, which is mediated (synthesized) in the theological (where, as pointed out above, the dialectic stops). Kant's critical spirituality, on the other hand, is opposed to empirical (sense-making perception) and to theology, because for Kant the world is thoroughly evil.[57] For Kant there are three cardinal principles: (1) human freedom of the will; (2) immortality of the soul; and (3) existence of God.[58] The role of God in Kant's critical spiritual philosophy is as the "guarantor of the moral law that emanates from pure reason."[59] In the absence of God, the world is a living hell.

We turn now to Horkheimer, who works out a different version of critical spirituality.

Horkheimer: Spiritual Activism

In Horkheimer's essays (in *Critique of Instrumental Reason*), there is a plea to return to a kind of spiritual activism, such as when Jesus overturned the tables of the money changers, or aligned himself with the poor and more marginalized, rather than with those more well off and in power. In Horkheimer's *Critique of Instrumental Reason*, several of the essays are explorations of various spirituality/religion constructs as they relate to business.

Theism and Atheism. In this 1963 essay, Horkheimer[60] points out "crimes committed in the name of God are a recurrent theme in the history of Christian Europe." Horkheimer's concern is that, over time, Christianity moved away from the founder's utterance. Unlike Buddhism, there is in the more contemporary Christianity a renewed pact with worldly wisdom that can be a "readiness for fanaticism," something that its founder was put to death for.[61] Horkheimer points out several facets that Christ as founder of a spirituality portrayed, for which he was put to death:

1. The last would be first.
2. Out of hope, not fear.
3. Being on the cross [of suffering] rather than putting the ruling order first.
4. Help the poor in spirit rather then being primarily oriented toward riches, power, prestige, or affairs of state.

Business spirituality seeks to reconcile Christianity with what by most accounts is a corrupt world: burning women accused of witchcraft as heretics; sending children to work before they could read; making and blessing bombs, and so on.[62] And, more so, in this age of Enron, Haliburton, and WorldCom, Horkheimer prefers the Christian spiritual path of Kierkegaard, who extolled suffering as a virtue. He is distrustful of the patchwork scholasticism (since the Monastic period, see summary above). Its barbaric foundation gives Christianity its most essential link to business. Hitler in World War II manipulated the masses using claims of "positive Christianity."

In contemporary work, this patchwork includes organizing spirituality around competitive business practices, servant leadership being hailed by Wal-Mart in its 1993, 1994, and 2002 annual reports—confusing servanthood with serving the business customer, and making acceptance of leader decisions a sign of one's spiritual maturity.[63] CEO Lee Scott writes, "Our founder Sam Walton, believed in servant leadership... wove it so skillfully into our culture that our Associates are naturally committed to community service with compassion and integrity."[64]

In the 2002 Wal-Mart Annual Report, the claim of Servant Leadership appears hypocritical, made in a year of record class action lawsuits against the corporation for various unethical practices. Horkheimer[65] seems nostalgic for "Talmudic spirit" in interpretations of the Torah. In other instances, the revival of the protestant work ethic degenerates into workaholism and performativity.

As Marx,[66] observing child and female sweatshop labor practices in the United States and the United Kingdom, put it, "Capital is dead labor, that, vampire-like, only lives by sucking living labor, and lives the more, the more labor it sucks. The time during which the laborer works is the time during which the capitalist consumes the labor-power he has purchased of him." To Horkheimer,[67] as with most other critical theorists, "each [wo]man's life had a meaning, not just the lives of the prominent."

Horkheimer emphasizes Martin Luther's hatred of scholasticism as the "Whore Reason." The difference between scholasticism and CT approaches to business spirituality is that scholastics glorify existing social conditions, whereas for CT, socioeconomic transformation means widening participation. Horkheimer[68] is skeptical of Luther, as well as Kant's[69] limitation of metaphysical speculation, which leaves reason free to room in commerce. With social Darwinism, people justify exploitation using theological and evolutionary terms. One ruthless competitive business practice, or competition among nations, becomes just as spiritual in its unfolding as any other, using trite comments, as "God's ways were peculiar."[70] Horkheimer concludes that with each phase of capitalism, theology and spirituality are adapted to fit the socioeconomic situation.

Horkheimer[71] describes that "The Spirit of the Gospels" as the thesis, but the antithesis of once militant atheism, has atrophied. Instead of dialectic synthesis, Christ "could not longer be distinguished from the radiant Being of the Neoplatonists." Atheists, in the main, adopted Nature-as-Eternal guideline of self-preservation. Their position was little different from social Darwinian spirituality. A rebel voice would post an antithesis more consistent with Christianity's founder and ask for "liberty and justice" for all.[72] The integration of business and spirit for theists and atheists, after the French Revolution, becomes an ideology of individual self-preservation.

"The new spirit" for Horkheimer[73] would improve the lot of workers, provide them more equitable share of the wealth, liberate them from brutal oppression under backward dictatorships, and build middle-class virtues for a new socioeconomic order, including a more active part in shaping society. For this to happen, the kinds of scholasticism spirituality where God and Son of God are as mythical as king and prince in a fairy tale would need revision. Horkheimer stresses that "without God one will try in vain to preserve absolute meaning."[74] Instead of love of the other as an abstraction, a dim historical memory, or empty talk, for Horkheimer it is part of action: a deconstructive resituation in which "various implications contained in this principle [would] be made explicit."[75] What directions could Christian love have today in business and society? For example, to eradicate injustice and world hunger. For Horkheimer, nihilistic works on political economy have equally empty rhetoric as scholasticism. To Horkheimer, Christ's speeches are much like those of Marx and Engels. Certainly, atheism is no longer providing the opposition. Rather, a new spirituality, a more honest theism focused on justice, ethical practices of answerability to the situation of workers and the poor, is called for.

The Soul. In Horkheimer's[76] 1967 essay on "The Soul," he develops the interplay of its scientific and theological conceptions. The idea of a soul that outlives the body is a development Horkheimer says is independent of scripture. Its roots are in ancient Greece, not in Judeo-Christian sources. Scholasticism overlays the Greek concept of soul onto visions of hell and heaven. Thus the duality of soul and corporeal (body) was established as the nonspatial and the spatial. In Islam and Pomponazzi (fifteenth century Europe), the heretical idea of a union of individual soul with world-spirit (world-soul) emerges among theologians, and is consistent with Hegel's dialectic doctrine. In Leibniz's view, the individual soul is a monad, an immaterial spirit essence: "The lower monads live vague, unspirited lives. Consciousness, spirit, and soul are essential attributes of the higher monads." But for Nietzsche, "we have a nervous system, but not a soul."[77] Horkheimer concludes that "'soul' in retrospect is becoming a pregnant concept expressing all that is opposed to the indifference of the subject who is ruled by technology and destined to be a mere client. Reason divorced from feeling is now becoming the opposite of *Anima* or soul."[78] Soul, then, stands beyond what science dismisses as transcending senses and outside what theology can provide. The problem for critical theorists is that soul is romanticized so that oppression, murder, Auschwitz and the Warsaw ghetto (and those of New York), the Vietnam war, and starvation are ignored, which leads Horkheimer to ask if God is also not paying attention, on a journey, or dead. We long for the spirit (or soul) that is so easily rejected in the rebellion of young writers. To keep alive the idea of spirit, to the critical theorist, means to also keep alive the skeptic's doubt regarding any alignment of spirituality and business in global capitalism.

The German Jews. The[79] 1961 essay, "The German Jews," points out that since the 1920s, pluralism has been on the decline. People are persecuted, even in democratic societies, for their religion, politics, nationality, or skin color. The plight of the Jews, for Horkheimer, is to overcome prejudice. He asks if the collective memory, and spirit, of this particular group has become so different and so embittered to further rupture unity of the people. The aim of democratic society is for groups with different beliefs and customs, or spirit, to be able to coexist peacefully. "Since the twenties of this century, however, the pluralist society has been in decline."[80]

Intense competition between individual entrepreneurs, now on a global scale, is leading to far-reaching uniformity. Yet, as in Germany, in Russia too the Jews were targeted, and more recently they are targeted for elimination in the Middle East. After 9/11, the diversity of cultural, religious, ethnic, and racial identity has lessened. Spirit has become less about "we" and more about the "I." The point here is that the forces of globalization and post-9/11 combine to exacerbate individualism.

Patterns of thought, association, inclination, and repugnance have developed for Catholics, Protestants, and Jews in ways that extend to business matters. Concrete thought-forms, gestures, and emotional reactions distinguish one spiritual practice from the other. Here, Horkheimer brings home his thesis: being combined into one, totalized spirituality is neither assimilation nor emancipation. It symbolizes a collapse of spiritual diversity. In the case of assimilation to the global empire, persecuted spiritual paths identify themselves with the dominant order, which means more highly conservative traits than majority culture. In the case of liberation, criticism lacks the grounded point of departure one finds in an orthodox community. The decline in diversity through assimilation or liberation constitutes its own form of spiritual abuse. That is, globalization has its sense of spirit, one that is acculturated worldwide. And this is what makes Horkheimer's essays so unique. He extends his criticism of business and society, as well as global capitalism, from the vantage point of Jewish heritage. And it is neither a "critico-negative spirit" nor a positive Christianity spirit, it is one admitting diversity, plurality, and tolerance.[81] Horkheimer argues, "The Zionist movement, with its refusal to trust any longer in the prospects of pluralism or of the civilization of the autonomous individual…is the radical yet resigned reaction of Judaism to the possibilities thrown open in the last century."[82]. The result is to allow opposition but not extermination.

Horkheimer[83] closes with an apocryphal story about Hegel. To paraphrase the story, Hegel presented a course on the development of ideas. Audiences came to hear Hegel expecting the mystery of the "Absolute" to be resolved. Instead, Hegel moved from Asiatic empires via slavery to Christian nations, and finally to the history of philosophy, beginning with logic.

Each work was discussed in terms of how the limitations of an absolute truth gave rise to the impulse for more inquiry. Expecting that the series on philosophical concept would culminate in Hegel's own discourse on the dialectic, the audience was disappointed when instead he began again with logic. "The story sounds like one from the Talmud, and the similarity is more than accidental."[84] Dialectic philosophy is part of Jewish tradition. What becomes explicit is only a moment in the process of thought striving toward truth, but never arriving.

Horkheimer turns to spirituality in his essay on "The Jews": "Yet the understanding of the Jews, of which we are speaking, depends on a spiritual change and the disappearance of the trauma" of the violence practiced by and on the Germans.[85] Converting the spirit of an anti-Semite into one who overcomes prejudice is part of the transformation. Demagogy took hold of Germany at a time of socioeconomic crisis. Anti-Semitism was peddled as propaganda of hatred. That is why critical theorists are so sensitive to injustice.

The End of the Fairy Tale of the Customer as King. Finally, the[86] 1964 essay from *Critique of Instrumental Reason*, "Feudal Lord, Customer, and Specialist: The End of the Fairy Tale of the Customer as King," brings together the business aspects of soul (spirit) in the other essays reviewed. Horkheimer expresses the irony that capitalism, having won freedom from the feudal king, has now made the customer the absolute ruler. In both, subordination and hierarchy are adopted. Business people accept the phrase "customer is king," as basic manners and civility in the market place. Suppressing the memory of feudal servanthood, with its pauperization and other economic limits, would be retrogressive. The suppression serves to let Western civilization claim "spiritual advantage over the rest of the world; the East, of course, challenges this view."[87] Worldwide, over 1 billion people live below the international poverty line, earning less than $1 per day.[88]

Today, hospitals and universities have adopted the "customer is king" terminology. Yet, if we compare the ethics of care in hospitals before patients became (insurance) customers, it will be seen that the medical business was radically different. Similarly, the corporatization of the university, where president is CEO, students are customers, and faculty perform to dashboard assessment indicators has made the university business radically different. I am skeptical of the idea that patients and students are considered customers in corporately managed versions of hospitals and universities.

In advanced capitalism, with its far-reaching uniformity, standardization of production, and consumption (e.g., Disneyfication, McDonaldization, Wal-Mart effect), the individual identity presupposes the social uniformity of the economic situation in which one is embedded. What I read in Horkheimer's essays is a distrust of the spiritual regression in the application of servant leadership, suspicion of "to serve the customer," and skepticism of a self-development centered positive spirituality version, which is so popular in contemporary business.

This is a theme that one finds in Horkheimer's work with Adorno. In the book, *Aspects of Sociology*, Horkheimer and Adorno say, "spiritual regression must be counted among the most threatening symptoms of total sociation."[89] He sees a danger in fascism aligning with spiritual regression because of "hypostasizing the ephemeral."[90] In other words, reifying some complex and dynamic phenomenon into something where the important differences, in this case, in spiritual traditions and practices, get truncated to some fundamental coherence. Horkheimer and Adorno critique Herbert Spencer for transforming spiritual freedom and equality into a legitimation of economic conservatism. Similarly, in the case of Hitler's fascism, spirituality and religious practice becomes a way to sort people for the Holocaust and to legitimize it. Further, in truncating spirituality to its most maniacal and diabolical terrorist practice, fascism accomplishes the Holocaust with progressive rationalization, standardization, and other facets of the division of labor (as a postmodern writer, Bauman has written about this persuasively). Part of the truncation of spirituality is to focus on subordinating ego interest to the social, or "common good," effectively talking people out of a more "critical sociology."[91] Here, a truncated spirituality means taking a myopic view, looking the other way, being the bystander to atrocity.

In particular, Horkheimer and Adorno[92] are concerned that in the conceptualization of the individual in eighteenth-century capitalism, there begins the substitution of the ethic of competition for the ethic of cooperation. It is the ethic of competition that results in instrumentalism and treating people as means, rather than in the more Kantian sense of humanity as an end unto itself. Instead of collaboration of mutual exchange, the individualistic competition ethic lends itself to the social Darwinian thesis inspired by Spencer (and Adam Smith) in Darwin's work.

The turn of Horkheimer and Adorno toward critiques of the culture industry is precisely to counter the illusion of economic competition as being progress, when in their view it is degenerative of cooperative exchange. Further, their critique of division of labor, its standardization, routinization, and individuation (standardized specialists) seems to me to anticipate George Ritzer's[93] McDonaldization thesis (i.e., that the Weberian dimension of rationalization have allowed a dehumanization to occur). The irony as Horkheimer and Adorno[94] point out is "the fewer the individuals, the more the individualism," because with individualism there is enthronement of competition and hierarchy. The individual becomes a free market cog. Horkheimer and Adorno also are skeptical of the way spirituality has been wrought in the Protestant ethic as a concept of moral compulsion to duty. In individualism, there is an ideal of equity and freedom of choice promised by the idol of market forces that is not realized in political economy self-determination.

Benjamin: Angel of History

Walter Benjamin was a Jew, a literary critic of German literature after his superb essay on Goethe spoiled all his chances to get into a PhD program in Germany, having critiqued the only academics doing Goethe and who might have served on his committee (Ardendt[95]). Benjamin was also fleeing Hitler. He believed that the Nazis were ready to close in on him, because the Gestapo had seized his Paris apartment and library. Benjamin got as far as the Franco-Spanish border, where a manuscript he was working on was confiscated from him, and that night Benjamin took his own life.[96] The very next day the guards relented and let the refugees cross the borders. Ironically, the Jews in Paris were simply shipped back to Germany if they were found to be political opponents.

Benjamin's path to critical spirituality is a unique surrealist experience of epic dialectic method. This comes forth in his incomplete "Arcades Project."[97] The flâneur (stroller, walker, and idler) strolls leisurely through the nineteenth-century Paris arcade. The arcade is the forerunner to the department store and the indoor mall, where one walks through faux nature without intention to buy, gazing the death of nature, deciphering visual images of what Horkheimer and Adorno called the culture industry. The poet, Goethe, informs Benjamin's critical spirituality, a poetic-angel's view of the world set down in an epic poem that would juxtapose primary documents, trading the historical roots of fascism and the economic battles in Europe. Benjamin's Goethean concept is that of an "*Ur*-phenomenon extracted from the pagan context of nature and brought into the Jewish contexts of history."[98] Benjamin is the flâneur-angel strolling through the crowds, turning his back to those crowds, looking backward as an "angel of history"[99] retrospectively looking not at some dialectic chain of events but at "one single catastrophe which keeps piling wreckage upon wreckage and hurls it in front of his feet."[100]

Benjamin's work on a dialectical method of history in his arcades project is concerned with fathoming an origin of the visual forms and the Paris arcades in socioeconomic facts, then it shows its unfolding and decline as a historical form of orality and the eruption of visuality as a medium of sensemaking.[101] Whereas, in earlier generations, history of oral generations was explained to people in terms of religious doctrine,[102] or "old traditional experiences of nature,"[103] Benjamin's dialectic method offered a way of awakening, as if from a dream to a visual nightmare. For Benjamin,[104] "The new, dialectical method of doing history presents itself a[s] the art of experiencing the present as waking world, a world to which that dream we name the past refers in some new visual truth." Each now is a now bursting into spacetime, casting its light onto what is present and what is past, coming together in a flash, and keeping dialectics at a standstill where a critical reading is founded.[105]

Benjamin[106] did his classic article "The Storyteller..." asserting that storytelling competencies have eroded, changed, and been destroyed forever by the new rhythms of work. Earlier, storytelling was tied to the crafts, to the rhythm of workers doing weaving and sewing, before they were forbidden to tell and listen to stories, and before they were divided and put under the noise of machines.

Fromm: The Absolute Spirit Gets Sick

Erich Fromm was a Jewish-German-American social psychologist. He joined the Frankfurt Institute in Critical Theory in 1930, moving to Columbia University in 1934 to escape Nazi persecution. In his doctoral work, Fromm studied with a rabbi, and was influenced by rabbis and Talmudic scholars in his family. He drew upon his knowledge of the Talmud and Torah in fashioning his theory of authority and personality. For example, in the Adam and Eve story, Fromm,[107] used his knowledge of the Talmud, but he departed from orthodox Judaism, when he fashioned a theory of existential angst, where Adam and Eve had learned independence from authoritarian moral values by taking independent action (eating the apple of the Tree of Knowledge). Adam and Eve had become aware of their nakedness, separateness from the universe, and powerlessness within a dominant society, resulting in their guilt and shame. To state another example, Fromm was inspired by the Torah in an interpretation of the story of Jonah. Jonah refused to be controlled and did not want to interfere in the affairs of Nineveh. For Fromm, the resistance to or escape from authoritarian and repressive socioeconomic structures was healthy. Fromm's[108] work includes a Talmudic interpretation of the Sabbath commandment, where work is a violation of a day of rest. "The Sabbath is the day of peace between man and nature; work is any kind of disturbance of the man-nature equilibrium."[109] The Sabbath, for Fromm, symbolizes a day of harmony between man and nature, as well as between man and man.[110]

In short, in terms of dialectic, Fromm's critical spirituality, informed by Talmud and Torah, is a Hegelian *Absolute Spirit* that has gotten mentally sick, and become neurotic.[111] In Hegelian dialectic, *Absolute Spirit* guides history in a rational path. But in Frommian *Absolute Spirit,* the road to liberation from self-emancipation from misperceptions never escapes repression. The struggle is to escape the love of one's chains and to love one's self. As Fromm[112] put it, "To love another person is only a virtue if it springs from this inner strength, but it is a vice if it is the expression of the basic inability [to] be oneself."

Conclusion and Implications

Benjamin, as well as Horkheimer, Fromm, and Adorno, critique Kant's ought (categorical imperative). Kant skirted the ethics of answerability. It was enough for Kant that we not lie or steal because of the Golden Rule. But, this was perverted in business ethics. It is now just a stakeholder theory, that we do not lie or steal from the corporation, that we treat that surrogate for market forces, the customer, as always right. Great, do you see how answerability becomes nothing but conviction ethics, and how that is enfolded into the stakeholders of the mind? God forbid if real stakeholders engaged in the dialogic and did direct democracy and asked for answerability. Fromm challenged authoritarian rule as an escape from freedom, be it in theology, the state, or corporation. Each of these CT scholars presents a version of a critical spirituality, one that dovetails with my review of spiritual abuse.

If my thesis is correct, CT founders have had an ambivalent conception of the relation of spirit and business. On one hand, they object to spiritual abuse, the way it plays a role in instrumental performativity, injustice, and oppression. On the other hand, there seems tacit recognition in the essays reviewed that a spirituality that seeks equality, social justice, and plurality is beneficial to business and society. For CT, the relation of spirit and business is dialectical. The thesis of positive spirituality with its emphasis on individualism is opposed by the antithesis of critical spirituality with its emphasis on social justice. In this view, critical spirituality is not a dismissal of all spirituality, it is merely incredulity to self-development individualism and abstract scholasticism. At issue is how is "love thy neighbor as thyself" put into practice?

Notes

1. Boje, D.M. 2000. Approaches to the study of spiritual capitalism. In Biberman, J., Whitty, M.D. (eds.), *Work & spirit*. Chicago, IL: University of Scranton Press. xxv–xxxii. At http://business.nmsu.edu/~dboje/conferences/IntrotoSpiritualCapitalism.html. (Last accessed Dec 3, 2007).
2. Boje, D.M. 2007a. Festivalism at work. Toward Ahimsa in production and consumption. In Biberman, J. and Whitty, M.D. (eds.), *At work: Spirituality matters*. Chicago, IL: University of Scranton Press. 93–110.
3. Boje, D.M. 2007b. Another view: Approaches to the study of spiritual/religiosity capitalism. In Biberman, J. and Whitty, M.D. (eds.), *At work: Spirituality matters*. Scranton, PA/London: University of Scranton Press. xxi–xxviii.

4. Boje, D.M. and Rosile, G.A. 2003. Towards festivalism: Or, can I be spiritual and still walk on the dark side? Presentation to academy of management, management spirituality and religion joint session with critical management studies.

5. Boje, D.M. 2007c. Story and spiritual leadership. Paper presentation to Vanguard University, Los Angeles on April 19 to the Judkins Institute for leadership studies.

6. For gifts of the spirit verses: 1 Corinthians 12:8–11, 27–31; 1 Corinthians 13:1–13; 1 Corinthians 14:26–39; 2 Corinthians 4:13; Acts 2: 4, 17; Ephesians 1: 17; Exodus 31:3; James 1:5–6; Mark 16:17–18; Romans 15:19.

7. Barkun, M. 1994. *Religion and the racist right: The origins of the Christian identity movement.* Chapel Hill: University of North Carolina Press.

8. Spencer, H. 1866. *Principles of biology.* 1. New York: Appleton and Company.

9. Blue, K. 1993. *Healing spiritual abuse.* Downers Grove: InterVarsity Press.

10. Boje, D.M. 2007c.

11. Burks, R. and Burks, V. 1992. *Damaged disciples: Casualties of authoritarian churches and the shepherding movement.* Grand Rapids, MI: Zondervan.

12. Enroth, R.M. 1994. *Recovering from churches that abuse.* Grand Rapids, MI: Zondervan.

13. Henke, D. 1996. Spiritual abuse. Online at The Watchman Epositor http://www.watchman.org/profile/abusepro.htm (last accessed September 5, 2007).

14. Johnson, D. and VanVondern, J. 1991. *Subtle power of spiritual abuse.* Minneapolis, MN: Bethany House.

15. Lawless, A.C. and Lawless, J.W. 1995. *The drift into deception: The eight characteristics of abusive Christianity.* Grand Rapids, MI: Kregel.

16. Spiritual abuse, at http://en.wikipedia.org/wiki/Spiritual_abuse (last accessed September 5, 2007).

17. Yeakley, F. 1988. *The discipling dilemma.* Nashville, TN: Gospel Advocate.

18. Enroth, R.M. 1994.

19. Lawless, A.C. and Lawless, J.W. 1995.

20. Henke, D. 1996.

21. Horkheimer, M. 1974. *Critique of instrumental reason.* O'Connell, M.J. (tran.). New York: Seabury Press (A continuum Book). First published in German in 1967.

22. Adorno, T.W. 1951/1974. *Minima moralia. Reflections from damaged life*s (First published in German in 1951.) London: New Left Books. 242.

23. Boje, D.M. (ed.). Forthcoming. Critical theory ethics for business and public administration. New Jersey: Information Age Press.

24. Boje, D.M. and Al Arkoubi, K. Forthcoming. Critical perspectives in management education. In Armstrong, S. and Fukami, C. (eds.), *Sage handbook of management learning, education and development.* London ; Thousand Oaks, CA: Sage.

25. Adorno, T.W. 2000/1963. *Problems of moral philosophy.* Schroder, T. (ed.). Livingstone, R. (trans.). Stanford, CA: Stanford University. 172.

26. Bakhtin, M.M. 1990. *Art and answerability.* Holquist, M. and Liapunov, V. (eds.). Liapunov, V. (trans. and notes), Brostrom, K. (supplement trans.). Austin, TX: University of Texas Press. From Bakhtin's first published article and his early 1920s notebooks.

27. Bakhtin, M.M. 1993. *Toward a philosophy of the act.* Liapunov, V. (trans. and notes). Holquist, M. and Liapunov, V. (eds.). Austin, TX: University of Texas Press. From Bakhtin's early 1920s notebooks. The 1993 edition is the first edition in English.

28. Ibid.

29. Bakhtin, M.M. 1990.

30. Bakhtin, M.M. 1993.

31. Ibid.

32. Ibid. 5–6.

33. Ibid. 6.

34. Weininger, D. 1995. Review of Wiggershaus's book *The Frankfurt school*. Boston Book Review. Last accessed on September 5, 2007 online at http://www.bookwire.com/bbr/politics/frankfurt-school.html

35. Wiggershaus, R. 1993. *The Frankfurt school: Its history, theories, and political significance*. Robertson, M. (trans.). Cambridge, MA: MIT Press.

36. Adorno, T.W. 1951/1974.

37. Adorno, T.W. 1977/1981. Cultural criticism and society. In *Prisms*. Weber, S. and Weber, S. (trans.). Cambridge, MA: MIT Press. 34. Translation modified. For the German version, see Kulturkritik und Gesellschaft. *Prismen*, vol. 10.1 of Gesammelte Werke, ed. Rolf Tiedemann. Frankfurt am Main: Suhrkamp, 1977. 11–30.

38. Claussen, D. 1997. Intellectual transfer: Theodor W. Adorno's American experience. *Duke Journals*, online essay (last accessed on September 5, 2007) at http://ngc.dukejournals.org/cgi/reprint/33/1_97/5.pdf.

39. Adorno, T.W. 1951/1974.

40. Kellner, D. 1995. Erich Fromm, Judaism, and the Frankfurt school. Online manuscript (last accessed on September 3, 2007) at http://www.gseis.ucla.edu/faculty/kellner/kellner.html.

41. Adorno, T.W. 1989. *Kierkegaard construction of the aesthetic*. Hullot-Kentor, R. (ed., trans., and foreword). Ninneapolis: University of Minnesota Press. xi.

42. Ibid. 90.

43. Ibid. 91.

44. Ibid. 92.

45. Ibid. 93.

46. Ibid. xix.

47. Ibid. 25.

48. Ibid. 99.

49. Ibid. 101.

50. Ibid. 104.

51. Ibid. 105.

52. Adorno, T.W. 2000/1963.

53. Ibid. 165.

54. Ibid. 148.

55. Ibid. 106.

56. Ibid. 48.

57. Ibid. 149.

58. Ibid. 67.

59. Ibid. 148.

60. Horkheimer, M. 1974. 34.

61. Ibid. 35.

62. Ibid. 39–40.

63. Boje, D.M. and Rosile, G.A. 2007. *Specters of Wal-Mart: A critical discourse analysis of stories of Sam Walton's ghost*.

64. Wal-Mart Annual Report. 2002. 12. See online annual reports (last accessed, September 3, 2007) at http://walmart.com.

65. Horkheimer, M. 1974. 37.

66. Marx, K. 1967 [1867]. Capital unabridged: vol. 1. *A critical analysis of capitalist production*. Engles, F. (ed.). Translated from German third edition by Samuel Moore and Edward Aveling 1967. New York: International Publishers. See chapter 10 *The working day*. 233.

67. Horkheimer, M. 1974. 38.

68. Ibid. 39.

69. Kant, I. 1785/1993. *Grounding for the metaphysics of morals: On a supposed right to lie because of philanthropic concerns.* Ellington, J.W. (trans.). Indianapolis, IN: Hackett Publishing Company. Published in 1785 in German; third edition published in 1993 in English.
70. Horkheimer, M. 1974. 39–40.
71. Ibid. 43.
72. Ibid. 43.
73. Ibid. 45–46.
74. Ibid. 46.
75. Ibid. 48.
76. Ibid.
77. Ibid. 55, 57.
78. Ibid. 60.
79. Ibid.
80. Ibid. 103.
81. Ibid. 109.
82. Ibid. 110.
83. Ibid.
84. Ibid. 113.
85. Ibid. 116.
86. Ibid.
87. Ibid. 135.
88. World Development Indicators. 2006. The World Bank. March at. http://web.worldbank.org/ (last accessed September 3, 2007).
89. Horkheimer, M. and Adorno, T.W. 1972/1956. *Aspects of sociology by the Frankfurt institute for social research.* Viertel, J. (trans.). Boston: Beacon Press. The 1972 English Translation from the 1956 German Soziologische Exkurse by Europlaishe Verlagsanstalt. 33.
90. Ibid. 30.
91. Ibid.
92. Ibid.
93. Ritzer, G. 1993/2002. *The McDonaldization of society.* Newbury Park, CA: Pine Forge.
94. Horkheimer, M. and Adorno, T.W. 1972/1956.
95. Arendt, H. 1955/1968. *Introduction to illuminations.* Arendt, H. (ed. and intro.), Zohn, H. (trans.). New York: Harcourt, Brace & World. 1–55.
96. Ibid. 18.
97. Benjamin, W. 1999. *The arcades project.* Eiland, H. and McLaughlin, K. (trans.). Cambridge, MA, London: Belknap Press of Harvard University Press.
98. Ibid. 462.
99. Ardendt, H. 1955/1968. 12.
100. Ibid. 12.
101. Benjamin, W. 1999. 462.
102. Ibid. 388.
103. Ibid. 447.
104. Ibid. 389.
105. Ibid. 463.
106. Benjamin, W. 1936/1955/1968. The storyteller: Reflections on the works of Nikolai Leskov. In Arendt, H. (ed. and intro.), Zohn, H. (trans.), *Illuminations.* New York: Harcourt, Brace & World. 83–110.
107. Fromm, E. 1951. *The forgotten language: An introduction to the understanding of dreams, fairy tales and myths.* New York: Rinehart and Company. 246.
108. Ibid.
109. Ibid. 244.

110. Ibid. 245.
111. Erich Fromm at http://en.wikipedia.org/wiki/Erich_Fromm (last accessed September 6, 2007).
112. Fromm, E. 1947. Man for himself: An inquiry into the psychology of ethics. New York: Rinehart and Company. 126.

CHAPTER ELEVEN

The Ethics of Spiritual Inclusion

KATHY LUND DEAN, CHARLES FORNACIARI, AND SCOTT R. SAFRANSKI

Introduction

To date, most work conducted in the spirituality and religion in the workplace (SRW) domain has adopted a "positive" tone regarding its role within organizations. Extant research by and large has accepted that SRW is good for organizations without examining where and how it might go awry—that employees will simply be spiritually expressive without threat or interference from either the organization or peers. The newest wave of SRW experiences, however, shows increasing disputes about SRW and how it is practiced. In this chapter, we argue that there is a practice of accepting and including spiritual selves into organizations and thus there must be an ethical means by which to do so. We define "inclusion" in this context as enabling different spiritual or religious expressions while being part of an organizational whole, and believe that inclusion in organizations is an ethical practice that requires tolerance, flexibility, and an orientation toward community.

On the basis of the growing numbers of SRW disputes, we cannot take for granted that managers and organizational members (1) know what to do inclusively; (2) want to be spiritually inclusive; (3) and/or will not use SRW for personal or organizational gain. We discuss a brief SRW history in the next section, and discuss further why SRW has become an ethics issue.

A Trajectory Toward Inclusion

As Morgan[1] notes, the "faith-at-work movement gestated for two decades in virtual secrecy before receiving widespread recognition. The wall began to deteriorate slowly, and with little notice, because religious employees [initially] tended to bring their faith to work in silence and were met with inattention by management." Early popular press articles (e.g., Conlin;[2] Gunther[3]) chronicled how spiritual and religious expressions had been growing significantly in workplace settings for years, and that the incidence was widespread enough to merit reporting.

Employees had begun moving into previously ignored and uncharted organizational territory, such as talking openly about spiritual beliefs, organizing prayer groups at work, and questioning organizational initiatives on the basis of negative spiritual or religious impact. Conlin[4] reports that organizations, eager to gain a hiring and retention advantage in the ultratight labor market of the late 1990s, jumped to offer outlets for SRW expression. Systematic academic coverage of the SRW phenomenon simply had not begun yet. Clearly, employee practice was leading organizational responses, academic research efforts, and overall attention.

In 1999, however, Mitroff and Denton's[5] groundbreaking book acknowledged the degree to which SRW had taken hold. The Management, Spirituality, and Religion (MSR) interest group within the Academy of Management was established and an explosion of SRW-related academic research began to emerge. To date, over 500 books and academic and popular press articles about this phenomenon have been published, and SRW no longer raises eyebrows.

While there is still some discussion on whether SRW is authentic and will last, or whether it will ultimately gain a "fad" status (e.g., Cavanagh;[6] Porth, Steingard, and McCall[7]), the literature generally regards SRW as a normal outgrowth of workplace trends, such as an aging workforce examining its legacy, employees spending more time than ever at work, and Generation Y-ers aiming at better life/work integration (Cash and Gray;[8] Dehler and Welsh;[9] Gogoi;[10] April 5; Ingersoll;[11] Lund Dean and Fornaciari[12]).

Given that the stream of SRW research has been steady, consistent, and broadly based over a number of academic disciplines for well over a decade (Lund Dean and Fornaciari[13]), it is perhaps more appropriate to ask not whether SRW is a transitory phenomenon, but rather to explore issues and implications from its widespread organizational existence. The next section explores both the current paradigm and what we believe to be fundamental ethical issues that the field has yet to address.

The Current SRW Research Paradigm
and Underaddressed Issues

Researchers overwhelmingly view the practice of SRW as being beneficial to both individuals and organizations. In general, two major paradigmatic assumptions are clearly present in SRW research (cf., noted collections such as Biberman and Whitty;[14] Giacalone and Jurkiewicz;[15] Williams[16]). At the individual level, the underlying view has been that pursuing spiritual and religious development allows for a "whole person," or an employee who is fully present in himself or herself, and consequently on the job. This leads to personal benefits ranging from heightened satisfaction, increased work performance, and improved well-being, to a more consistent relationship with a higher power. Likewise, at the organizational level, the underlying assumption is that allowing or encouraging SRW is either "just good business" (e.g., it is the morally right thing to do, or it honors the unique nature of individuals comprising our workforce) or is "good for business" (e.g., it leads to improvements in the bottom line or is a powerful recruitment tool in a competitive job environment).

As noted earlier, these two positive norms explicitly and implicitly dominate the SRW paradigm, and any "negatives" within the research have typically revolved around concerns like obstacles to successful implementation of SRW practices within individuals and firms (for a review, please see Lund Dean and Fornaciari[17]). However, although SRW is now firmly established as an expression of employees seeking meaning and fulfillment at work, we argue that four questions arise as inherent by-products of a paradigm that speaks only of the positive SRW outcomes.

First, we must ask about the moral implications of the organization as a whole, or key members of its senior management, proselytizing to its employees or advocating a particular religious or spiritual orientation as part of its ongoing operations, or in implicitly making it a condition of employment. For example, Riverview Community Bank in Minnesota is run openly on evangelical Christian principles. Employees pray together at meetings and evangelism is a central part of its operations. While Riverview states that its position is to always hire the most qualified person for the job and promotions are strictly based on merit, it also acknowledges that it has not had to actually operationalize potential faith versus practice issues relating to Jews or Muslims applying for employment.[18] Situations such as this lead us to ask how we can draw the distinction between a firm's desire to operate how it best sees fit and an employee's desire to be left alone on matters regarding spirituality.

Second, the current SRW paradigm is quiet about providing guidance on how a firm may accommodate an individual's right to express himself or herself spiritually as he or she best sees fit when those practices involve proscribed behaviors such as proselytizing or engaging in actions based on spiritual/religious beliefs that may be disruptive to the firm, other employees, or its customers. For example, how does a firm respond to a group of forty Muslim employees' request to leave a production line at the same time for one of their daily prayers?[19] While situations such as this are most often perceived as legal problems that are frequently resolved in the courts using an "accommodation versus cost" test, the deeper moral issue is where and how does the line get drawn between the firm's right to make a profit, the individual's right to freedom of religious expression and the responsibilities that imbue to both parties in the pursuit of their rights?

A third question breaches moral issues between allowing SRW in organizations for its own sake versus using it as an instrumental tool for enhancing the firm's performance. In short, can firms, and should firms, use religion and spirituality as a tool for enhancing performance-related goals, or just allow it for its own sake?[20,21,22,23] This question begs discussion in similar veins to the one above, in that there exist rights and responsibilities on both sides of the employer/employee relationship. Sheep[24] describes the perceived tension and trade-off succinctly:

> While I do not dispute that societies have a legitimate interest in the cost-efficient production of firms (an egoistic/instrumental concern), I maintain that societies have at least as great an interest in their social responsibility (a benevolent/moral concern) to contribute toward rather than erode the social capital of organizational members as parts of larger communities...these two concepts are *complementary* and do not necessarily conflict. (Italics in original).

Finally, the SRW paradigm currently provides little direction on how individuals of different faiths should interact with the religious rights of others who may have very different worldviews and beliefs.

Do employees have to honor or accept other faiths as legitimate? Again, while the courts have made decisions holding firms accoun for *not* preventing overt acts of employee discrimination and harassment by other employees due to religious issues,[25] perhaps the deeper ethical question here concerns individual motivations and behaviors that may not reach the level of overt harassment but operate on a much subtler level, such as shunning those who disagree religiously, speaking derogatorily behind their back, or excluding them from committees or groups.

SRW is an organizational fact, but the inherently "positive" viewpoint of SRW fails to acknowledge some of the major conflicts that it may engender between individuals and within organizations. Fundamentally, there are four questions (discussed later) that concern employees wishing to express themselves on their own terms, within their own faith traditions—whose faith expressions may put them at odds with others. The underlying concern is the idea of either individuals or firms using faith in an attempt to shape or force others to engage in their perception of "right behaviors." In this context SRW is no longer simply a private issue of personal growth, and by definition any discussion of "right behaviors" is an exploration of ethical values and norms.

The potential for conflict is significant. Employees appear to no longer be reticent about expressing their spiritual needs and so the "treading lightly" phase is over. As a result, in the past ten years, complaints involving religious rights in the workplace have increased rapidly, along with an increase in U.S. Equal Employment Opportunity Commission (EEOC) and court filings. While comprising a relatively small percentage of all EEOC claims, religious discrimination actions have increased faster than virtually any other type, with roughly 45 percent growth between 1992 and 2005.[26,27] We may also be sure that disputes that have been elevated to a legal status are only a portion of all the SRW disputes experienced.

SRW's fundamental tenets of authenticity and personal responsibility, along with a practical application guideline suggested by an early U.S. Supreme Court ruling, may provide guidance for resolving serious ethical dilemmas as SRW continues to grow. The decision, *Pickering v Board of Education* (1968), essentially ruled that an organization must balance its own needs against those of the employee without burdening either side with regard to religious accommodations within the workplace. Using insights gained from how SRW disputes are currently legally resolved, we argue that organizations and managers who are alert to the ethical aspects of SRW dispute resolution can foster greater SRW inclusion by broadening the letter and spirit of *Pickering*.

Thus, the next section of this chapter reports on the ways organizations are struggling with operationalizations on a daily basis—how to include SRW expressions that are authentic and fair but may pit employee versus employee or employee versus organizational policy. These struggles can be seen as variants of one of two major ethical issues. The first is how organizations should accommodate SRW without "using" spiritual or religious expression as an organizational instrument (or, employee versus organization), and the second is how to resolve competing employee claims of "rightness" when certain belief systems clash (or, employee versus employee). We end the chapter with a discussion of how the parties in a SRW dispute are beholden to the "balancing" concept that *Pickering* suggests.

SRW Without Instrumentality:
Two-Way Respect

Cases in which religious beliefs run into direct conflict with work requirements have been around for some time. In one of the earliest cases of this kind of conflict, *Pickering v Board of Education*, the court established a key principle when it ruled, in essence, that the burden on employees must be balanced against the need of the employer (in this case a school district) to provide efficient delivery of services.[28]

Pickering's "balancing test" principle is evident in many recent cases of SRW conflict. Across the country, disputes involving pharmacists who refuse to fill prescriptions for either "Plan B" or the emergency "morning after" contraception pill, or birth control in general, are increasing. In 2005, Heather Williams worked as a part-time pharmacist at a Target store in Missouri. For five years she had refused to fill prescriptions for Plan B, and also refused to refer clients to pharmacists or physicians willing to fill those prescriptions. After Target received complaints that another pharmacist refused to fill the same kind of prescription at another Missouri location, Target implemented a new policy that required pharmacists to agree to either fill or, alternatively, refer such prescriptions to other pharmacists. Williams was fired after refusing to agree to the policy.[29]

Other pharmacists in at least ten other states have similarly refused to offer patients these pills on religious grounds and have lost their jobs[30,31] while large pharmacy chains struggle to find a workable balance.

Walgreens, Wal-Mart, and CVS all have policies in place wherein if one pharmacist does not want to fill the prescription, there will be others available to do so. Williams' religious belief system did not allow her to comply with offering these medications, yet legally patients have a right to obtain medication prescribed by their physician, and pharmacies have a right to stock and sell them.

Sexual orientation as part of respecting organizational diversity is a particularly fruitful area of disagreement. In a well-publicized case, a Hewlett-Packard (H-P) employee was fired for posting what were considered to be "hateful" Christian Bible verses when H-P added sexual orientation to their diversity policy. Multiple attempts to accommodate the employee's beliefs failed and the court upheld his firing, because of a Title VII duty to protect other employees from a hostile workplace environment.[32,33] This decision is consistent with the Supreme Court understanding of an employer's *de minimus* ("just enough") duty to accommodate religious needs. If the demand by the employee requires an accommodation that would conflict with another employee's rights, that would be considered an undue hardship for the employer and, therefore, not required.[34]

In another case, a Christian employee working for AT&T refused to sign an employee certificate requiring him to "respect and value" differences, including those of sexual orientation,[35] which resulted in his dismissal. Unlike in H-P's case, the court found in favor of this employee because of differences in how the organization responded to essentially the same issue. In the latter case, the employee had stated that while he was unwilling to "respect and value" a gay sexual orientation, "he would not discriminate or harass any employee on any basis." When AT&T would not consider any changes to the handbook language that might have allowed the employee to sign the statement, the court decided it had not made sufficient effort to accommodate the employee's religious needs.[36]

In an attempt to manage SRW fairly across multiple faith traditions, some large organizations have formed "affinity groups" that are sanctioned by the organization, given space to meet, and sometimes even allotted a budget from the organization. Affinity groups self-form around a common theme or need; all groups are judged equally valid and are given the same resources. While in theory affinity groups seem like an ideal inclusion solution, results have been mixed. They have worked extremely well for Intel, whose groups include traditional religious faiths as well as the "Recent College Graduates" group, the "Gay, Lesbian, and Transgendered" group, and the "Parents" group.[37]

They have not worked so well at Coca-Cola, whose spokesperson refuses to speak to outsiders about them and asserts that such groups are in the unsanctioned "underground," or at General Motors (GM), where religious groups are not included in GM's sanctioned affinity groups.[38] While affinity groups have generally not been among litigated parties (except at GM, where a Christian group sued to gain access to affinity group status and lost [*Moranski v General Motors*, 2005]), they represent in this context avenues of expression within an organization as a whole, coexisting with varied success due to fundamental ideological differences.

SRW between Individuals: Whose Right Is Right?

Judiciaries are being asked increasingly to decide whose belief system may in effect trump another's when those belief systems clash. In some cases, conflicts are worked out informally, among employees themselves. In others, such disputes must be adjudicated. Although in a judicial setting we see an individual versus an organization, the disputes are at the root individual differences that cannot be resolved and the organization is forced to choose a side that is subsequently tested in the courts. Illustrative cases abound.

Cummins[39] reports on a Christian woman who came to her job wearing a sizable button with a color photo of a fetus, indicating that her religious tradition "required her to be a witness against abortion." When her co-workers complained, managers worked out three potential accommodations, all three of which the employee refused. She was fired, and she subsequently sued her firm but lost the lawsuit when the court decided that offering three "reasonable" options was consistent with employer responsibility.

In the aftermath of September 11, the EEOC established a new discrimination category, tracking disputes that involve those who "are or are perceived to be Arab, Muslim, Middle Eastern, South Asian or Sikh."[40] Reports of harassment against Muslims for religious expressions such as adhering to their prayers or for wearing the *hijab* (traditional head scarf) in the workplace are increasing at a faster rate than religious complaints as a whole.[41,42,43] In most cases, managers have failed to stop the harassment, and in some cases managers participated in it.[44,45] For example, when an Afghani employee of a meat company was repeatedly harassed by his co-workers for his Islamic beliefs, the court found that the organization's managers had a duty to protect him.[46]

In Minneapolis, Muslim cashiers had refused to scan pork products for Target customers because of their religious restriction against pork. Initially, Target simply asked other cashiers to run the product across their scanners for them, but when customers and other employees complained, Target moved the Muslim employees out of the cashier's jobs altogether and into different positions.[47]

Although not in an employment context, a recent lawsuit at Southern Illinois University at Carbondale (SIU) is emblematic of these types of disputes. In April 2005, the Christian Legal Society (CLS) chapter at SIU sued the university after their student group charter was revoked due to another student's complaint that CLS had discriminated against homosexuals by denying them membership. Student leaders in CLS claim a religious imperative to deny practicing homosexuals entrance and leadership opportunities in the group while the other student claims an equal right to join CLS regardless of sexual orientation—a belief consistent with SIU's own antidiscrimination policy.

In May 2007, CLS and SIU agreed on a settlement clearly in CLS' favor: the university reestablished CLS as a recognized student group, paid its legal costs, established a $10,000 scholarship fund for CLS to administer, and agreed to allow CLS to deny homosexuals membership.[48,49] In its decision, an appeals court found that the university did not clearly state any laws it believed CLS violated and that CLS' policy fell outside the demands of SIU's own antidiscrimination policy.[50] Thus, in this instance, one group's beliefs allowing them to discriminate trumped another's belief that this was wrong.

Going Forward: Ethical Practices
for Managing SRW Issues

Workplace expression of religious and spiritual beliefs will become much more commonplace and will appear in many more types of organizations in the coming years if we take its current trajectory outward even modestly. Steadfastly secular organizations, including financial institutions and parts of the federal government, all have sanctioned religious subgroups.[51,52] Mainly in the United States, there is also a growing emphasis on practicing informal religions as well as personal spirituality unconnected to a specific religion.[53] The likelihood that SRW conflicts will arise is growing commensurate with the ever-growing demands for recognition from traditional and immigrant religions, new religions, and personal spiritual journeys. Atkinson[54] warns us that "there is no such thing as a fringe religion when the workplace is concerned" and notes that a "request by a Wiccan to have Halloween day off may be…laughed at by supervisors, but if the request is serious, it should be taken seriously."

The Supreme Court has established that Title VII protects strongly held beliefs that are not tied to any religious tradition and even provides protection to those who do not believe in the existence of God.[55] In 1944, with *United States v Ballard,* the Supreme Court decided that lower courts were not to determine a faith tradition's "comprehensibility," but rather to determine whether one held beliefs sincerely and in the "individual's own scheme of things."[56] Although this takes a valuation burden off employers, it can complicate SRW matters significantly. If an employee decides that he or she wants to have his or her own religion, and believes it with conviction, the employer may have to accommodate that.[57] There is a rather bizarre example that blurs the line between reality and fiction; in a 1997 episode of the television series "Seinfeld," the character George Costanza self-proclaimed the "Festivus" holiday, which, according to a posting in Wikipedia, some people now celebrate in varying degrees of seriousness![58]

A potential and significant challenge for SRW dispute resolution is the politicization occurring mainly in the United States. Jerry Falwell's legacy is the firm grip that religious issues have on American politics. It may be more likely that employees will take disputes over religious rights to court as groups begin to provide financial and other resources. A Tehama County (California) social service agency employee wanted to hold prayer sessions in meeting rooms but the agency only allowed him to use lunchrooms and outdoor areas. When the employee sued, the lawsuit was financed by the Pacific Justice Institute—a religious-liberty organization.[59] Ultimately, a court found that the county had made a reasonable accommodation in sanctioning specific agency space for his prayer sessions.

Although the increase in EEOC complaints, formal legal complaints, and the religious combativeness evident in the United States may be discouraging, there is hope for managing diverse spiritual expression in ethical and inclusive ways. In an analysis of why firms pursue particular discrimination lawsuit responses, James and Wooten[60] identified four distinct resolution paths associated with the type of alleged discrimination. One of their findings was that religious discrimination disputes were handled with the least aggressive, retaliatory, and public path.

These researchers note that religious discrimination claims seemed not to inspire the kind of anger, fear, and mobilization efforts that characterized claims of sexual harassment and race discrimination. Borrowing from Argyris,[61] James and Wooten found fewer threat-rigidity response behaviors such as vehement denial and obstruction when firms resolve religious discrimination complaints. Thus, even if SRW complaints go as far as filing a legal complaint, SRW problems do not appear to be the ones that are most personally or organizationally corrosive.

Although its future is uncertain, The Workplace Religious Freedom Act of 2005, introduced in the U.S. Senate by a bipartisan slate, would amend Title VII of the 1964 Civil Rights Act to make it easier for employees to obtain "reasonable accommodations" for their SRW expression. The text of the Act defines more precisely what "undue hardship" means and has ratcheted up how that term may be used in terms of how big a burden employers must demonstrate. In essence, the Act would make it more difficult for employers to deny accommodations. While speculative, it is reasonable to expect that employers would work more closely with employees who have SRW requests rather than face the increased legislative scrutiny such an amendment would provide.

Based on the above evidence and illustrative cases, *Pickering*'s balance principle represents an ethical norm and as such demands authentic flexibility on *both* sides of the employment relationship. Ethical and inclusive SRW practice demands that managers and employees approach SRW expressions mindful of others and the potential impacts those expressions may have on peers and co-workers. Purely legalistic solutions, meaning jury decisions or legal settlements, will suffice only for short-term, episodic solutions. Legalistic solutions also have limited use because learning and healing are necessarily in an *ex poste* way—law moves after behavioral precedent. As King[62] notes,

> ...[Courts] generally concluded that the employee's claim to violation of First Amendment speech or religious freedom was not violated by the employer's need to promote workplace order, decorum, or efficiency. When the employer has demonstrated a willingness to accommodate an employee's need to exercise or express religious or spiritual practices in the public workplace, the court system is not obligated to pursue further options.

As King and other cases suggest, an employer's willingness to work with employees' spiritual expressive needs in an authentic, respectful way is a crucial consideration in resolving SRW disputes. But, *Pickering*'s "undue hardship" clause must also apply to individuals for SRW to be practiced inclusively and ethically, even though employees may not consider that "balancing" burden to be theirs. For example, employees' willingness to engage with the negative impacts their expressions have on others is crucial: consider the outcomes of the H-P case and the button-wearing employee case.

We suggest four dialogical questions between employee and employer when a SRW dispute arises:

- What is the essence of the spiritual or religious expression? What message is crucial to get across to others, or to what principle is it crucial to adhere?
- Are there multiple, authentic ways to get the message across or adhere to principles?
- If so, which way best balances the employee's expressive needs with others' freedoms of expression and belief as well as with organizational needs and limitations?
- If not, what are the remaining options for both parties?

Considering the illustrative cases we have either included in this chapter or read about, we believe if both employee and employer whittle down to the core principle or faith-based imperative and *discuss* options for expressing it, we would have fewer disputes to read about as legal episodes. For example, what did it mean to the button-wearing employee to be a "witness against abortion"? What was the essence of that message? Clarification could have meant better options suggested by the employer, or having the employee reconsider any of the three accommodative options consistent with her beliefs. In another example, why does GM *not* include religious groups in its sanctioned affinity groups? What message is the organization trying to get across? Understanding the root of GM's resistance, perhaps in dialogue between executive management and worker representatives, could lead to much more creative possibilities for all sanctioned groups.

Referring once again to James and Wooten,[63] they note that the longer a dispute takes to resolve, the more inflexible, rigid, and conservative the parties become. Those are not desirable qualities when discussing any dispute, and especially one as deeply personal as SRW. And, it is important to note the fourth question above—there may be instances of SRW expression that simply cannot be resolved. Even in that event, we believe that authentic dialogue to understand each one's position could make ending the employment relationship less destructive.

Thus, managing SRW expressions ethically demands that all organizational members avoid taking an inflexible stance and that they both openly acknowledge the rights and responsibilities of their respective positions. If an employee asks for an accommodation for religious reasons, ethical practice requires that the employer make a good faith effort to find one. Employees, too, have a responsibility to express themselves without believing that they are their own islands, and to understand that others may and do disagree with their faith-based beliefs.

While there is no guarantee that this stance will avoid court disputes or an EEOC filing, staking out an inflexible position or assuming that a request is simply not legitimate is an unethical approach. Given the "Festivus" example above, Cash and Gray[64] warn against trying to determine the legitimacy or seriousness of an employee's belief. Managing SRW in an increasingly pluralistic society demands discipline and an eye on the big picture. Sheep[65] reminds us that we live in a "society of organizations" wherein we are beholden to each other not just within our current organization but within the society of work as a whole. Ethical management of SRW expression is imperative to maintaining the connections that make us whole.

Notes

1. Morgan, J.F. 2005. Religion at work: A legal quagmire. *Managerial Law*, 47 (3/4): 249 [247–259].
2. Conlin, M. 1999. Religion in the workplace. *Business Week*, November 1.
3. Gunther, M. 2001. God and business. *Fortune*, July 9.
4. Conlin, M. 1999.
5. Mitroff, I. and Denton, E. 1999. *A spiritual audit of corporate America: A hard look at spirituality, religion, and values in the workplace.* San Francisco: Jossey-Bass.
6. Cavanagh, G.F. 2003. Religion and spirituality in business: Obstacles and opportunities. In Williams, O.F. (ed.), *Business, religion, and spirituality: A new synthesis.* Notre Dame: University of Notre Dame.
7. Porth, S.J., Steingard, D., and McCall, J. 2003. Spirituality and business: The latest management fad or the next breakthrough? In Williams, O.F. (ed.), *Business, religion, and spirituality: A new synthesis.* Notre Dame: University of Notre Dame.
8. Cash, K.C., and Gray, G.R. 2000. A framework for accommodating religion and spirituality in the workplace. *Academy of Management Executive*, 14 (3): 124–134.
9. Dehler, G.E. and Welsh, M.A. 2003. The experience of work: Spirituality and the new workplace. In Giacalone, R.A. and Jurkiewicz C.L. (eds.), *Handbook of workplace spirituality and organizational performance.* Armonk, NY: M.E. Sharpe.

10. Gogoi, P. 2005. A little bit of corporate soul. *Business Week Online*, April 5.

11. Ingersoll, R.E. 2003. Spiritual wellness in the workplace. In Giacalone, R.A. and Jurkiewicz, C.L. (eds.), *Handbook of workplace spirituality and organizational performance*. Armonk, NY: M.E. Sharpe.

12. Lund Dean, K., and Fornaciari, C.J. 2007. Empirical research in management, spirituality, and religion during its founding years. *Journal of Management, Spirituality, and Religion*, 4 (1): 3–34.

13. Ibid.

14. Biberman, J. and Whitty, M.D. 2004. Overview. In Biberman, J. and Whitty, M.D. (eds.), *Work and spirit: A reader of new spiritual paradigms for organizations*. Scranton, PA: University of Scranton Press.

15. Giacalone, R.A. and Jurkiewicz, C.L. 2003. Preface. In Giacalone, R.A. and Jurkiewicz, C.L. (eds.), *Handbook of workplace spirituality and organizational performance*. Armonk, NY: M.E. Sharpe.

16. Williams, O.F. 2003. Introduction. In Williams, O.F. (ed.), *Business, religion and spirituality: A new synthesis*. Notre Dame, Indiana: University of Notre Dame Press.

17. Lund Dean, K. and Fornaciari, C.J. 2007.

18. Shorto, R. 2004. Faith at work. *New York Times Magazine*. October 31: 40–46, 62, 66, 69.

19. Estreicher, S. and Gray, M.J. 2006. Religion and the U.S. workplace. *Human Rights*, 33 (3): 7–20, 24.

20. Driver, M. 2005. From empty speech to full speech? Reconceptualizing spirituality in organizations based on a psychoanalytically-grounded understanding of the self. *Human Relations*, 58 (9): 1091–1110.

21. Brown, R.B. 2003. Organizational spirituality: The sceptic's version. *Organization* 10 (2): 393–400.

22. Jackson, B. 2001. *Management gurus and management fashion: A dramatistic inquiry*. London: Routledge.

23. Kamoche, K. 2003. Organizational spiritualism: Toward a critical analysis. Paper presented at the Academy of Management. Seattle.

24. Sheep, M.L. 2006. Nurturing the whole person: The ethics of workplace spirituality in a society of organizations. *Journal of Business Ethics*, 66 (4): 368–369 [357–375].

25. Estreicher, S. and Gray, M.J. 2006. Religion and the U.S. workplace. *Human Rights*, 33 (3): 17–20, 24.

26. Atkinson, W. 2004. Religion in the workplace: Faith vs. liability. *Risk Management*, 41 (12): 18–23.

27. Grensing-Pophal, L. 2006. Religion in the workplace. *Credit Union Management*, 29 (10): 36–40.

28. King, S.M. 2007. Religion, spirituality, and the workplace: Challenges for public administration. *Public Administration Review*, 67 (1): 103–114.

29. Mannies, J. 2006. "Pill" dispute here costs pharmacist her job. *St. Louis Post-Dispatch*, January 27, http://www.stltoday.com. (Last accessed July 24, 2007).

30. Stein, Rob. 2005. Pharmacists' rights at the front of new debate. *The Washington Post*, March 28, http://www.washingtonpost.com/wp-dyn/articles/A5490-2005Mar27_2.html. (Last accessed July 24, 2007).

31. Schoeff, M. Jr., 2006. Bill seeks to expand right to religious expression at work. *Workforce Management*, 85 (4): 3.

32. Clark, M. 2004. Religion vs. sexual orientation. *HR Magazine*, 49 (8): 54.

33. Lund Dean, K. and Safranski, S.R. Forthcoming. No harm, no foul? Organizational intervention in workplace spirituality. *International Journal of Public Administration*.

34. Atkinson, W. 2004. 22.

35. Clark, M. 2004. 56.

36. Ibid. 56.

37. Shorto, R. 2004. 62.
38. Ibid. 47, 62.
39. Cummins, H.J. 2007. Religion-work disputes creating new challenges. *Deseret Morning News*, April 1, B9.
40. Semuels, A. 2006. Workplace bias against Muslims, Arabs on rise. *Los Angeles Times*, October 3, C1; http://www.adc.org/index.php?id = 2973. (Last accessed July 24, 2007).
41. Ibid.
42. Anonymous. 2007. Illinois law school to recognize Christian student group. http://www. firstamendmentcenter.org/news.aspx?id=18590. (Last accessed July 24, 2007).
43. Eastman, H. 2006. Religion in the office: Prayer books and law books. *Washington Business Journal.* August 11, http://washington.bizjournals.com/washington. (Last accessed July 23, 2007).
44. Anonymous. 2007.
45. Estreicher, S. and Gray, M.J. 2006.
46. Ibid.
47. Cummins, H.J. 2007.
48. Bartlett, T. 2007. Pennies from heaven. *Chronicle of Higher Education*, July 6, http://chronicle. com/temp/email2.php?id=2d4yHzzFhKhBBfq6typhfHsdjBk6jSdb. (Last accessed July 20, 2007).
49. http://www.telladf.org/UserDocs/CLS-SIUsettlement.pdf. (Last accessed July 20, 2007).
50. Anonymous. 2007.
51. Shorto, R. 2004.
52. King, S.M. 2007.
53. Cash, K.C. and Gray, G.R. 2000.
54. Atkinson, W. 2004. 23.
55. Morgan, J.F. 2005. 252–253.
56. Cash, K.C. and Gray, G.R. 2000. 126–127.
57. Grensing-Pophal, L. 2006.
58. Ibid. 38–39.
59. Egelko, B. 2006. Public employee loses religious freedom case: Tehama County's limits on evangelical Christian upheld. *San Francisco Chronicle*, May 2, B-2.
60. James, E.H. and Wooten, L.P. 2006. Diversity crises: How firms manage discrimination lawsuits. *Academy of Management Journal*, 49 (6): 1103–1118.
61. Argyris, C. 1990. *Overcoming organizational defenses*. Boston: Allyn & Bacon.
62. King, S.M. 2007. 106.
63. James, E.H. and Wooten, L.P. 2006. 1115.
64. Cash, K.C. and Gray, G.R. 2000.
65. Sheep, M.L. 2006. 357.

CHAPTER TWELVE

Teaching about Spirituality and Work: Experiential Exercises for Management Educators

ROBERT MARX, JUDI NEAL,
KAREN MANZ, AND CHARLES MANZ

Spirituality and work have been increasingly linked together by management educators and researchers as a promising approach to workplace improvement. In recent years, the burgeoning number of conferences, books, and scholarly articles on this topic has begun to establish spirituality and work as a mainstream topic in the management classroom. From early writings,[1,2,3,4] which introduced the spiritual side of work to management educators, to more recent works that have attempted to establish meaningful definitions and models of spirituality at work,[5,6,7,8] the interest and enthusiasm for applying spiritual values to affect solutions to business problems and to enhance quality of life for organization members continue to grow.

Perhaps a telling measure of the maturation of the concept of spirituality in academic circles is the number of management journals devoting special issues to this topic. Most recently, *Leadership Quarterly* published a special issue[9] entitled *Toward a Paradigm of Spiritual Leadership*, and the *International Journal of Organizational Analysis* published a special edition on Spirituality in Organizations.[10] The *Journal of Management,*[11] *Spirituality, and Religion* has devoted an issue to Virtues in Organizations.

Scholarship in this domain now includes articles reviewing the development of scales to measure spirituality[12] and the empirical outcome research of Duchon and Plowman,[13] which identified that work units with higher scores on scales of spirituality exhibited higher performance data than their lower-scoring counterparts. Far-reaching conceptual papers by authors such as Pearce, Waldman, and Csikszentmihalyi[14] propose a theoretical model and a research agenda for studying virtuous leadership.

There are also numerous published anecdotal reports that support some of the promising empirical and conceptual works underway. Aburdene[15] examines the example of Australia's ANZ Bank, which was transformed from a least-preferred employer to an employer of choice in four years, and also won the Bank of the Year Award for three years running and the 2004 International Spirit at Work Award after creating a novel program based on spiritual tools to improve employee satisfaction.

In a body of related work that attempts to understand the role of positive organizational phenomena—which represents the best of the human condition in organizations—Kim Cameron, Jane Dutton, and Robert Quinn are spearheading an effort to explore existing empirical research and stimulate further emphasis in this perspective. In their book *Positive Organizational Scholarship*[16] they point out that the positive side of organizational life has received little attention from management scholars when compared to the emphasis on traditional research on organizational dysfunction and problem resolution.

While management scientists continue to refine and develop definitions, theories, models, and empirical studies, management educators and trainers face the enduring problem of introducing the concepts of spirituality and work to students of management and organizational employees who are likely to view work from a financial performance and competition paradigm rather than from a frame of reference that incorporates a spiritual view.

Although scholars and consultants might find the idea of combining spirituality and work a fruitful undertaking for improving organizations, this blending is not a "natural" combination for most practicing managers or students of business. For many, an introduction to the concept of spirituality in the management classroom is their first institutional exposure to these ideas.

When the concept of spirituality at work is introduced in the management classroom, a predictable response often occurs. That is, one or more participants remark that the lofty moral and ethical intentions of a spiritually assisted workplace are often in direct opposition to the harsh financial realities of the marketplace, where the bottom-line performance measures govern corporate survival. Although common sense might view these perspectives as antithetical, recent research findings suggest otherwise. In the book *Positive Organizational Scholarship*,[17] the authors investigate the impact of "goodness" and "positive human potential" on organizational outcomes. More specifically, they contrast the world of work typified by greed, manipulation, and wealth creation with another kind of work environment emphasizing appreciation, virtuousness, and human well-being. Scholarly researchers investigating the former worldview study problem solving and competitive strategies while those with the latter worldview examine "theories of excellence...positive deviance...and positive spirals of flourishing."[18]

On the basis of the concept of positive psychology,[19] Cameron's own research on virtuousness and performance[20] indicated that when perceptions of virtuousness in organizations are high, the organizations enjoy higher levels of profitability than comparable organizations with lower levels of perceived virtuousness. What makes these findings even more impressive is the fact that the data were collected from organizations that had recently engaged in downsizing. Cameron[21] goes on to show that virtuousness in organizations can amplify or foster escalating positive consequences[22] and buffer the organization against the negative outcomes of organizational events, such as downsizing, "by enhancing resiliency, solidarity, and sense of efficacy."[23,24]

Mitroff and Denton's seminal book on workplace spirituality[25] includes a definition of spirituality that emphasizes virtues, and states that spirituality is inextricably connected to virtues such as "caring, hope, kindness, love, and optimism." The concept of virtuousness may offer a methodology for initiating a classroom conversation about spirituality, which honors the diversity of spiritual sources among individuals yet aligns co-workers on activities that can lend to the "social betterment" of the organization.[26] As Krishnakumar and Neck[27] state, "The spiritual freedom model" of spiritual expression at work "represents the implementation where people in an organization are encouraged to express their views of spirituality. Here the organization doesn't establish any particular spiritual principle as common to all its employees." The challenge, according to Thompson,[28] is to connect the diverse spiritual paths of individual employees to a common set of beneficial outcomes for the organization.

In our exploration of the best ways to introduce the topic of spirituality in the workplace to business school students, we have come to believe that language is the first issue for the management educator to address. The challenge is how to bridge the gap between the personal, internal, and private language of individual spirituality and the inclusive and public language of the classroom and of the working world. Manz, Marx, Neal, and Manz[29] have emphasized the importance of language for creating an inclusive working definition of spirituality. They suggest that using the language of "virtues" and "organizational virtuousness" can be an effective way to introduce this topic in the classroom.

Nevertheless, it can be a formidable challenge for management educators to introduce the topic of spirituality and work to a room full of engineers, accountants, blue-collar supervisors, results-driven MBA students, and busy executives whose attention is usually focused on "more pressing matters."

However, once a theoretical and empirical basis for challenging the notion of the incompatibility of organizational virtuosity and high levels of organizational performance is established, students are more prepared to engage in the process of reconciling virtuous behavior in the organization with a bottom line. Thus, it is helpful to provide a brief lecturette on the positive results connected to spirituality and virtuousness in the workplace as a way of establishing some credibility and relevance for students before inviting them to participate in experiential exercises.

The Public Face of Spirituality at Work

One approach to introducing the concept of spirituality at work to the management classroom is to use a sequence of exercises that begin to explore the nature of the workplace, what it is like to work in it currently, and what it might become in the future. By examining the organization first, we have often been able to gain a consensus in the class for the need to improve the quality of work life and the level of effectiveness.

Following are two examples of exercises that can be used to introduce students to the value of exploring the link between spirituality and the workplace.

"The Messenger": A Powerful Video Case
of Spirituality in the Workplace

Video has been shown to impact classroom learning in a number of beneficial ways, including the heightening of affective arousal toward the subject matter[30] and orienting the learner on what is to be focused in the video segment.[31] By motivating and arousing students' interest in the topic to be learned, video segments have been shown to make students more responsive to content-based instructions that follow.[32] When used effectively, video segments increase both motivation and comprehension.[33,34]

One video segment that has been shown to successfully introduce the concept of Spirituality at Work into the management classroom is the January 4, 2001 edition of ABC's *Nightline*, which featured Dr. Fred Epstein, a New York pediatric surgeon.[35] Moderated by *Nightline* correspondent Ted Koppel, the segment depicts the transition of Epstein from his lifelong attraction to high-tech surgical techniques through a paradigm shift that forever altered how he practiced medicine. As the thoughtful surgeon reads a poem that he reviewed from a dying patient, he stops at a line, "take my trembling hand and warm it with your touch." With a tear in his eye he asks, "How many trembling hands have I not held?"

Without giving up his appreciation of technology, Epstein applies his new insights to completely revamp his practice, which now includes parents wearing scrubs and bringing their child into the operating room and even holding the anesthetic mask over the child's face so that the last image seen by the child before succumbing to the anesthetic slumber is the parents. Although the video only uses the word "spirit" occasionally, it is the expression of spirit that permeates the story. The learnings from "The Messenger" emphasize the ability of a technically driven professional to transcend the limitations of the mechanics of medicine and integrate it into a creative, inspirational, and meaningful way of recognizing the humanity of his patients, his colleagues, and himself.

While this video uses the medical profession as its backdrop, it is the integration of technology and humanity that ties the segment more broadly to the business classroom. Even though systematic empirical research has not been undertaken regarding the specific effects of this segment on student performance outcomes,[36] numerous anecdotal reports of its successful use have been received.

Perhaps one of the reasons for the usefulness of this story in initiating productive discussions about spirit at work lies in the absence of a specific spiritual source. This avoids the problem of appearing to promote a particular religious or ethical perspective. While the boy's poem served as the inspiration to Dr. Fred Epstein, there is no advocacy of poetry as a tool that will necessarily move others in a similar way. Rather, students' acceptance of a poem's message as a breakthrough for the surgeon gives class members the permission to revisit their own breakthrough moments at school or work and examine how such insights might be used for their own personal growth and potentially beneficial workplace outcomes.

"The Messenger" is used here as only one example of numerous other possible stories and videos that can provide a potent and concrete classroom example of spiritual behavior at work. Such examples can effectively initiate a discussion on the concept of spirituality at work and blend nicely with experiential activities and frameworks such as those discussed by Barnett, Krell, and Sendry;[37] Mitroff and Denton;[38] and Krishnakumar and Neck.[39] Concepts and case examples from the spirituality at work literature can be effective at the end of a discussion that is stimulated by videos or stories. Students can then be asked to identify specific actions that they might undertake to impact their own work situation in a similar manner.

Spiritual Virtues in the Workplace Exercise

This exercise begins with a set of virtues, which may be based on a number of sources. In addition to the virtues already mentioned by Mitroff and Denton,[40] Cameron[41] suggests forgiveness, optimism, hope, compassion, and integrity, while Manz, Manz, Marx, and Neck[42] add faith, courage, integrity, justice, and wisdom.

The procedure for the spiritual virtues in the workplace exercise begins with the facilitator selecting a set of five virtues (i.e., integrity, compassion, courage, optimism, and wisdom). Posters displaying a single word in large bold print corresponding with each of the five virtues are placed on the walls in separate locations around the room. Participants are asked to view the list of selected virtues and select one that has proved particularly problematic for them in their own workplace. Participants write about their situation on a large post-it note, describing how the absence of this virtue impacted their own organization. When this is done, everyone affixes their post-it note onto the poster displaying the name of their chosen virtue. Participants stand near the poster bearing the virtue of their choice, reading about the situations of others as they are posted. When all participants have completed their post-it stories and are standing beside the appropriate poster, everyone at each poster is asked to form into a subgroup. Each "virtue group" is then given thirty to forty-five minutes to meet (separate from the other groups) and share the examples/stories they listed on their post-its and to create a five-minute role-play that clearly depicts the conflict posed by the juxtaposition of a situation based on a business value and their chosen virtue. For example, participants in the "compassion" group frequently act out the downsizing of a competent employee, while showing little regard for the impact of the action on the individual but focusing on the fiscal savings to the firm that the firing will accomplish.

Role plays may be an amalgamation of several stories with a common theme or may be based largely on one participant's example. Following the role-play, the group is responsible for facilitating a discussion among all the remaining groups on what was observed in the role-play and how their conflict might realistically be reconciled in a more compassionate workplace. Using the feedback received and insights gained during this discussion, the "Virtue Team" huddles briefly and performs a shortened, revised version of their role-play, which includes ways that an organization might embrace virtuous activity without sacrificing its bottom line. As each team presents their role-plays, the concept of virtuous organizational activity can be elicited in an engaging way that offers several examples of organizational deficits in virtuousness and how these scenarios can be reasonably resolved.

When this exercise is combined with a case in a video segment that affords a positive example of spirituality at work, we have observed that the participants feel grounded by the emerging examples of organizational virtuousness and lack thereof, and they feel ready to examine their own possible personal spiritual sources. Rather than viewing spirituality at work as a completely religious or mystical concept, participants are primed to build on these activities, to explore organizationally beneficial spiritual behaviors from a common ground, and to further examine their own spiritual roots and how they are manifested in their own behavior at work.

Private Sources of Spiritual Behavior at Work

After watching a video segment rich in examples of spirituality at work and then identifying and enacting organizational scenarios that depict a less than adequate implementation of virtuousness at work, the stage is set to examine the more private spiritual worlds of the participants in the class. Interesting questions arise. What is the diversity of sources that contribute to the individual's path that must ultimately merge with the sources of others to produce congruent beneficial outcomes for the organization? To what degree does religion connect with spirituality, given the many religious and nonreligious differences inherent in the participants in a classroom or organizational setting? What frameworks can be useful for helping participants examine their own spiritual roots and paths while remaining tolerant and inclusive to the plethora of perspectives that will be mentioned during these activities, including those that base their organizational performance on ethical, scientific, legal, economic, and other "nonspiritual" sources?

Here we will share three experiential exercises that have been successfully used by management educators to help individuals explore this aspect of spirituality in their lives, which is not often tapped in the secular world of business or in business education settings.

Brainstorming the Relationship between Spirituality and Religion

This exercise begins by stating to the class that there is a lot of confusion about how to appropriately address spirituality in the workplace because some people are concerned that the topic implies a focus on religion. We then make it clear that we are not talking about religion and explain that it is important to understand the differences in the terms used. We write the word "Spirituality" on one blackboard or flip chart and the word "Religion" on another. Then we brainstorm. Ample time is allowed for clarification.

As each person calls out a word or phrase, we ask them which column it goes in. At first the words are pretty clear, but pretty quickly we get into words that are not so clearly delineated, such as "community" or "love." We encourage students to discuss and debate these words to find out what people mean, and usually someone says, "I think they go in both columns." So then we create a third category of terms that fit both spirituality and religion. The discussion helps people to become aware of any biases or stereotypes that they might have in regard to either concept. By the end of this brainstorming exercise, people are more comfortable with the idea of spirituality, in part because they have helped define it. Then we can begin a discussion of what spirituality in the workplace might mean and how it might be practiced.

Spiritual Perception, Awareness, and Practice Exercise

Barnett, Krell, and Sundry[43] bemoan the lack of available tools for business school faculty who wish to teach about spirituality. They have developed a framework that offers students a set of categories for examining their spiritual path, including mystical, personal, ritual, and a related continuum of public to private regarding how their chosen spiritual path is experienced. They also describe a three-part experiential exercise for introducing spirituality at work into the management classroom. The first part asks the participants to think about a time when they have been feeling particularly spiritual. This part is kept private. In part two, participants are asked to think about someone they know or have met whom they believe to be a very spiritual person, and why he or she is considered so. This part is shared. The final part asks how the approaches to spiritual development used by them and the person they identified in part two are different. The answer to this question is shared with the instructor in a journal entry.

Spiritual Lifeline Exercise

The final exercise in this sequence is one that should be used after the group has built a sense of trust, safety, and connectedness. It is the most personal of all the exercises we have offered, but it is also the one that allows the student or participant to truly integrate his or her own spiritual journey with his or her career journey.

This exercise allows the student to reflect on significant events in his or her spiritual life and career life. Often we keep these two parts of our lives separate. By creating lifelines for one's spiritual path and for one's career path, participants can begin to examine how these parts of life may actually overlap.

Each person is asked to symbolically portray on a lifeline the "critical spiritual events" and the "critical work events" in their lives. They are instructed to not use words; they should use only drawings or symbols. Artistic ability is actually a hindrance in this exercise, because artists spend too much time on the aesthetics instead of unfolding their life story. Participants are told to keep the symbols simple, but make them identifiable enough so that they know what significant event the symbols stand for. If there is time, the instructor may ask the participants to portray where they think their spiritual path and their career path may be going in the future. (Note: this part of the exercise works best when people can go to someplace where they can be quietly reflective and alone, ideally in or near nature.) This takes about twenty minutes.

The next part of the exercise is to have participants share their lifelines with each other. If the group is small, everyone shares their drawings with the entire group. It helps to create an environment of deeply respectful listening. If the group is large, people form groups of two to three and at least twenty to twenty-five minutes are spent to share the drawings among them. At the end of this time, two or three volunteers share their drawings with the whole group.

We have used these exercises in undergraduate and graduate business classes, in church groups, at business conferences, and with executive groups at strategic planning retreats. It seems to work well with any group, although it is a little more difficult with those who have not had much experience in life or in work.

One caveat to be considered in all of these experiential exercises is the instructor's responsibility to maintain inclusivity of language, such that each person's private terminology for describing the sources of their inspiration to work for the common good through the expression of positive workplace outcomes (such as trust, creativity, or courage) is honored. Manz, Marx, Neal, and Manz[44] discuss the necessity of including the nonspiritually-based language of science, law, ethics, and so on for those who do not espouse spiritual sources for their workplace behavior yet agree that a common set of beneficial "social betterment" outcomes for the organization is a worthwhile pursuit.

Summary and Conclusion

Interest in understanding how spirituality can enhance the workplace continues to grow.[45,46,47] Notably, the recent introduction of the discipline of positive organizational scholarship[48] provides theoretical and empirical work that attempts to understand and evaluate the importance of virtuousness and performance,[49] courageous principled action,[50] and fostering meaningfulness in working and at the workplace.[51] Positive organizational scholarship also offers organizational scholars who are trying to understand the concept of spirituality at work a number of promising avenues for exploration.

In the meantime, proponents who consider spirituality at work as a potentially powerful beneficial force in organizations have begun to include such concepts in the traditional business school curricula. While scholars have developed a number of provocative theories and some promising empirical findings, classroom instructors and organizational practitioners struggle to find experiential exercises that can impact modern students and business people while walking the treacherous borders between person and organization, public and private values, religious and spiritual language, and more.

In this chapter we have introduced several classroom-tested activities that might be used to accomplish this objective. While our support for the usefulness of these exercises is primarily anecdotal, we have found them to be consistently effective learning tools in a variety of management educational settings.

Similarly, the order of the exercises has yet to be evaluated regarding whether the emphasis on organizational level considerations should precede the focus on personal and individual considerations or vice versa. However, our experience tells us that it is easier to start with the more abstract organizational experiences, and once trust and safety have been created people become more comfortable with exploring the more personal aspects of spirituality in the workplace. While we await careful, empirical analysis of these activities, participant feedback has been largely supportive.

Notes

1. Neal, J. 1997. Spirituality in management education: A guide to resources. *Journal of Management Education*, 21(1): 121–139.
2. Neal, J. 1998. Teaching with soul: Support for the management educator. *Journal of Management Systems*, 10(4): 73–90.
3. Bolman, L.G. and Deal, T.E. 1995. *Leading with soul: An uncommon journey of spirit.* San Francisco: Jossey-Bass.
4. Naylor, T.H., Willimon, W.H., and Osterberg, R. 1996. *The search for meaning in the workplace.* Nashville, TN: Abingdon Press.
5. Biberman, J. and Whitty, M.D. 2000. *Work & spirit: A reader of new spiritual paradigms for organizations.* Scranton, PA: University of Scranton Press.
6. Barnett, C.K., Krell, T.C., and Sendry, J. 2000. Learning to learn about spirituality: A categorical approach to introducing the topic into management courses. *Journal of Management Education*, 24(5): 562–579.
7. Krishnakumar, K. and Neck, C.P. 2002. The "what," "why," and "how" of spirituality in the workplace. *Journal of Managerial Psychology*, 17: 153–164.
8. Mitroff, I. and Denton, E. 1999. *A spiritual audit of corporate America: Multiple designs for fostering spirituality in the workplace.* San Francisco: Jossey-Bass.
9. *The Leadership Quarterly.* 2005. Special issue: Toward a paradigm of Spiritual Leadership. Vol. 16.
10. *International Journal of Organizational Analysis.* 2005. 13(1).Edited by Karen Klenke.
11. *Journal of Management, Spirituality, and Religion.* 2006. Manz, Charles C., Cameron, Kim. S., Manz, Karen P., and Marx, Robert D. (Guest Editors), Special issue on virtues in organizations. 3(1,2).
12. Fornaciari, C.J., Sherlock, J.J., Ritchie, W.J., and Lund Dean, K. 2005. Scale development practices in the measurement of spirituality. *International Journal of Organizational Analysis*, 13(1): 28–49.

13. Duchon, D. and Plowman, D.A. 2005. Nurturing the spirit at work: Impact on work unit performance. *Leadership Quarterly*, 16: 807–833.
14. Pearce, C.L., Waldman, D.A., and Csikszentmihalyi. Forthcoming. *Virtuous leadership: A theoretical model and research agenda.* Vol. 3.
15. Aburdene, P. 2005. *Megatrends 2010: The rise of conscious capitalism.* Charlottesville, VA: Hampton Roads Publishing.
16. Cameron, K.S. 2003. Organizational virtuousness and performance. In Cameron, K.S., Dutton, J.E., and Quinn, R.E. (eds.), *Positive organizational scholarship.* San Francisco, Berrett-Koehler.
17. Ibid.
18. Ibid. 4.
19. Seligman, M.E.P. and Csikszentmihalyi, M. 2000. Positive psychology: An introduction. *American Psychologist*, 55: 5–14.
20. Cameron, K.S. 2003.
21. Ibid.
22. Cooperrider, D.L. 2000. Positive image, positive action: The affirmative basis of organizing. In Cooperrider, D.L., Sorensen, P.F., Whitney, D., and Yaeger, T.F. (eds.), *Appreciative inquiry.* Champaign, IL; Stripes. 29–53.
23. Cameron, K.S. 2003. 62.
24. Masten, A.S., Hubbard, J.J., Gest, S.D., Tellegen, A., Garmezy, N., and Ramirez, M. 1999. Competence in the context of adversity: Pathways to reliance and maladaptation from childhood to late adolescence. *Development and Psychopathology*, 11: 143–169.
25. Mitroff, I. and Denton, E. 1999.
26. Cameron, K.S. 2003.
27. Krishnakumar, K. and Neck, C.P. 2002.
28. Thompson, W.D. 2000. Can you train people to be spiritual? *Training and Development*, 54: 18–19.
29. Manz, K.P., Marx. R.D., Neal, J., and Manz, C.C. 2006. The language of virtues: Toward and inclusive approach for integrating spirituality in management education. Journal of Management Spirituality and Religion, 3(1,2): 104–125.
30. Hannafin, J.J. 1986. Motivational aspects of lesson orientation during CBI, paper presented at the annual meeting of the American Educational Research Association, Washington, DC, April.
31. Hooper, S. and Hannafin, M.J. 1991. Psychological perspectives on emerging instructional technologies: a critical analysis. *Educational Psychologist*, 26(1): 69–95.
32. Keller, J. and Suzuki, K. 1988. Using the ARCS motivation model in courseware design. In Jonassen, D. (ed.), *Instructional designs for microcomputer courseware.* Hillsdale, NJ: Erlbaum Association. 401–434.
33. Keys, B. and Wolfe, J. 1988. Management education and development current issues are emerging trends. *Journal of Management*, 14(2): 205–229.
34. Marx, R.D. and Frost, P.S. 1998. Toward optimal use of video in management education. Examining the evidence. *Journal of Management Development*, 17(4): 243–250.
35. Marx, R.D., Manz, C.C., Manz, K.P., Cameron, K. 2003. Teaching about spirituality and work: a powerful video segment for the management classroom. OBTC National Conference, Western New England College, Springfield, MA. June 11–14.
36. Marx, R.D. et al. 2003.
37. Barnett, C.K., Krell, T.C., and Sendry, J. 2000.
38. Mitroff, I. and Denton, E. 1999.
39. Krishnakumar, K. and Neck, C.P. 2002.
40. Mitroff, I. and Denton, E. 1999.
41. Cameron, K.S. 2003.

42. Manz, C.C., Manz, K.P., Marx, R., and Neck, C.P. 2001. *The wisdom of solomon at work: Ancient virtues for living and leading today.* San Francisco, CA: Berrett-Koehler.
43. Barnett, C.K., Krell, T.C., and Sendry, J. 2000.
44. Manz, K.P., Marx. R.D., Neal, J., and Manz, C.C. Forthcoming
45. Roberson, W. 2004. *Life and livelihood: A handbook for spirituality at work.* New York: Morehouse Publishing.
46. Twigg, N.W. 2004. Transformational leadership: The effects of spirituality and religious orientation, proceedings, annual meeting of the Federation of Business Disciplines (FBD), South Western Academy of Management (SWAM), Orlando, FLA, March 3–6.
47. Manz, K.P. et al. 2006.
48. Cameron, K.S. 2003.
49. Ibid.
50. Worline, M.C. and Quinn, R.W. 2003. Courageous principled action. In Cameron, K.S., Dutton, J.E., and Quinn, R.E. (eds.), *Positive organizational scholarship*. San Francisco: Berrett-Koehler.
51. Pratt, M.G. and Ashforth, B.E. 2003. Fostering meaningfulness in working and at work. In Cameron, K.S., Dutton, J.E., and Quinn, R.E. (eds.), *Positive organizational scholarship*. San Francisco: Berrett-Koehler.

CHAPTER THIRTEEN

Future Directions

Len Tischler and Jerry Biberman

The chapters in this book have explored current issues and practices of applying spirituality in a variety of organizations and situations. They have also explored concerns that have been raised about these issues and practices. While most of the chapters have stayed within the existing positivistic paradigm, some begin to at least push on or test the boundaries of the paradigm.

In this concluding chapter we will examine the need to expand spirituality in organizations, and the model we used in chapter one to describe it, into nonlinear areas. We will also look at whether, in order to do so, it is necessary to come up with a totally new paradigm, or, conversely, whether it is possible to do so within the confines of the current paradigm. We will conclude by speculating how the model we presented could be expanded, and will attempt to answer the question of what an "enlightened" organization would look like.

As we wrote in the opening chapter, the research and writing on workplace spirituality to date has remained pretty much grounded in the prevailing linear positivist social science paradigm, which emphasizes the importance of objectivity and the tools and approaches of the scientific method.

As Hawkins[1] points out, this linear positivistic approach is an extension of the Newtonian scientific paradigm, which values content over context and which fails to adequately address spiritual experiences or concepts. Specifically, the approach does not adequately address transcendence, nor does it adequately address nonlinear influences.

As we mentioned in chapter one, Wilber's model, in talking about interior states and experiences and about levels and lines, attempts to bridge this gap or go beyond a strict positivist approach. However, Wilber defends his model in a linear way, and mostly cites linear research and concepts in explaining the elements of his model.[2,3,4] Sandra Waddock[5] argues that spirituality, emotion, and community have received little attention in management thinking, research and practice,[6] calling spirituality the "ghost in the machine."[7]

If indeed there is a need to expand our model into nonlinear areas, the question then becomes whether, in order to do so, it is necessary to come up with a totally new paradigm, or, conversely, whether it is possible to do so within the confines of the current paradigm. We will now examine these questions.

Arguments For and Against Remaining within the Confines of the Current Paradigm

By remaining within the current paradigm, researchers would share a common and commonly accepted vocabulary and methodology, a nomological net, within which to conduct research and evaluate and report their findings. Researchers would thus be able to relate their concepts and research findings to other research being conducted and reported. This would make it easier for their findings to be presented at existing conferences and published in existing and peer-reviewed journals and other publishing outlets, and thus make it easier for the researcher's work to be accepted as contributing to the field, and for the researcher to receive tenure and promotion at her or his academic institution.

However, by remaining within the confines of the current paradigm, researchers remain trapped in the constraints (many of which are, admittedly, self-imposed) of that paradigm. By adhering to the social scientific paradigm, researchers are forced to reduce their concepts to linear concepts that can be observed and measured using instruments that are validated according to accepted (within the paradigm) methodologies. Thus, we have found that very little extant research has addressed transcendence or nonlinear influences.

Arguments For and Against
Developing a New Paradigm

By developing a new paradigm, researchers would be able to go beyond the perceived restraints of the existing paradigm. They would be better able to address spiritual experiences or concepts such as transcendence and other nonlinear concepts.

However, by creating a new paradigm, researchers would no longer share a common and commonly accepted vocabulary and methodology with which to conduct research and evaluate and report their findings. They would thus, at least initially, find it more difficult to relate their concepts and research findings to other research being conducted and reported. This would make it more difficult for their findings to be presented at existing conferences and published in existing and peer-reviewed journals and other publishing outlets. This would, at least initially, make it more difficult for the "paradigm pioneer's"[8] work to be accepted as contributing to the field, and for the paradigm pioneer to receive tenure and promotion at her or his academic institution.

Expanding the Model

Whether or not we stay within the existing paradigm or create a new paradigm, we still need to expand the concepts of the model we presented in our first chapter to incorporate transcendence and other nonlinear concepts. At the least, we need to incorporate Wilber's[9,10,11] notions of levels and lines of human development that we described in our opening chapter and expand them to incorporate not just the individual, but also the work unit, whole organization, and society. We would thus need a model consisting of progressively transcending and inclusive developmental levels of consciousness at all four levels. We would also need to expand the "measures" used in the model from the three general categories presented in our original model to the twenty-four lines of development described by Wilber.

Toward a New Nonlinear Paradigm

To move the model into a new nonlinear paradigm, we would need to develop a nonlinear way of conceptualizing such contextual (as opposed to content) concepts as transcendence, unity consciousness, and egolessness, and how to apply these concepts to not only the individual, but also the work unit, whole organization, and society as a whole. Such a model would need to move beyond the two-dimensional representation of three dimensions that we presented in chapter one to more of a holonic or holographic model containing overlapping dimensions, which would be too difficult to illustrate in a two-dimensional format for this book.

Since we cannot illustrate the entire model here, we would like to raise the question of what the highest level—unity consciousness or transcendence—might look like for the individual, work unit, whole organization, and society.

Biberman and Whitty[12] speculated about how a "spiritual" individual and organization might behave. They speculated that persons operating from a spiritual paradigm perspective would be open to change, have a sense of purpose and meaning in their life, appreciate how they are connected with a greater whole, and have individual understanding and expression of their own spirituality. In contrast to a scarcity belief, they possess what has been referred to as an "abundance" mentality—a belief that there are abundant resources available to all, so that there is no need to compete for them. They would also be more likely to trust others, share information, and work in concert with teams and coworkers to accomplish mutual objectives. They would empower their coworkers and people below them in the organization hierarchy. They would be more likely to use intuition and emotions in reaching decisions. They would also be more likely to use win-win collaborative strategies in conflict situations.

Biberman and Whitty[13] further speculated that organizations that operate from the spiritual paradigm would be expected to have flatter structures and a greater openness to change. Their belief in abundant resources would lead to greater interconnectedness and cooperation among organization units and empowerment of workers at all levels of the organization. Rather than believing in the preservation of the self at all costs, these organizations would be more concerned with existing in harmony with their environment, and would thus be more supportive of the ecology and environment and more concerned with meeting the needs of internal and external customers. These organizations would be more likely to encourage creative thinking and cohesion in the working of its units to establish and accomplish mutually agreed missions and objectives for the organization. We would postulate similar qualities at the levels of the work unit and society.

Going a step further, we would postulate that at all four levels, individual to society, "support of nature" would be an inherent, nonlinear feature of spirituality. We know in personal and business life that even when we are very well planned, things often work out differently than our plans called for. Groups and organizations find this too. When we investigate, we often find that there were certain things about the environment that we couldn't predict or control. Spiritual people talk of the "support of nature," of gaining support for their desires more easily as they grow spiritually. Support of nature is a concept that implies that nonlinear, usually "objectively" unobservable and nonverifiable, forces exist in one's environment (context) and, to the extent of spiritual development, are more or less supportive of one's life.[14]

Questions

Several questions still remain to be answered: Is a "spiritual" person or organization the same as an "enlightened" person or organization that is operating from unity consciousness? Would higher consciousness exhibit a different set of behaviors at each of the levels? If so, how could we conceptualize and measure higher consciousness at each level? The answers to these questions will help to move us into a new paradigm for understanding spirituality in business in a nonlinear contextual way.

Further, we would raise the following questions: Does spirituality or enlightenment reside only in individuals or also in groups, organizations, and societies? Does an organization's spirituality, for example, depend on the number of people within it who are deeply spiritual, or on the founder being spiritual and setting the example, or on culture? Or can its spirituality exist separately from individuals within the organization?

For example, how can we distinguish that green and socially responsible organizations are spiritual and that others are not? At what point do such behaviors become attached to the spirituality domain and why? That is, although growth in spirituality would seem to lead people to act more responsibly, people can act responsibly without being particularly spiritual. Alternatively, some religions preach that by acting responsibly one can gain entrance to heaven—can grow spiritually. Which of these is true? Does outer behavior lead to spiritual growth or does spiritual growth lead to outer behavior—or both?

Does support of nature exist? Are there other nonlinear forces that affect us? Can we measure such nonlinear effects? In addition to the individual level, can they occur at the levels of the group, organization, or society?

This book has brought out many ideas related to spirituality and its growth. There remain many more to ferret out.

Notes

1. Hawkins, D.R. 2002. *Power vs. force*, Carlsbad, CA: Hay House.
2. Wilber, K. 2000. *A brief history of everything.* Boston: Shambala.
3. Wilber, K. 2001. *Sex, ecology, spirituality: The spirit of evolution.* 2nd rev. ed. Boston: Shambala.
4. Wilber, K. 2005. Leadership Workshop, Boulder, CO, July.
5. Waddock, S.A. 1999, Linking community and spirit: A commentary and some propositions. *Journal of organizational change management,* 12(4): 323–344.
6. Ibid. 334.
7. Ibid. 335.
8. Barker, Joel A. 1989. *Discovering the future: The business of paradigms.* St. Paul, MN: ILI Press.
9. Wilber, K. 2000.
10. Wilber, K. 2001.
11. Wilber, K. 2005.
12. Biberman, J. and Whitty, M. 1997. A postmodern spiritual future for work. *Journal of Organizational Change Management,* 10(2): 130–138.
13. Ibid.
14. Mahesh Yogi, M. 1996. http://www.maharishi-india.org/institutions/i3/vedic_science.html. (Last accessed Sept 15, 2007).